Vegas Vignettes

Coming of Age in the *Real* Sin City

Mike Soskin

Edited by Saul Isler

Cover design by Susan J. Sullivan

ISBN-9781983020261

To my father, Frank Soskin,
who, in learning I was going into the business,
gave me these words of wisdom:
"Protect yourself at all times
and keep your eyes and ears open
and your mouth shut."

Acknowledgements

I want to thank my editor, Saul Isler, an author and a friend of many decades. I was about to stop writing this book as I was not too thrilled with its possibilities. He read the first part and told me, “You have some good stuff here,” so I plodded on for another year. Then there was my wife Cheryl, who read every word as I progressed and offered invaluable insight to the content. She also nudged me along when I faltered. I also thank Susan J. Sullivan who created the cover of this book and worked long hours to help bring the book to life. I owe a great deal to Pat Amundson, a former "Teacher of the Year" in the Washington State school system, which is no mean feat. She was the first to read the manuscript, forgave me for the profanities and told me, “This is written in your voice, don't let anybody change it." Words I clung to as I moved along. And thanks to my good friend, Gary Jezek, whose opinion I solicited and knew nothing at all about Las Vegas. He finished it and asked to read it again. That was invaluable encouragement. Finally, many thanks to John DeLuca, owner of Statewide Investigations, who set some things straight and made valuable contributions.

VegasVignettes

Behind the Tables, Behind the Scenes 1950-1996

Preface

The Mob is dead. Long live the Mob. Some things never die and anything related to Las Vegas prior to the 1980's consisted of the Mob, and the Mob and the Mob. The internet is rife with "historians" and other individuals who claim they knew this Mobster, that one, and had personal knowledge of goings on that can never be confirmed. Some are figments of the imagination of the writer and some are downright hilarious. For example, a man claiming to have been a bartender at the Desert Inn in the '50s was serving Frank Sinatra and Sam "Momo" Giancana at the bar early one morning and they invited him into a conversation concerning the takeover of a casino, and how to skim the proceeds for the Mob. The movie the "Godfather" made these guys folk heroes and television continues to glorify them. Now they have a "Mob Museum" in Las Vegas which dotes on the past. They even have a picture of my father on the wall somewhere in there and he was far from being a Mobster. Las Vegas never would have become what it is without the Mob, that is certain. They were the only people in the country who knew what it took to operate a casino and nobody else could have kickstarted the industry in the only place in the USA where it was legal. Hats off to the Mob.

The Mob Museum pays homage to people like Tony "the Ant" Spilotro, whose claim to fame was putting some guy's head in a vise and squeezing it until his eyes popped out, and a whole list of other fellows who led the justice department on a merry chase. This is not what this book is about. If you are looking for various events in the history of the mob, you will be disappointed.

As a young man I had contact with some of these individuals simply because my father worked for them, and I was friendly with some of their kids. I had occasion to meet a few of the more "famous" gentlemen, but only on a social level. I dated the daughter of one of the major owners of the Desert Inn when I was in my early 20's, and recall being in his home while he was playing gin rummy with a friend. He coughed up a wad of phlegm, spit it on the floor, and ground it into the carpet with his shoe. On another occasion, when it looked like his daughter and I might get serious, he gave me some fatherly advice. He put his arm around me and said (quote) "Whatever you do, stay outta the can."

This was the life I grew up in, and really didn't know any different. If you want to know what it was like to come of age in this environment, and subsequently wind up in the industry, you will find some interesting facts here. If you're looking for Mob history, you have only to go to the Internet.

Everything you read here actually happened. It's not "based on actual events," these *were* actual events. In some cases, I have not used names, as I want to avoid embarrassment to any possible survivors or their progeny. The names that are used are genuine. I may have been off a bit in chronology, but not by much.

As it happens, I have what I believe is the distinction of working in six major resorts that no longer exist. These include the Desert Inn, the Thunderbird, the Dunes, the Stardust, the Sands and the Frontier. I also worked at the Tropicana, Circus Circus and the Flamingo, all of which are still operating. I have an overall picture of the industry from the Mob era to the corporate. I also had an interest in, and ran the gaming in, an off-Strip hotel casino and truck stop for over 10 years. It's now called "The Wild, Wild West" and belongs to Station Casinos.

If you are curious about what it was like to live and work in Las Vegas during those times this will offer you a rare look from the inside.

Prologue; Whidbey Island, Washington, 2018

I don't live in Las Vegas anymore. After almost 50 years I decided to leave the place where I grew up, worked nearly 45 years in the casino industry, raised my family and led what I thought to be a normal existence. Somewhere along the line it ceased to be home. There will always be part of me connected to Las Vegas, not the Las Vegas of today, but the town that grew from a small dusty backwater with legal gambling, into a metropolis of nearly three million, where in every direction you can see an endless sea of tile roofs, and every vestige of the small pristine city that I remember has disappeared.

Moving to a new area is never easy. Especially when you don't know anyone, the way of life and the people are completely different than what you've always known. As time progresses you meet neighbors, forge friendships and become established in your new community. The people for the most part, are intently curious about Las Vegas, the questions never seem to stop, and after my reciting an experience or two the unfailing response is "you should write a book." I'm not a writer, so I never really entertained the idea. Yet the questions kept coming, and whenever a show about Las Vegas or the Mob aired on TV invariably someone would mention it to me and ask me if this was how it was.

I began to watch some of the programs and documentaries but, after one episode of "Breaking Vegas," I swore I'd never watch another. "Breaking Vegas" is a travesty, so bad it's embarrassing, yet people believed what they had viewed. Some of the documentaries aired on "American Justice" were quite well done and reasonably accurate. I remember relating to my wife and some guests an incident that concerned a prominent Las Vegas citizen, an incident that no one was aware of. It was one of the first computer scams, maybe the biggest, and involved the father of a famous movie actor and some accomplices whose names were never mentioned. The father was later convicted of gunning down a federal judge and was in prison for life. He died in a super max facility on March 15, 2007. He was also a card cheat and an integral part of this particular scam, along with his wife and a crew that they had assembled. Two days later, "American Justice" aired a documentary that concerned everything I told these people, along with the names that had not been previously mentioned anywhere publicly. I was amazed at the accuracy of their report. The timing from my personal point of view was great, yet there was so much it didn't mention, mainly the Las Vegas scam, how it was uncovered and how it actually worked. It was a fluke that it was discovered at all.

By now I was beginning to be flooded with flashbacks, literally hundreds of incidents that took place in my years in the industry. Each story I told brought back memories of others, and they built upon themselves until I began to realize that maybe I had knowledge of things that people really are interested in; yet to me they were part of everyday living.

A friend of my wife, a long-time Las Vegas resident, recently married, came to visit. As it happens, her husband is a cinematographer who had just finished filming a documentary for the History Channel entitled "Las Vegas, An Unconventional History" They had interviews with several entertainers, some casino people and they did well with what they had to work with. The "Mobsters" they interviewed were nothing more than ex-cons, petty burglars and street thugs. The closest they ever came to the Mob was sitting around a particular pizza parlor waiting for a real wise guy to come in and nod hello to them. After all those years nobody was around to contradict them. After dinner one night we talked into the late evening about Las Vegas, how it grew and things that happened over so many years. When the evening waned, they were wide eyed, almost stunned. He remarked, "I wish we had known about you before we started filming, we had trouble finding anyone who could relate to anything prior to 1970." Then he added the usual remark, "You should write a book." I wasn't convinced, yet I must admit that I began jotting down some reminders of things I knew of and experienced. I still felt like it wouldn't really elicit any interest. It was the "coffee table" books that did it. The large colorful books with all the old pictures, the entertainers, "old" Las Vegas, dates replete with stories of the way things were. These were mostly written by "historians," who in my opinion are people who study archives, talk to people, and then establish themselves as experts.

My friends in Las Vegas were constantly sending me these publications as they surfaced, and I admit I enjoyed looking at the pictures, familiar sights and people who no longer exist. I recognized a lot of faces and even saw myself pictured on page 70 of "Las Vegas, Then and Now," driving down the Strip in my 1958 Impala convertible. I had no idea the picture was taken. The picture, under a magnifying light was definitely me, beside the fact that I had the only yellow Impala convertible in town. I began to notice some discrepancies in the text of the books, mostly dealing with chronology, the dates, events, and personal interjections. I began to realize that no one really knows the difference, and if they've been around long enough to see this, they really don't care.

To be truthful, I don't know why I care, but I do. To quote the great Andy Rooney, from his book "My War," "I attended a symposium of distinguished historians in Chicago in 1994. Some of them were in their '60s, marginally too young to have served in World War II. I was in awe of their intellectuality until they started lecturing specifically about the war I knew. If you break your leg and go to a doctor who knows all about broken legs but has never broken his own, you know just a little bit about broken legs that the doctor does not. I thought about that listening to the historians. They had read and studied all about the war for years and had a great grasp of the overall picture. There was only one advantage I had over them. I was there when it happened. On several occasions I've actually ended up convinced that my memory serves history better than the historians. They can write their books, I'll write mine." I have decided to write mine.

To the best of my knowledge, no one has ever written about what it was like to grow up in Las Vegas, work in the gambling industry when the "Mob" still ran the casinos and be a part of the small group of people that kept the dice moving, the cards flying, and the wheels spinning. I was part of this group at age 21.

So, come back with me, if you will, to a time and place so unique that it will never exist again.

Vegas Vignettes

1. The Journey West

The "City of Los Angeles" was known as a "streamliner," one of a few elite trains that covered the USA from coast to coast. Jet travel by air had yet to be introduced and cross-country air travel was, by today's standards slow and expensive. The trains for the most part had Pullman sleeping accommodations, dining cars, complete with cocktail service, and other amenities, but no private bathrooms. In the early 1950s they were still a primary mode of travel for cross-country passengers.

I had taken a commuter train from Cleveland, boarded the City of Los Angeles in Chicago, and was on my way West to join my family in our new home. I carried two suitcases, one contained my underwear and socks and two kosher salamis given to me by my aunt and uncle for my father. Seems there was no such thing as a delicatessen where I was headed. The salamis disappeared the first night out. The case has never been solved and I'm sure the statute of limitations has long expired by now. The aroma, (which is a gentle term at best), remained. and tantalized my dad for weeks. After two days and nights, stops at cities like Omaha and Grand Island, Nebraska, Cheyenne and Laramie Wyoming, Ogden and Salt Lake City, and so many smaller towns in between, I arrived at my new home, Las Vegas Nevada. It was 11:20 PM on Aug 18th 1950. I was fourteen years old.

I picked up my bags and made my way into the Union Station, which became the site of the Union Plaza Hotel in later years. After the hugs and kisses we drove down Fremont Street, which was to be known later as "Glitter Gulch," and headed for home. I recall a few blocks of brightly lit signs and the old "Howdy Pardner." Cowboy sign, on the Pioneer Club, decked out with a ten-gallon hat and an animated arm destined to wave forever. Then Fremont Street became downtown, a block of JC Penney, Ronzone's, Sears and Roebuck, the El Cortez Hotel, and the Outdoorsman, the only sporting goods store in town. The whole thing encompassed six blocks (casinos included). After that were a couple of used car lots, (one set into a copse of Mesquite trees), a few seedy motels, and darkness. The few scattered lights and streetlamps were muted by the surrounding dark and to a boy who had never been west of Cleveland it was almost surreal.

Our home was on Peyton Drive, two blocks south of Charleston Blvd., the only east/west artery that continued west past 5th Street, known as the Strip. After 5th, it became the Tonopah Highway and ultimately, after 500 miles of the most inhospitable terrain in the United States, arrived in Reno.

The next morning, I awoke to bright sunshine, which was to be the norm for the next 48 years. I stood in our kitchen and looked across the backyard bordered by a chain link fence that ran the length of the street. Should you climb that fence and start walking you would encounter nothing but desert all the way to Albuquerque. It was the end of the eastern border of Las Vegas. I opened the door and the heat hit me like a hammer. I could never have conceived that kind of heat, and the steady hum of the swamp coolers on the houses made it seem as though the heat were alive. When I commented on it. my folks told me it was a "dry heat," which was a common statement made by anyone who moves to the desert and tries to justify the move to friends and family still in the east. It, quite frankly, was bullshit. Heat is heat and the kind that can give you second degree burns if you touch the handle of a car door or walk on cement with no shoes is debilitating, I don't care how "dry" it is.

That afternoon my mother took us to the Desert Inn for lunch, she wanted me to see where my father worked as a casino boss., and also see the part of town known as the "Strip." When we got into the car I noticed that the steering wheel, made of hard plastic in those days, had a cloth cover stretched over it-this eliminated getting severely burned by the heat inside the car. It didn't take me long to notice the absence of traffic lights; there were only two in the whole city at the time. One at the corner of 5th and Fremont and the other at the end of Fremont street where it dead-ended at Main street-right in front of the Union Pacific train depot where I had arrived.

The Strip itself was a narrow two-lane road bordered by desert on both sides, drifts of sand swirling along with the cars, and an occasional tumbleweed. This caused us to get a bit dusty; without air conditioning you had to keep the windows open. The Club Bingo, which eventually became the Sahara Hotel, was the first Club on the Strip. Across and down about half a block, was the El Rancho Vegas with a swimming pool right out on the Strip. To get to the casino and restaurant you had to walk past the pool. Directly across the street was the comparatively new Thunderbird hotel and that was it until you came to the Desert Inn. The Last Frontier Hotel was directly across the Strip from the Desert Inn and the remainder of the Strip was empty desert for quite a way down the road.

The Frontier also had the pool right out on the Strip with riding stables and a mock western village to the rear. Many a day we would rent horses and ride down the Strip, return to the Frontier, tie the reins to an oleander bush and jump in the pool. From the Desert Inn it was a long way to the Flamingo with nothing but desert and a small motel or two and The Grace Hayes Lodge, (a local nightspot), in between. Grace Hayes was the mother of Peter Lind Hayes, a popular singer and entertainer. The Flamingo was considered "way out on the edge of town." It wasn't unusual to see a buckboard ringed with pots, pans and other paraphernalia parked in front of the Desert Inn. The horses, (or mules), were boarded across the street at the Frontier stables. Once you were past the Flamingo Hotel you were on your way to Los Angeles, traveling a dangerous two lanes all the way. Hardly anyone would attempt to drive it in daylight in the summer, those that did generally had several containers of water just in case. Those that didn't were just plain crazy. There were no cell phones to depend on, and you could go hours without seeing another car or truck.

2. The Big Bosses

Arriving at the DI (as the Desert Inn was referred to), I recall walking into cool, quiet luxury. The entrance and lobby were polished flagstone, the casino was to the right. It was the first time I had been in a casino, and it certainly wasn't going to be the last. Looking back, I sometimes wonder if that first impression had a hand in my decision to enter the gambling business, (the "racket" as it was referred to by insiders). Please bear in mind that the casino consisted of five crap tables, four Blackjack games and two Roulette wheels. The ceiling was low, and there was a quiet, intense atmosphere. The slots were a minor consideration in those days and I would guess that the DI had maybe 150. These machines were one-coin machines, and the jackpots would fall from a glass enclosure right into the coin tray, (generally followed by a scream). They were really thought of as a diversion for the ladies while their husbands were at the Craps tables. These were the major casinos of the world. With the exception of Monte Carlo, Nevada was the only venue in the world where you could gamble legally.

Once we were seated in the Cactus Room, the main restaurant which looked out onto the pool area, several of the "bosses" came over and said hello to my mother and to us, the kids. These were guys you read about in all the newspaper articles about gangsters going to Las Vegas and becoming "legitimate citizens." They were dressed well and had what seemed to be plastic smiles on their faces, their demeanor bordering on giddy. When I mentioned this to my mother she told me that these gentlemen weren't adjusted to the fact that they didn't have to worry about a raid, or going to jail on a daily basis, and they were still getting used to being in "heaven." My mother never wasted words. Our lunch, of course, was "compliments of the casino" (hence the word "comps") and my first exposure to the Las Vegas lifestyle for those fortunate enough to be involved with the casinos.

At the table next to us, having a bloody rare steak for lunch was Morris Kleinman, one of the big bosses, and a known Mobster. He was a rough and tumble individual, and a mean and nasty drunk. He was an ex-fighter and when he had few drinks in him there was no telling what he would do. One night, Marshall Caifano, a.k.a. "Johnny Marshall," was sitting at the casino bar. Caifano was a high-ranking mobster in the Chicago outfit and was a cold-blooded killer. Morris went over and tried to pick a fight with him. The other owners and security hustled him away. Ruby Kolod, one of the major partners, was heard saying to Morris, "are you crazy?"

It was a few years later that Marshall Caifano was put in the new book of "excluded persons" and not allowed in any casino, or in Las Vegas, for that matter. Anyway, as we sat there having lunch, Nick "Peanuts" Donalfo walked over to say hello, and asked Morris what he was eating. Morris replied, "A customer."

These guys were outwardly wonderful and welcoming to customers, but in reality, they considered them the enemy. When a table or the whole place was losing, the moaning and groaning, cursing and kicking was something to behold. When I would walk into the casino to see my father, if I saw a game with black chips ($100) in front of every player, I kept on walking.

Years later, when I was dealing, a player won a substantial amount of money, picked up his chips and headed for the cashier's cage. One of the owners, who had been watching, muttered under his breath, "cocksucker." The pit boss smiled and said to me, "The gentleman came in to play and the "cocksucker" won. If he would have lost, he would still have been a gentleman.

3. Armed Robbery; Not a Good Idea

I remember the day that Carmen "Minnie" Cardillo's wife dropped him at our home in Cleveland. He and my dad got into our 1949 Buick and headed West to Las Vegas to see if there was housing available, and to get the general idea of what it would be like to live there. The Desert Inn was nearing completion, and they were both offered positions in the new establishment. My father worked weekends in the illegal clubs on the outskirts of Cleveland. The two most famous were the Mounds and the Pettibone. The Mounds Club was the scene of an armed robbery that made all the papers. A crew of armed and masked men herded everyone against the walls - the men had to drop their pants, (they spared the ladies this indignity), and they made off with a huge amount of money and Stripped the patrons of their cash and jewelry. These desperadoes could have picked a much softer spot to pull a robbery. The robbers were never apprehended, (by the police, that is), rumor had it they would have been much better off if they had. The owners of these establishments administered their own brand of justice, (such as being deposited in Lake Erie with cement stockings). When a raid was imminent, they always got tipped off, and by the time the police arrived the patrons would be playing ping-pong in tuxedos or scattered at the bars and playing gin rummy at several tables. The gaming tables sunk into the floor, nobody ever looked under the rugs. No wonder the Cleveland "outfit" was so anxious to become legal and get wealthy without worrying about the authorities.

When I learned that we would be moving to Las Vegas I spent hours in the school library trying to get some idea of what was to be my new home. There wasn't much information available, some info on Boulder (Hoover) Dam some 32 miles away, and really nothing else of value. It was literally considered the wild west, Reno being the major city in Nevada. The only highway east was Route 66 and there was no four-lane road anywhere, except the one that connected Las Vegas and Boulder City, all 30 miles of it. Cars weren't air conditioned in 1950 and there were long stretches of desert between services, if you were to break down and didn't have an ample supply of water it could be fatal. If you stopped for gas, bought a snack and asked for a glass of water, you were charged for it. Sometimes the water cost more than a gallon of gas. Such was the life I entered. To a 14-year-old who had known nothing but the cultured confines of Cleveland Heights, Ohio, it was a shock, to say the least.

4. Lunchtime; Las Vegas Style

Lunch time at Las Vegas High was like lunchtime at any other high school, except there was no school cafeteria. As a result, you either brought your lunch or patronized a nearby restaurant. There was a hot dog and sandwich hut across the street or some restaurants close by. Most people brought their lunch-the usual fare: PBJ's a banana, apple-whatever mother packed the night before.

There was one exception; Jack Binion. Jacks' family owned the world-famous Horseshoe Casino a few blocks away and Jack would go there to eat. He had permission to bring four friends every day, no menu restrictions, meaning that whoever made it to the "Shoe," as we called it, dined on steak while those less fortunate ate baloney or the like. This, of course, resulted in a stampede to get to the car when the bell rang. It was first come first served and the first four (unless a previous commitment was made) were the lucky ones. Everyone connived ways to get out of class prior to the bell so as to get a head start. The waitresses wouldn't accept a tip either. Mr. Binion took care of everything.

Then one day for some reason, only one or two showed up to try for lunch at the "Shoe." After some investigating I found that a few of the guys in our group were going to the El Cortez casino, just a few blocks away. Probing further I learned there was a booth for six, at the very end of the coffee shop, in a corner right next to the door to the kitchen. The booth was always available because nobody wanted to sit where a squeaky door opened every few seconds, and the noise from the kitchen roared out. When the door swung open the booth was practically invisible to the rest of the room. Seems the waitress on that station (her name was "Jezebel" (or at least that's what it said on her name tag) had a little something going on the side. If you put a silver dollar on the edge of the table-a real silver dollar, no four quarters or two halves, she would stand in the corner and when the door to the kitchen opened she would lift up her dress and show us her "patootie" as she called it. She didn't wear underwear. This was not a real long exposure, just a brief flash, but bear in mind that this was 1951, and to 15- and 16-year-old boys at that time, this was a revelation, the sun and the moon.

Try to picture, as the word got out, 12 or so teens crammed into a booth for six, some eating lunch, some faking it, with their eyes bugging out, afraid to blink lest they miss it. Once in a while we would even get two performances, for an extra silver dollar of course. The conversation on the way back to school was highly animated. Here it was, the *Real Thing*, right in front of our eyes.

Outside of a rapidly repulsed grope in the back seat of a car, or some of the animated "little dirty comics" which showed such stalwarts as Popeye or Batman in sexual situations, none of us had any experience with "patootie," and Olive Oyl wasn't much to look at. Then one day Jezebel was gone. No one knew whether she quit or got fired but the noontime rush to Binions' resumed. I'm sure most of us will always remember Jezebel, our first real exposure to the commodity that brought down dynasties, ruined careers, threatened national leaders and generally is the motivating factor in the world as we know it. Frankly, it is one of the main factors in the functioning of the gaming industry.

5. The Birds and the Bees; Lessons in Love

There was only one whorehouse in old Las Vegas. It was called Roxie's and was located off the Boulder Highway in an area called "four-mile" or Pittman. There wasn't a building or business on the highway and forget about streetlights. It was set off the road in a clump of trees and visible by a lone bulb that sat over the door. The word around town was that it was partially owned by the sheriff, one Glen Jones. Newspaper publisher Hank Greenspun was able to get him on tape stating that the place would stay open "as long as they continued to pay him." I guess that constitutes ownership with minimum investment. On occasion they would conduct a "raid" to make things look good. Greenspun got word of an impending "raid" and sent a photographer in on the tails of the law officers. When the flashbulbs started popping several "pillars of the community" leaped over the top of the bar and crouched down behind. The picture showed just their heads as they were on their way down. It looked like a shooting gallery with two heads as targets. One was a prominent attorney and the other a judge. The picture appeared in the morning paper and gave everyone a chuckle.

Roxie's was off limits to military personnel from Nellis AFB and of course to those who were underage. But that didn't keep us from trying. There were two bouncers at the door and they questioned anyone they didn't know. We would let our beards grow, (those of us who were so blessed), and turned our collars up but it was to no avail. After our second try we were unceremoniously ushered out to the parking lot with a couple of slaps to the face and a kick in the ass. That left us with nowhere to go for illicit female companionship.

Then we found out about Searchlight. Searchlight was off the beaten path about 60 miles from Las Vegas on the road that would someday become the main road to Laughlin and Bullhead City, many many years later. There were two clubs in Searchlight that we heard about, the El Rey and the Crystal Club. Both were supposed to be brothels. One night we pooled our money and sent Grant Day into the Monte Carlo club, (downtown Las Vegas) to make one bet. If we won we would be off to Searchlight, if we lost, it would be an early evening. (Grant would one day own the biggest office supply business in Las Vegas, at the corner of Main and Charleston.)

The Monte Carlo club was the only casino in town that had women dealers (Blackjack only). We went to school with their daughters and had been to their homes on occasion. They dealt sitting down on stools, the only place in town that did so, and never once questioned our ages or notified the pit boss even though they knew us. Seems that every time we sent our money in we came out with double (or quadruple) depending on the amount we started with. Grant would say "all I know is that I put the money up, she smiles at me and pays me every time." Then four teenagers would hurtle through the darkness on their way to Searchlight. The first time we walked into the El Ray club we were the only customers. Outside of the bar and a Blackjack table plus a few slots that should have been in a museum even then, there was nothing. The bartender knew exactly why we were there and saved us the embarrassment of asking about the girls by motioning to a door at the back of the room. The door opened and a woman came out and invited us back. I was sure she must have been the madam, but as it turned out she was the youngest of the four women that were there at the time. To say they were matronly was stretching it a little. However, they were quite nice and talked to us like we were grown men. They would talk about sports, fishing, or any number of things. Finally, we learned the menu. To just get laid was five bucks. We had heard that five bucks at Roxie's would get you 15 minutes. If your time ran out it was five more bucks or you had to dismount.

We made several trips to Searchlight over the ensuing months, and it became something to look forward to. Then EJ ruined it for all of us. One night there was a commotion where the rooms were located and the bartender and bouncer went running back. One of the "rules" of the establishment was that the lady had to wash the customers penis with warm soapy water, held in a basin. This accomplished two things; hygiene, and artfully done would save wear and tear on the old "money maker," probably reducing the strokes by a third. Well, she was a little too artful with EJ, and being a healthy teen, he ejaculated into the basin. Now he wanted his money back, and they refused. They offered him a reduction to the price of a "hand job" which I believe was two bucks. He still refused and, being a little drunk, started a ruckus. The result was that we were told to leave and not return. This applied to the other club in Searchlight, too. EJ went on to marry his high school sweetheart and raise a family. He became the slot manager at the Horseshoe Club. Many years later, after getting off work he went home, shot his sleeping wife in the head and turned the gun on himself. No one, to the best of my knowledge, ever knew why.

6. Some Facts about Las Vegas in 1950

In 1950, the population of Las Vegas was 22,000. The population of the whole state of Nevada was purported to be 147,000 (I think they included the sheep). There were no dial telephones. If you wanted to make a call you picked up the receiver and the operator would say "Number, Please?" You would repeat the number you were calling and they would connect you. Our number was 3779R. Many of the operators were high school girls, and they knew everything that was going on because they listened in on anything that might be interesting. Sometimes we knew the operator by her voice and exchanged gossip. Dial phones were introduced near the end of 1954, I was overseas for 18 months and called home upon my arrival in San Francisco. The operator told me there was no such number as 3779R in Las Vegas, I felt like I was in the Twilight Zone until we finally got it straightened out. The new (and only) prefix was Dudley, followed by four digits.

There was no television. The rest of the country had been enjoying television for at least five years, but Las Vegas was not to get TV until 1953.

Then it was local with local advertising. It took about two years to finally get network broadcasting, though limited. I remember when it was announced that television was imminent, Sears and Roebuck was the only place you could buy one. They had models in the window and people would stand and stare at the test pattern.

With only those two traffic lights in the city, you could get from one end of town to the other in a matter of minutes. Then the roads would dwindle off into the open desert. The few small neighborhoods were scattered, with Huntridge being the oldest and most established. The main residential area was downtown where most of the prominent residents lived. I had a friend whose mother had some chickens in her backyard, and he killed a bobcat that liked chicken, supposedly with a two by four. His picture was in the newspaper, and he endured a lot of ribbing. His home was 400 yards behind the Ford agency, which was located on 5th Street, the busiest street in town. It was 5th Street that became the Strip at the intersection of San Francisco Street, (eventually to become Sahara Avenue).

There was one high school in town, Las Vegas High (of course). There were about 900 students. The rest of the school district was made up of two grammar schools (the high school was a four-year school) and one grammar school under construction. Las Vegas high got its first baseball program in 1951. Since the closest other high school was in Basic (Now Henderson) and was much smaller, most of the football and basketball competition came from California. In the state basketball tournament in 1950 Las Vegas played a game with Lincoln County. Lincoln County only had five boys on the team, so the five-foul rule was waived. Las Vegas did subsequently compete well against the much larger California schools.

Some other facts about Las Vegas at that time: The limit all over town was $200 on Blackjack, and $500 on the Craps in most places on the Strip. Benny Binion at the Horseshoe club would take any bet as long as it was your first bet and all cash. Hereafter, on that particular play, that was your limit. A few of the Strip hotels had certain customers who could bet $500 on the Blackjack games, but it was a rarity. I can remember a customer from Dallas would sit at the Flamingo and bet two hands, with a $500-dollar bill on each. He had a stack of $1000 bills in front of him as a reserve. The minimum wager on the Strip was $1. Downtown had several places where you could bet as little as 50 cents. The old Boulder Club (which would become part of the Horseshoe), even had a 10-cent Blackjack game where they dealt real dimes. Dealing on that table was probably the most demeaning job in town. I heard someone comment that the dealer on that game had a look on his face like he was "sniffing a barrel full of assholes," quote, unquote.

7. A "Leg Up" on American Teens

In 1947, the Wildcat Lair opened in downtown Las Vegas, around 4th and Stewart. It was a youth center for high school kids and, every Friday and Saturday night, dances were held. A guy at the door checked your breath as you came in and he knew all the tricks. If you sucked in instead of blowing out, you were automatically barred for the night. He was about 5ft. 5 inches tall, stocky and was tough as nails. Some of the guys found out the hard way. His name was Mickey, and nobody argued with Mickey. If you wanted in to the "Lair" you had to do your drinking later in the evening. On the Friday or Saturday dance nights, one of the entertainers appearing on the Strip would come down to the Lair and sing a few numbers for us between shows. We had the privilege of dancing to the live voices of such greats as Patti Page, Joni James, the Ink Spots, Kay Starr, Nat "King" Cole and others. They would do a few numbers for us, then jump into the hotel limo and go back and do the second show at the hotel. It was really a decent thing for them to do.

Las Vegas was literally a cultural wasteland. I had studied classical piano in Cleveland for a few years prior to moving west, and my mother tried to find a piano teacher so I could continue my studies. The closest thing she could find was Buddy Grover, who played in a trio at the Desert Inn lounge. He was a great guy, but he didn't have it for the classics. End of studies.

8. The Boulder Highway Speedway

The Boulder Highway that connected Las Vegas to Boulder City was the only four-lane stretch of road within 500 miles of Las Vegas. There weren't many freeways in Los Angeles at the time. If you wanted to drive from San Diego to Los Angeles your only option was highway 101, or the Pacific Coast Highway, as it was called. It was two-way, two-lane traffic all the way and you had to slow down for such Beach Cities as Long Beach, Laguna Beach and Huntington Beach.

The Boulder Highway was four lanes, separated by a wide median, and from the end of Fremont Street (the main drag in Las Vegas) to Boulder City, there wasn't a single building. Nothing. There were three roads that ran into the highway from Las Vegas, They were barely paved, and there were stop signs at the intersection. On the other side of the highway, Lake Mead Road ran all the way to the Lake. So here was a wide four-lane highway without a single building in sight, no lights or stop signs to slow you down and there was no speed limit in Nevada. The Binion family had an armor-plated Cadillac limousine with an engine as big my dresser, and with Barbara, the oldest daughter driving, we would load it up and be at the Lake, swimming, in 15 minutes. On weekends, we would race cars on the highway in the Railroad Pass area, and the police would come out and watch the races. If a car happened to be on the way to Boulder City, we would stop the races and wave them through. I don't have to describe what the highway is today. As for the armor plate on the limousine, it was to protect Benny Binion, who returned to Texas to surrender and serve a jail sentence. He left their Bonanza road home in a caravan of bodyguards. There were a few people in Dallas who felt they had a score to settle with Benny.

He served 3 1/2 years in jail. The day before he was to arrive home, I was playing Poker at their home, and went to use the upstairs bathroom. I lifted up the seat, and underneath the seat was a sign that said "Goodie, Goodie, daddy's home."

9. A Las Vegas First

There were very few restaurants in Las Vegas, and no Chinese restaurant. Some of the residents probably never had eaten Chinese food and had no idea what it was like. Fong's Gardens opened in 1951 and was the first and only Chinese restaurant in town. I lived within walking distance and, at 15 years of age, got a job as a busboy there. The place was an immediate success. In the back-storage area by the kitchen were huge containers of Chung King products. Chop Suey, Lo Mein, Won Ton Soup, etc. When someone ordered Chop Suey off the menu, for example, they got Chung King. They would just heat it up and serve it. Everyone raved about the food, saying it was the best Chinese food they ever tasted. In most cases it was the ONLY Chinese food they ever tasted. Nobody knew the difference.

The place stayed open for decades. And the owner, Ah Fong made a fortune in real estate, and gave back to the community in a big way, with grants to the new university and other charities. A few years later, The Sands hotel followed suit with a Chinese menu in the coffee shop. The food was excellent and every time a Chinese restaurant opened it was rumored that they had the chef from the Sands.

10. Lum's Ranch

Lum and Abner was a famous radio show that ran from 1931 to 1954. Besides being famous for the radio program, they also made at least seven movies. If you lived in America, you knew Lum and Abner. The part of Lum was played by one Chester "Chet" Lauck who was a frequent visitor to Las Vegas. Chet Lauck bought a ranch way out in the desert, past the mining community of Blue Diamond. The pavement (if you could call it that) ended at Blue Diamond, and the next several miles to the ranch was dirt road, barely graded. The ranch, which he named the "Bar Nothing," was set at the base of towering cliffs which changed color hourly as the sun moved. From an opening in the cliffs, a cold, clear spring ran through the property. Chet dammed the spring and created the larger of two lakes that turned the ranch into a beautiful greenbelt. The larger lake (which we called the upper lake) was quite large, with an island in the middle, and a small wooden dock with a canoe and paddles. Chet named it Lake Harriet, after his wife. The water was cold and crystal clear, and he stocked it with Bluegill and Largemouth Bass. The stream ran out of the upper lake into a smaller lake, the "lower lake," surrounded by weeping willow trees whose branches hung out over the water. It, too, was stocked with fish, and beneath the branches were huge bass, much larger than the fish in the upper lake. Add the many wild ducks and other waterfowl, and this was probably the most picturesque location in Southern Nevada.

At the outflow of the upper lake they installed a water turbine that generated electricity for the ranch house, which was a sprawling, beautiful building. The water that ran from the lower lake was diverted to irrigate several acres, which grew hay for the horses. This was truly a magical place. Chet had a girlfriend named Betty Boyle, an attractive blond who owned the Desert Inn ladies shop, and lived with her mother, right next door my family. One day my dad told me that we were invited to the ranch by Mr. Lauck, and, bring your fishing rod. I couldn't imagine where you would fish in the middle of the desert between Las Vegas and Los Angeles. I took my best friend, Danny Kolod, whose dad was a major owner of the Desert Inn, and we all drove out to the ranch. We fished, swam, and had a fabulous time. We were offered horses to ride, but we were too busy catching fish. I was stunned by the beauty of the place, and Chet told us that we had permission to visit any time, please take home some fish, because he was hardly ever there, and there were too many fish. For a fifteen-year old, this was paradise. The only problem was getting there, because we were too young to drive, and we didn't know anyone who could take us. Once we even took Danny's brother's car without his knowledge and headed for the ranch. When we returned you can say that the "heat was on".

The place had a strong draw for us. Nick "Peanuts" Donalfo "worked" at the Desert Inn, (he "represented" some gentlemen from back east) and he had a teenage daughter named Ginger. She was a freckled redhead with a good head on her shoulders, and, unbeknownst to Danny and me, she was supposedly being paid five dollars a day to follow us around and keep us out of trouble. She was hard to shake. We all hung around the DI pool in the summertime, and she was with us all the time.

One day we decided to hitch hike to Blue Diamond and walk to the ranch from there. Which was not too smart as we were in bathing suits and clogs which offered little protection in the desert summer. We got a ride just outside of town from the driver of a big rig semi who was headed to Blue Diamond. Ginger rode up front with the driver, and Danny and I rode on the coupling between the cab and the trailer, right between the exhaust stacks. It was so hot that Danny got woozy and I was holding onto him for dear life. When we arrived at the Blue Diamond Mine, one of the supervisors offered to drive us to the ranch in his pickup. We accepted, and when we got to the ranch we couldn't wait to get into the cold water-we almost drank the lake dry, as we didn't take any water with us.

After several hours of swimming and fishing, (Chet had fishing rods for guests) we decided we'd better start back. The plan was to walk the several miles to Blue Diamond, use a phone and call home for someone to come and pick us up, which really wouldn't sit too well but we had no other way unless we could get a ride from someone going to Las Vegas. We started walking on the dirt road and hadn't gone very far when one of my shoes broke and wouldn't stay on my foot. The temperature had to be at least 115, the road was so hot you couldn't touch it with your hand let alone walk on it, and we had no water. I tried to walk, sliding my foot with the shoe on the bottom, but it didn't work, and I wasn't about to take off my bathing suit and wrap it around my foot, as Danny suggested. The situation looked serious, when behind us on the road appeared a cloud of dust, from which a black Cadillac limousine appeared. It stopped when we waved, and in the back seat sat Jake Kozloff, the owner of the Frontier Hotel, and Cliff Jones, the lieutenant governor of the State of Nevada. I sat up front with the chauffeur, and Ginger and Danny sat on the jump seats in the back. They took us to the Frontier, which was across the street (Strip) from the Desert Inn. We didn't know the road went further than the ranch, and we had no idea where they were coming from. They probably bought a couple million acres that the Bureau of Land Management was willing to sell.

Chet Lauck sold the ranch in 1954 to Vera Krupp, heiress of the Krupp munitions fortune from WWII, who had just purchased the Frontier Hotel. She in turn sold it to Fletcher Jones, who owned car dealerships. He then sold it to Summa Corporation (Howard Hughes) which then donated it for a State Park. When I see the pictures of the state park today, it brings back a flood of memories from growing up in Las Vegas. Years later, Ginger married a superior court judge in Los Angeles, Robert Fratianne. They had five children, one of whom was Linda Fratianne, the famous figure skating champion and silver medal winner in the 1980 Winter Olympics.

Danny Kolod died in a boating accident on Lake Mead in 1958. His body was never recovered.

11. The Messiah, He Has Risen

In the summer of 1952, Jesus Christ checked into the Desert Inn. One night at dinner my dad told us all about him. He was a perfect replica of his namesake, and he caused quite a stir. He walked around in a flowing white robe and wore sandals on his feet. This is in the days when people came into casinos fashionably dressed. I remember my dad telling us about a guy that came into the Desert Inn dressed "like a bum." He was wearing khaki pants, a polo shirt and tennis shoes. That should give you some idea of what it was like in the early '50s in the Strip casinos. They didn't know what to make of him, until somebody recognized him. It was Howard Hughes, years before he became a recluse. Strange, you could walk into the casino in a bathing suit and a terry cloth shirt, and nobody would look twice. But Hughes, in khakis and a polo shirt looked like a "bum."

Anyway, back to Jesus. He established credit for check cashing, and when they called his bank in Los Angeles they found that he indeed had an account under the name of Jesus Christ, and that a check for $10,000 would clear without a problem. He only wanted to cash $2500, but when a casino checks an account in order to cash a check, they always use at least twice the amount to be cashed when they would make their inquiry to the bank. He cashed the check, (signed Jesus Christ) and immediately went to the Craps table and "fired it up" (gaming speak for betting high). The next day a friend and I were at the pool at the DI, hoping to get a glimpse of Jesus. Sure enough, there was a murmur among the people at the pool, and here he came, white flowing robe, sandals, long hair and beard. He looked like the real thing. He removed his robe and jumped into the pool. When he got out, he got a lounge chair, and laid in the sun. The show was over, for us, anyway.

Several months later a casino customer sent my dad a lengthy clipping from the LA paper. Jesus had a cult out in the hills around Los Angeles. In the '50s, LA was a literal paradise, and you didn't have to go very far out of town to find solitude. Tie that in with the weather, and you had a lot of cults, goofball Messiahs, and whatever. Nobody really paid much attention to them. After all, California was referred to as the "land of fruits and nuts."

Jesus had a large house where his flock resided, and in order to join his group and accompany him to heaven, you had to sign over everything you own to Jesus Christ. He then headed to Las Vegas because he had never experienced sin firsthand, and as a result, didn't know how to "fight it" here on Earth. That was okay with the cult, but he also began to initiate a few of the wives to "celestial delights" in his bedroom. He told them that they would experience ecstasy far beyond any banal earthly couplings that they had experienced in the past. He was a busy man, and sometimes "blessed" them two at a time. This didn't sit too well with some of the husbands, and they planted dynamite under the floor of his bedroom and blew him back to where he came from. I was only 16 at the time, and I don't remember the final disposition of the event. Knowing what it was like at that time, I'd have to say that nobody went to jail.

12. The Federal Bureau of Investigation

The landmark apartments were among the first luxury apartments in Las Vegas. They were close to the construction site of the ill-fated Landmark Hotel. Two cocktail waitresses from the Flamingo were sharing an apartment there. "Sam" lived downstairs and a redhead, "Vanessa" lived upstairs.

I was kind of dating Sam and would "drop over on occasion" (sailor speak for "any port in a storm"). Seems their rent was being paid by two thugs from New York. I never knew whether they were real mobsters or wannnabes. These guys were the jealous type and insisted that the girls would not fool around while they were gone. These were two stupid guys.

I stopped by one night and Sam wasn't home, but I got invited upstairs for milk and cookies with the redhead. I was very low key and never liked anyone to know my business, which drove the pit manager and the shift manager insane. The next night I went to work and was put on an empty (dead) blackjack table. The two nosy managers converged on me with huge grins, said nothing and just stared at me. Finally, the shift manager reached up and plucked at the corner of my mouth, and said to Dick Mead, the pit manager, "It looks like a red hair to me." I knew that she came in and shot off her mouth and the word had got to them. I went ballistic, and by the time I got a break I was out of control. When I went to the coffee shop employees' area, she was there. I called her some vile names and, in front of 20 people, I threatened to put her out in the desert with Russian Louis. I cooled off after that and regretted acting like a hot-headed 23-year-old.

Three days later, Vanessa disappeared. She left clothes in the closet, money in the bank, her car and motorcycle in the garage. Months later her parents came and got her things. I don't know if she ever surfaced. After she was gone a few weeks, a man who asked my name and handed me the business card of an FBI special agent and told me to be in his office at 10AM the next morning approached me. At our meeting he asked my relationship with Vanessa and told me he had witnesses to the fact that I threatened to introduce her to Russian Louis. He reminded me that I could be in serious trouble, told me not to leave town, and ended the meeting. I asked him if I could go across the dam into Arizona as my boat was at a marina a few miles into Arizona, and I fished on my days off. He asked if I had ever taken her on the boat and I told him, "No chance." He told me they would notify me if they wanted to see me again. I never heard from them again and I don't know the outcome. My father once told me "lose your head and your ass goes with it"

He was right again.

13. A Day at the Races

In 1947, a gentleman by the name of Joe Smoot hitched a ride to Las Vegas with Hank Greenspun, a New York attorney, decorated world war two officer, and future founder of the Las Vegas Sun. He also ran for governor, but that's another story.

Joe Smoot had visions of a horse racing mecca in Las Vegas and visions of promoting a race track. His credentials included being involved with successful ventures as Santa Anita, Hialeah, and Gulfstream, although it wasn't noted that he was booted out of all three, way before they opened. He had a team of smooth talkers, and one of his associates was a man by the name of Paul Revere Williams. A fitting name for a horse track promoter.

Anyway, Smoot and his associates managed to raise over 2.5 million dollars from the residents of Las Vegas to begin construction of Las Vegas Park. Subsequently the venture was plagued by forgery, embezzlement, a cast including a Senator, a bankruptcy referee and a federal judge. Senator Pat McCarran posed with Smoot in front of the project and was accused of receiving $8000 in cash from him in a room at the Thunderbird Hotel.

The Park did open, but failure of tote boards, poor attendance and lack of interest made sure it didn't stay open long. They ran a few motorcycle races, tried quarter horses, then closed. Old Joe was subsequently charged with felony embezzlement along with his associates, and two others were charged with felony forgery. There were a lot of unhappy investors. In an attempt to track some of the money, a Federal judge asked Joe why he couldn't account for over $500,000 in cash that was missing. Joe replied "you ever try to bribe a politician with a check?" That even brought a chuckle from those who were bamboozled. Awaiting indictment, Joe, who claimed he was broke, got a job as a shill for $8 a day at a downtown casino. It was rumored that Joe knew that if he left Las Vegas he could become a counterpart of Russian Louis, knowing that Las Vegas was an "open city" to the Mob, meaning that they couldn't kill anybody there. Russian Louis Strauss was a Mobster who disappeared and was never seen again as per ex-Teamsters president, Jimmy Hoffa, creating years of conjecture as to where he wound up. The indictment never came down, and Joe, who was living in a room (free) at the MGM, died of natural causes at the age of 71. Later, Greenspun said that on the way out to Las Vegas in 1946, Joe confided that he didn't think a Las Vegas racetrack would be successful.

Some of the local humor said that the horses they were going to run were descendants of the noble steeds ridden by Paul Revere and his fellow minute men in the Revolution. There were also those who said they *were* the same horses. The track was dismantled, and the site wound up as part of the convention center, the Las Vegas Hilton International hotel, and the Las Vegas Country Club. It should be noted that when they began to tear up the base of the grandstand there were literally hundreds of rattlesnakes underneath taking advantage of the shade. There were more snakes than there were people coming to the track.

14. A Noted Scientist, in the Flesh

Robert E. Lee was the next charlatan to invade Las Vegas, and this time it got personal. My father announced one day that we had a guest coming for dinner. My mother had spread a special table in the living room, (we had no formal dining room), and spent the day cooking. When we asked who the guest was, my dad told us that it was a scientist by the name of Robert E. Lee, who was mentioned in the "Who's Who" of science and had perfected a process of extracting oil from old capped wells, or even "dry" holes that the big companies had given up on. He had approached a couple of the major owners of the Desert Inn, and after showing them his "credentials" told them that he was coming into the area to reclaim some old wells and drill a few new ones where he was certain that a humungous amount of oil lay under the ground. Supposedly, he had documents from petro-geologists that showed a gazillion barrels of oil lying right there within reach of those who were willing to invest.

Now, let me explain something. The owners of these casinos at that time were experts at gaming, and the expertise stopped right there. They had a huge respect for anyone who made a living outside of gambling, and therefore thought that if you weren't in the "racket" you had to be an honest person. Of course, they probably had never been conned because that's a risky business for a con artist. There were easier targets. Some of the big owners thought this was the greatest opportunity they had ever been presented with and decided to invest. They passed the info out to a few of the key personnel and gave them the chance to buy in. My dad decided it was worth the chance and made an investment. Robert E. had set up an account at one of the local banks, under some lofty heading, and the money was to be deposited to the account. They never asked the bank to check it out.

At dinner that night Robert E. gave my brother, my sister and I some advice on how to study science and make it a career. My mother and father beamed at the attention he was sending our way. I was only 16 and I knew that this "fascinating" individual was full of shit. However, what does a dopey teenager know about these things? My opinion, (about him being full of shit), fell on deaf ears.

Robert E. was a pudgy white-haired man in his '50s and his old "down home" country manner was to put everyone at ease.

The next day I went into the school library and spent an hour looking into scientists and didn't find Robert E. Lee. The librarian said she never heard of a "Who's Who" in science. They did drill a well, (supposedly), about two miles out of town right near the Los Angeles highway. It was no more than half a mile from where the Mandalay Bay sits at this time. But you couldn't see the city from there in 1952. My friend Danny's dad was one of the larger investors in the venture, so one afternoon Danny and I got into his Ford convertible and drove out to see the well. We turned off the dirt road, drove in a cloud of dust to where an old pickup truck sat in front of an old rusty oil rig that was pumping up and down. The rig was enclosed by a chain link fence and in the bed of this old truck, that had most of the paint chipped off, sat a cowboy in an old beat up chair. He had his feet up on an orange crate, showing off his cowboy boots and had his ten-gallon hat pulled down over his face. Beside him was a large, oil can, the type they used on the old railroad. When we got out and slammed the car door, he awoke and sat up. We told him who we were and asked him when he thought the gusher would come in. He said he didn't know. He's paid by the day to sit by the well and when it started to squeak, to squirt some oil on the moving parts. We couldn't get close enough to see the hole, but it was probably only a few feet deep. We drove back to town, and Danny told his dad what we had seen. His dad told him the same thing my dad told me. This story ended as expected. Among curses and threats everybody realized that they'd been had. Robert E. Lee was nowhere to be found and neither was the money. I don't know how much longer the rig pumped, but the cowboy didn't hang around and the rig sat there for years until the town started to grow.

Naturally, the word got out, and there was a lot of conjecture as to how long it would take to introduce Robert E. Lee to Russian Louis Strauss. I was afraid to bring it up to my dad and I really don't remember them catching up with Robert E. Lee.

Maybe it was a good lesson for these guys who thought that anyone who was not in the racket must be honorable.

15. Mobster No. 1; John Roselli

One night I was at work at the Palace Station and was told that a woman standing outside the pit wanted to talk to me. I figured that it must be a comp request or something of that nature, so I walked over to her and asked what I could do for her. She replied, "Don't you recognize me? I looked closely and saw a plump middle-aged woman who hadn't aged very well, and I had no idea who she could be. I was getting a little agitated, as I was busy and had no time for games. She then remarked, "I don't get out much since John's been gone." I said "John?" At which she looked around as if the FBI was trailing her, and whispered "John Roselli, I'm Carol." Then it dawned on me.

She was working at the gift counter in the Desert Inn lobby when she was 15 or 16 years old. That's where she met John Roselli. Roselli was the Mob's main man in Las Vegas and Los Angeles. He looked like all the suave Mafiosi, white hair, slender, dressed to kill (no pun intended) and deeply tanned. She was a beautiful blond girl with a pleasant demeanor. Roselli was a ladies' man and, from what I heard, in spite of his impeccable manners, could get nasty if he got jealous. Roselli got involved in some highly sensitive doings and it was said that the Kennedy Administration offered him a contract to kill Fidel Castro. All this is a matter of record so I'll forego a lot of detail and suffice it to say that there was talk that he was involved in the Kennedy assassination. He was going to be deported at one time by the justice department, but Italy refused to take him back. Somehow, he remained in the US. He was not a solid citizen.

In the mid '60s I heard that Carol, barely 17 at the time, and John had become an item, with the blessing of Carol's mother, with whom she lived. In truth, I had seen the three of them out together several times. At first, I thought he was romancing the mother, but it wasn't that way. Soon they were seen around town as a couple. Roselli was in his sixties, yet her mother encouraged the relationship. Carol made a pass at me at the Desert Inn in 1958, I told her she was pretty, but I wasn't prepared to go to jail. That didn't stop Roselli. Anyway, I don't know how long this love affair lasted, but it wasn't a short one. To sum it up, John Roselli was discovered in a 55-gallon drum that had broken loose from its anchor in a bay near Miami. He had been strangled, shot and since he wouldn't fit in the drum in one piece, they cut his legs off. Of course, there was speculation as to whether they cut his legs off before or after they killed him.

In my conversation with Carol, all she could talk about was her days with "John" and she was evidently happy that she had someone to talk to who remembered her only claim to fame. She still lived with her aged mother and never married. After she left, I remember thinking "what a sad situation."

16. Bartender's Delight

Frank Musso opened an Italian restaurant and bar just a few hundred feet from the entrance to the Sands Hotel in the 1950s. Frank was an accomplished chef and did the cooking when the place first opened. It became a huge success, and not only was an eating establishment, it also became an after-hours hangout for casino workers and celebrities. After 1AM, the bar was always full and food was served until the wee hours. The place became so successful that Frank hired some top chefs and began to pursue his favorite pastimes, betting horses and shooting Craps at the Desert Inn. He had a motor home, and often went to Del Mar, near San Diego, for weeks at a time, to play the horses. The place was so successful that it took seven years before it went under. Frank lost the whole building with his business, and his two bartenders with his head waiter and Maître D'' opened the Golden Steer Steakhouse in 1958. I believe it's still open; the oldest steakhouse in Las Vegas.

Frank took his motor home and headed for California. When he returned he lived in his motor home behind the Golden Steer, and, went to work for his ex-employees as a host. To their credit they saw that he had free eats and a small income. It was the least they could do. If it weren't for him, they wouldn't have become financially secure. I'm told that there were a couple of small casinos opened on the site of Musso's, then it became a Denny's. I guess that the property is now part of the Venetian Hotel. This wasn't an unusual story in the Las Vegas that I knew in the '50s, '60s and '70s.

17. Breaking In; Learning to Deal

"Gaming Industry" was a term used by the media and government agencies as the town began to grow. To those of us who earned our living in it, it was referred to as "the Racket" or "the Business." There were very few of us in the late '50s and there was no such thing as a dealer school. If one wanted to learn to deal and get into the "Business" he would either need to have "juice" (connections) or start downtown as a shill which paid eight dollars a day and if someone took a liking to you they would let you "break in" or learn to deal, but on your own time with no pay.

Dealers who came down from Reno and Lake Tahoe (where gambling was almost amateur and loosely-run compared to Las Vegas) were called "drifters," and didn't easily find work. That, of course, was going to change in a hurry. Most of the work force in the newer places were those who had worked in the illegal spots in the east and had connections or relatives in the Mob. There was an undercurrent of resentment against the newcomers from the locals who had worked in the older casinos for years.

18. Indentured Servitude

In the mid 1960s, dealer schools began to pop up all over town. The government was subsidizing people for jobs training, the money going directly to the schools. Everywhere there was a storefront in a Strip mall there was a dealer school. Most of the instructors couldn't deal themselves, and the quality of the people coming out of the schools was dismal. Most couldn't find work, and they kept coming out of the schools like a conveyor belt. A few of the schools were owned by the proprietors of a couple of downtown casinos and offered "job placement." They would take anyone who could walk and chew gum at the same time, and "place" them in their casinos.

In order to be employed, they had to sign a contract saying they would stay at the casino for one year, at shill's wages, $8 a day, and forego benefits for the first year. This was tantamount to indentured servitude.

There was a waitress in the steak house at the Frontier, whose husband was "placed" in the Las Vegas Club, and signed the contract. They were both from Germany and had two children. He worked two jobs, one as a busboy, and went to the dealer school. After 10 months in that downtown casino, he was offered a job at a Strip casino. Of course, he took the job as it meant a huge raise for him and benefits down the road. He gave notice and took the new job. After a week he was served papers to the effect that he broke a legal contract, and he had to go back to the Las Vegas Club and finish his sentence. The club owners were wealthy men. They had no end of people waiting to sign, yet they wanted to make an example of this man.

It left a bad taste in everybody's mouth. I don't recall whether he was able to return to the Strip job. The same people approached me years later and told me they could save me a lot of money. They would supply me with dealers, and just before their benefits were to kick in, I could terminate them, and they would send me a bunch more. I told them that I found the practice despicable, and I offered a raise to my dealers every year, as long as they were with me. They thought I was crazy. They didn't have to support a family or stand behind a table for a living.

19. A.K.A.

Working in the casinos in those days, one had to get used to working with people who were known strictly by their nicknames. There were many I knew for years without ever knowing their real names. For example, "Shortnose" Elsner, "Big Nose," "Maische," "Pearshape," "Tomato Face," (pronounced "Tomata Face"), "Santa Claus," "Sleepout Louie" Levinson, and "Kid Tarzan," or "Tarz." "Tarz" was six-four, 350 lbs., and not a muscle in his whole body. He got the name because he had a high voice and a lisp. "Three Craps a Loser" came out "Twee Cwaps a Wooza."

There were "Blow Me Down" Fatica, (he looked like Popeye), "Slick" Rosta, "Mushmouth" Unrot, "Hercules" or "Herk," "Bathhouse Sammy," "Muscles," "Beanie" Kirschbaum, "Potato Joe" Bednarz, "Peanuts" Danolfo, (The little kids called him "Penis"), "Tata" Bailus, "Harry the Turk," "Art the Greek," "George the Greek," "No-No" Siani, "Grasshopper" Thacker, "Water Bill," "Ice Pick Willie" Alderman, (who got the name by putting an ice pick in a person's ear then smashing it in with his fist), "Peterhead" West, "Suitcase" Murphy, "Eddie the Camel Rider," "Twinkletoes," "Scratch" DiFlorentis, "Hickey," "Tony the Ant," "Bananas," "Ying Yang," Irwin "Prune Face" Gordon, (also known as "Liverlips"), "Keno Slim," "Big Fritz," "Kewpie" Rich, (he looked just like a Kewpie doll), "Carney" Krausnik, "Shmeese" Solomon, "Socks," "Pitzy" Manheim, "Tut" Penny, "Money" Blank, (his wife referred to him as "Total"), "Eight Pounder," "Cocky" Powers, "Botts," "Jam Up," "Cans" Jones, a boss at the Desert Inn known as "Humpy." When asking for a loan, we would say, "Lend me $50, I'll pay you back when Humpy straightens up."

Bobby "The Hunch" Krauthammer (a dwarf, not a hunchback) was a sharp little guy with "connections" to the wise guys. Ying Yang's real name was Chuckie Nourse. He was in his mid-30s, with a shock of blond hair, Alfalfa style, and a ruddy complexion. He had an exuberant personality, always smiling and laughing, and he never shut up. Hence Ying Yang. Everybody referred to him as Yang.

As more and more Asians came to town it was amusing to watch the reaction of some of the Chinese when they heard him called

"Yang." They would study him with a perplexed look, and he knew they were staring at him and he would just smile. The dealers and floor men played a lot of golf, and they all had a roll of tape in their golf bags with Ying Yang written on it. They would make sure he saw it on the outside of the bag, as a threat to tape his mouth shut. It didn't help. He was diagnosed with cancer in 1969, went outside with his two dogs, leaned up against his tool shed and blew his head off with a shotgun.

"Shmeese" Solomon was an ex-featherweight boxer from Cleveland. He wasn't very good, and as a result, soaked up a lot of leather. He would tell people that he quit boxing because he was having trouble with his hands. When they would ask what was wrong with his hands, he would reply, "The referees kept stepping on them."

They taught him how to deal Blackjack, and, put him to work at the Desert Inn. If he had any players on his game you needed three pit bosses to watch him. Finally, one day he was standing on an empty table, and a customer sat down. Shmeese shuffled the cards, and dealt out six hands, five of which were to empty seats. That was it. He had two choices, get in shape and make a comeback, or retire. They got him a job dealing in some small joint out in the sticks one day a week. On his day off he would go in and write down his schedule so he wouldn't forget.

Irwin "Pruneface" Gordon took a fall for some Mobster and did time in prison. He was rewarded with a job at the Dunes Hotel, as the Baccarat Manager. Irwin was a real creep, he was one of those guys you're referring to when you say "You can take the man out of the prison, but you can't take the prison out of the man." They say his face got those lines from Bubba pushing it into a pillow.

One slow night in the Sands Baccarat, I was sitting on a stool, when "Scratch" DiFlorentis walked into the pit, came over to me, opened his shirt and stuck his big fat stomach an inch from my nose, and said "look what she did to me." He looked like he had four belly buttons. Seems he and his wife had a little spat, and she shot him 3 times in the stomach. He survived, and they kissed and made up. I figure the bullets couldn't penetrate the pasta.

20. Superstitions and Eccentricities

Almost all gamblers are superstitious. Some wear certain clothes or jewelry such as a lucky ring, a lucky hat, a religious amulet or even certain underwear (or lack thereof).

The Chinese used to bring a cricket in a small wooden box or cage and set it tight on the table. No one took exception to this unless, of course, they started to win. Then it was "Sir, we don't allow insects or animals in our casino." The cricket was banished to a purse or a dark pocket.

If someone brought a rabbit's foot to the table (which was permissible) and started a lucky streak some of the pit bosses would squirm like they had poison ivy. Of course, every hex had a counter hex and most of the Pit bosses in the hotels were armed to the teeth. They had paraphernalia from the deep Amazon rain forests, Indian medicine men and shamans. A good deal of these bosses were what we called "actors." If the casino was losing, or a customer got lucky and the big boss was around, they would go into contortions and grimaces worthy of the silver screen.

Those who really couldn't stand a winner were called "bleeders." They would curse, throw pencils. In one case, a pit boss at the Flamingo, by the name of Gans, kicked a wastebasket so hard it took off like a rocket, and hit a pit boss in the dice pit. Furthermore, there were those that took their black magic to another level and would stop at nothing short of human sacrifice to assure that no customer would ever win a bet. Remember that these gentlemen were used to working in places where the customer never left with any money, by design. Consequently, the sight of players with chips in their possession was a real trauma.

21. Dempsey Foster

Dempsey Foster took superstition to a new level. Dempsey worked in the Blackjack pit at the Flamingo hotel in the '50s and '60s. His defense against the Gods of Fortune was a little subtler. He was a fatherly looking figure, dapper, with white hair and a sharp nose. He had a low shoulder and was always pulling his suit jacket up to where he felt it should be. He had a way of looking up instead of directly at you and was very friendly to the customers, who never suspected his ulterior motives.

Dempsey would walk into the pit at exactly 15 minutes to 7, when his shift actually started. He would put his newspaper in the drawer, and then go to the Roulette wheel. If there was no game he would take the ball and put it in the number 21, which was red. If a game was in progress he would wait until the ball fell, then when the dealer had paid the bets and was ready to spin again he would reach in and place the ball in 21.

Next, he would go to the desk in the middle of the pit and take out all the matches, find the porter and have him replace them with new cartons. Having done away with the unlucky matches, he would proceed to each Blackjack table and turn all the half dollars with the heads facing to the front. When this ritual was completed, he'd head back to the Roulette and wait for the new dealer to come into the pit. Back in those days the Roulette dealers considered themselves specialists, and the old timers had their personal Roulette balls, made out of ivory (eventually replaced by plastics as the old veterans faded into the desert sunset). The ivory balls were kept in small jars of Vaseline which were opened at the wheel, the balls wiped off and put into play. The outgoing dealer would take his balls with him. Dempsey would take a sealed envelope out of his pocket, open it and ceremoniously remove a red handkerchief and give the balls another cleaning.

Only at that point was he ready to go to work.

Dempsey had a horse. The horse lived in Reno and Dempsey in Las Vegas. He carried a picture of the horse and would show it to customers, employees or anyone who feigned interest. He would explain, "I haven't seen the horse in twelve years, but I send a check for $40 every month for his board, (a tidy sum in those days). Every year the people send me a picture so I can see how he's doing. Forty dollars a month for 12 years is nearly $6000." You could buy a horse for $100. I'm sure the picture cost nothing.

It was customary when a dealer left a game for a break to say "good luck" to the player; standard practice in all the casinos. On one disastrous night for the house, Dempsey couldn't take it anymore. He took a few of us aside and said "You shouldn't be wishing these players good luck. They're the enemy and we are in the hands of the enemy. It's me you should be wishing good luck."

After the word got around whenever we would get off the table we would look directly at him and say "good luck" none too softly. The players would get quizzical looks on their faces but we persisted until one day Chester Simms, the casino manager, happened by and witnessed it. Chester was a scary guy with a booming, deep voice you could hear throughout the whole building. (Harry James, the bandleader married to Betty Grable called Chester the "great white father"). We of course told him that we were merely doing what we were told to do. Chester took Dempsey aside and murmured, (a murmur you could hear downtown), "What the fuck are you trying to do? Do you want to try to get your old job back?" After that incident, Dempsey referred to the dealers as "disruptive elements."

But the best was yet to come. Along with the horse, he owned a canary named "Baby Butch" and, according to Dempsey, this bird was able to do things that normal canaries couldn't do.

Baby Butch responded to his name and when Dempsey and his wife would have a little spat they would communicate by writing notes to the canary. For example, "Baby Butch, tell Helen I have to work on my day off this week". The note would then be placed in the cage. Upon seeing the note his wife would respond in the same fashion Dempsey swore that when his wife would go to the cage, the bird would "turn his ass to her."

One night I walked in the front door to go to work. In those days there was no time clock, and you could park wherever you pleased. I looked into the Blackjack pit and saw Dempsey standing there with the biggest and blackest pair of wraparound goggles I've ever seen.

They covered half his face. Trying to be nice, I asked if he had an eye infection and his only reply was a brief shake of the head and "It's too terrible to mention."

It didn't take long to find out that Helen had left the cage open and Baby Butch made a break for it out the front door. After an afternoon of frantic searching, Dempsey had to come to work; hence the dark glasses to mask his grief. The next day he ran an ad offering a $500 reward to anyone finding a canary that answered to "Baby Butch."

Well, at that time you could buy a canary at Woolworth's five and dime for a dollar, and they even gave you a cardboard cage to take it home. Friday night, Labor Day weekend, I came to work and as I drove in I noticed two people standing outside the front door of the casino with bird cages in their hands. It seems they were at the end of a long line of individuals, each with a birdcage containing a canary. Dempsey's wife had directed the respondents to the ad to the Flamingo Hotel Blackjack pit. Let's face it, $500 was an awful lot of money in 1959, and for a buck you had a chance to claim it. It was the best gamble in town at the time. Chester Simms walked into the casino and saw what looked like an extra- terrestrial standing at the end of the pit talking to a canary in a cage, with a whole line of hopefuls waiting their turn. Chester was "Black Irish" with a dark countenance, a shock of white hair and black horned rim glasses. At that moment he went pale.

Remember, these casinos were small by today's standards. The Flamingo had seven Blackjack tables, two Roulette wheels and five crap tables, so this line took up a lot of room. With a roar he sent security to march the hopefuls out the front door along with Dempsey and instructions not to come back in until his tragedy was resolved, giving him 24 hours to accomplish it.

Some of the dealers, loud enough for Dempsey to hear, threatened to take a shotgun into his neighborhood and ice the bird.

Finally, the circus died down. Baby Butch never surfaced, nobody got the reward, Woolworths reordered a load of canaries thinking there was a new fad and, surprisingly, Dempsey didn't lose his job. There were those that lost theirs for a lot less.

Dempsey used to cringe when the players would innocently bend the cards. The casinos used standard "Bee" cards in those days and you could buy them in any gaming supply. They were changed quite often on the tables. He would complain that the players treat the cards as if they are made out of aluminum. Hence, if the player in the 5th seat would bend the cards while picking them up Dempsey would dart in out of nowhere and whisper in a dealer's ear, "aluminum on five," then dart back out. This was the cue for the dealer to make a production out of straightening the cards.

My good friend and co-worker Jim Hysell bought a boat from Dempsey, a 14-footer with a 25-HP outboard engine. You had to put the engine on for each use, and it steered from the back. Dempsey swore he never used the boat, but he'd had it customized. He had a couple of guys put the boat on sawhorses upside down and paint the bottom black and light orange like a checkerboard. His rationale was that it would "confuse the fish."

One morning after work at 4AM we hitched the boat to Jim's car and headed to Lake Mead for a few hours fishing; the maiden voyage, so to speak. We got to the lake at daybreak, hung the motor on the back and left the dock. When we got outside the harbor, Jim said to me "hang on, I'm going to open it up and it should really fly." I was sitting in front facing forward when he hit the throttle. The boat leaped forward and instantly I saw Lake Mead coming at my face. The water almost came over the bow into the boat. We stopped and tried again. Same thing. Every time the boat got over a few miles an hour the bow would head straight down, like a submarine going into a crash dive. Came to find out that the boat had a "hook" or a "bow" in the bottom and that's just the way it was.

Dempsey refused to give Jim his money back saying we must have done something to cause it. He had loaned us a couple of life jackets, (we had to promise not to get them wet), and we refused to return them to him. This was a feud that simmered for years. Dempsey never got his lifejackets, and Jim had a boat that raced across the water at seven miles per hour.

Jim was one of the dealers who threatened to whack Baby Butch.

22. The Deer Brothers

There were two brothers who were pit bosses at the Thunderbird Hotel in the late '50s and '60s. Both were highly capable and well respected by their peers. The oldest was Bill, a bit on the superstitious side. He was a tall distinguished-looking man with graying hair and a slim build; additionally, he possessed the means to stop losing streaks in their tracks. For example, when the dice were passing, (meaning the patrons were winning and the shooter had held the dice for a long time), the house was in desperate need of the dice to fall on a seven, thus the winning roll would be over. In this situation he would casually walk to the end of the table in the direction that the dice were being thrown and stand there with his arms folded against his chest. He would then surreptitiously slide his thumb under his glasses and place it on the lower lid of his right eye. As the dice tumbled down the table toward him, he would pull down his eyelid exposing the whole white of the eye, red veins and all, affixed at the dice. This was known as the "evil eye." It was supposed to have stopped many a "hand", (parlance for a long roll). When the employees knew it was imminent they would try to stop and watch. That bulging eyeball was quite a sight.

However, if that failed to stem the tide, he had an ace in the hole, used only in the most extreme circumstances. In his jacket pocket was an old Indian arrowhead. When it was needed he would slip it into his palm and again assume the arms folded position at the end of the table. When the dice were approaching he would whip his arm down and point the arrowhead at the dice, his arm shaking and rigid. In the commotion and noise no one noticed it, with the exception of the workers nearby. It got many a laugh.

There were other ways to stop losing streaks more familiar to those in the business. You could walk through any casino in town and on every podium, in every pit, you would see a salt shaker. When things were going bad for the house a boss would walk in a circle around the pit and shake a trail of salt as he went, covering the whole area. Some came to work with a pocket full of pennies and when games were losing, they'd take a walk outside the pit and throw pennies under the losing tables. You could always tell if they had a bad night when they started vacuuming in the early mornings on the graveyard shift. It would sound like machine gun fire when the sweepers sucked up those pennies.

23. Cape Canaveral in Miniature

The more vindictive pit bosses had a flair for the spectacular. They would take the offending dice and place the whole set in an ashtray on the desk. There are five dice in each set. They would light a match and set the unlucky cubes ablaze. The results were spectacular. A hissing noise would follow and a thin streak of flame resembling a laser. would shoot up in excess of 25 feet. Dice are extremely flammable and the show lasted just a few seconds, however the after effects lingered for quite some time. The area would fill with noxious fumes which burned your nose, eyes and if you breathed any it would cause extreme pain in the throat. One would think that they would either evacuate the area or the customers would leave on their own. However, if the replacement dice continued to go against the house, you could pump mustard gas into the casino and nobody would budge. They would stand there with handkerchiefs or a wet cocktail napkin over their face and continue to play.

24. The Flood

This brings to mind an incident I witnessed at the Showboat Hotel and casino. It had the largest bowling alley in town with 36 lanes, and along with a bingo parlor, made it a popular place for locals. One afternoon the valley got hit by huge thunderstorms, and a wall of water rolled down Fremont street and began to swirl around in the Showboat parking lot. The casino was on street level, (5 steps down from the bowling alley and bingo hall), and the water started coming in the door. As the water level started to increase, Security announced over the intercom that the casino would be closing temporarily. The table games stopped in a matter of minutes, the slots were another story. Unwilling to give up their favorite machines most of the local matrons climbed onto stools and kept right on pulling the handles. This was dangerous because there was a serious risk of severe electrical shock, or worse. When the water reached a depth of about a foot, the ladies completely ignored the warning, nonchalantly puffing on their cigarettes and kept playing. I can recall standing on the upper steps leading to the casino floor and watching security guards lifting women out of the stools and taking them to the upper level. Those that protested and were not too overweight, were taken out still sitting on the stools. The fat ones had to wade through the water to the steps. Some protested long and loud knowing they would get a complimentary lunch or dinner out of it to quiet them down.

25. A Match Made in Heaven

It's a proven fact that people engrossed in games of chance are impervious to everything going on around them. They have no conception of time, and the only thing that would move them is a fire, and then they would have to see it themselves.

The Fremont Hotel card room featured a game called Pangingi, or Pan. Quite a few local women fell victim to this disease and it wasn't unusual to see irate husbands storming in during the early morning hours and dragging their wives out. Bodily. At the Flamingo hotel in 1959 a wedding party checked into the hotel. The bride, still in her wedding gown, with the groom, came into the casino and sat at a Blackjack table. The bride (young and pretty) had never played and had to be shown what to do. After a few minutes the groom went to make sure the bags were taken to their room, and the bride kept playing. She was totally mesmerized. The free champagne exacerbated the situation. She sat for hours betting $1 a pop and her new husband couldn't even get her to go to dinner. Three times during the night he tried to get her to come to bed and they began to argue.

Finally, at about 3AM (she was one of about three players in the whole place) he came out and physically dragged her off of the stool, which fell with a crash. They screamed at each other and security had to get between them to keep it from becoming violent. Her father came to assist and they finally got her to the room. They were not there the next night. Nobody asked about it because it wasn't an unusual event. I wonder how long the marriage lasted.

26. Is There a Doctor in the House?

On a busy Saturday night at the Tropicana Hotel a man at the Craps table collapsed. He lay prostrate on the floor and a call went out for a doctor. As it happened there was a doctor and his wife sitting at a Blackjack table not 15 feet away. (this was in 1965 and the casinos were still quite small).

The doctor leaped up from the table, identified himself as a doctor, and began CPR with chest compressions. Meanwhile the dice kept moving, the Blackjack dealer kept the game going, people walked around the man and the doctor and it was business as usual.

Outside of an occasional tsk-tsk, or "How awful!" nobody paid any attention at all. When the doctor got down on the floor he called to his wife and told her to play his hand for him. For the next several minutes she would call out to him, for example, "you have fifteen and the dealer has a face card showing" he would yell back, "Hit it." or whatever his decision was, and never missed a compression, he was totally focused on what he was doing. When security arrived with oxygen and an ambulance was called the doctor put his coat back on and got back on the Blackjack stool. When they wheeled the man out, I don't think anyone even took notice. I never heard anyone ask about his condition. This also was not unusual.

When people are engrossed in gambling nothing else matters. That's why it's been noted in many cases gambling is a form of therapy. When you're engrossed in it you don't think of your pain or your problems, no matter how serious. You escape for however long your money holds out.

27. Denizens of the Alley

Downtown Las Vegas was a series of gambling clubs that encompassed two blocks of Fremont Street. There were very few hotel rooms. The Horseshoe Club was actually located in the Apache Hotel which boasted a few rooms and was a little on the seedy side. The Fremont was the first real hotel casino in the downtown area boasting a full-service casino and somewhat comfortable accommodations. There were 447 rooms and suites. In the rear was an alley for deliveries and garbage pickup, etc. It was also connected to a few narrow side alleys.

There was a transient population that took up residence in this particular area. They lived in cardboard boxes, portable tents, even slept under the dumpsters. They were a motley, unwashed bunch who stayed drunk, downing whatever they could get their hands on and causing trouble and embarrassment to the club owners. On busy nights, when they weren't easily spotted, they would filter into the casinos where they would look for chips on the floor, cigarette butts, try to mooch a meal or the money for one which they would immediately use for cheap wine. Some even would snatch chips, usually from a dice table. If detected, they'd run out the back door.

One poor fellow, not "playing with a full deck," would sometimes run into the Horseshoe, jump up on a chair and start reading from the Bible, reminding all the sinners where they were headed in the hereafter. As soon as these miscreants were spotted, they would be grabbed by security and, none to gently, hustled out the back door. The security guards always made sure they left with a souvenir of their Las Vegas casino experience, i.e., a fat lip, a black eye, loose teeth or broken bones. But it was their way of survival so they persisted in spite of the repercussions.

28. The Promotion

In the early sixties the Fremont Hotel ran a promotion, a drawing for a brand-new Cadillac. According to Nevada law everyone who came in was entitled to one ticket, whether they gambled or not. Of course, if you gambled on the tables or the slots, you earned extra tickets which were deposited in a huge bin by the side entrance. There were always tickets on the floor or the sidewalk that were inadvertently dropped by people who were drunk, recently lost their money, or plain didn't think they had a chance. The Nevada Gaming Control Board kept a hard eye on these promotions to make sure they were being handled properly, gamblers being suspicious by nature.

Came the night of the big drawing and in front of a crowd, the winning ticket was drawn, you did not have to be present to win. Nobody claimed the prize so the winning number was posted in the lobby and also the newspaper. Two days later the winning ticket showed up . . . in the grubby hands of one of the alley denizens.

Now this was a real dilemma for management. Here was a guy with no money, no driver's license, no address, no nothing but the winning ticket. Of course, he took the cash alternative which was, I believe, $10,000. They *had* to pay him, which raised the concerns over what he would do with the money. After a somber meeting the bosses decided to put him in a hotel suite, with complimentary room service, which would at least keep the money in the hotel and perhaps get him drunk enough to come down and lose some of it back.

Once ensconced in the lap of luxury, he then invited all his fellow vagrants to join him in celebrating his good fortune. The wine and spirits flowed freely for several days. Word had it that none of the guests took advantage of the bathing facilities and the lobby was rife with the great unwashed, stumbling in and out and making a public spectacle. Finally, it got to the point where the bosses realized that the food and beverage cost was going to exceed the amount of the prize money (if he still had it) should the situation persist much longer. He had refused to put the cash in safekeeping in the cashier's cage. They told him that unless he started gambling they were going to put him out of the suite and send him on his merry way, money or no. At this, he got highly insulted, took the rest of the money (supposedly about $6000) went across the street to the Horseshoe Club and over the next 12 hours lost every penny of it. When the Horseshoe bosses were sure that he had no more money on his person, they unceremoniously dumped him back where he originally came from. There was revelry for days behind the clubs.

Remember that, to these guys Manischewitz was like Dom Perignon, and the money he gave to the bathless bunch bought a lot of alcohol. Everyone in town had a great laugh over it (especially the Binions who owned the Horseshoe). I don’t recall whether the Fremont ever had another promotion.

29. A Minor Mix-up

The Flamingo Hotel had white $100 chips. They were so old they were warped and worn smooth. They were called “hot stamp” chips, meaning the denomination was stamped into the face of the chip instead of a round colored insert in the center. They were cheap to make and as far as I know they were the only hot stamp $100 chips in town. On busy nights with heavy action they would bring out a rack of these chips ($10,000,) and put them on the “apron” of the Roulette wheel. That way, if a game needed chips in a hurry they would merely move the chips to the game.

There was very loose oversight in those days. The practice ended a few years later. One busy night the white $100 chips were stacked on the apron and, during the course of the hot, hectic evening, with mountains of ten-cent chips being played, the chips got mixed in with the $100 white chips that were practically identical. All the Roulette chips, lacking a designation, were then ten cents unless otherwise indicated by a marker button on the rim of the wheel.

This resulted in a 20-cent wager possibly being paid $7000 instead of $7. Even with 2 or three $100 chips mixed in a stack of 10 cent chips a huge overpay was certain. You could cash out a small amount of $100 at the cashier’s cage without any verification.

Finally, a dealer realized the error and pandemonium ensued. They stopped the game and went through the players’ chips and all the unused white wheel chips. When the smoke cleared there were four $100 chips missing. I suppose the player noticed the discrepancy in the chips and stuck them in his pocket.

30. Everyone Knows the Game Is Crooked But, It's the only Game in Town

As long as there are casinos there will always be gamblers who spend all their waking hours figuring ways to cheat them. Back in the '50s and '60s it was a constant threat, especially on the table games. The slots weren't a prime target because the jackpots were minuscule compared to today. The machines were thought of as a diversion for women whose husbands were busy on the Craps and Blackjack tables.

That brings up the question, Did the casinos cheat? The answer is yes and no. Some, but not all were cheating, but the chances of an average individual being cheated was slim.

To begin with, consider how the game of Blackjack was dealt at the time. There was one deck, no discard rack. Used cards were placed face up on the bottom of the deck, in sequence so the hands could be backed up in case of a dispute. When the dealer had a face card or an ace showing he would look underneath the card to see if he had an ace, or a ten if the up card was an ace. There was a proper way to do this to prevent someone from seeing your hole card. Knowing the hole card really wasn't a huge advantage; it could help a little, but not enough to swing the odds to your favor. It was easy for a dealer to "tip" his hole card with hand movements or eye signals, etc.

Most of the casinos that were cheating, (or "busting out" as it was referred to), did so on rare occasion when it looked like the house might book a big loss. In a play that lasted for hours they may cheat once or twice in key situations, a big double down or split for example. There were however, some that went after everybody. In the end as state Gaming Control began asserting themselves and regulating the industry, this practice is what brought them down. Some of the larger places that were closed were the Silver Slipper and the Royal Nevada. Other places knowing that closing was imminent, fell victim to fires of suspicious origin. Among these was the oldest hotel on the Strip, the El Rancho Vegas and the fairly new Desert Spa. There were a few major casinos that struck deals with

Gaming Control in order to keep their licenses. Had it been publicized that these famous places were caught cheating, Las Vegas may not have risen to the heights it was to achieve in the future.

Bear in mind there were no Video cameras or high-tech devices in those days, so any evidence to be recorded was on 8- or 16-millimeter film with a movie camera. This was a huge problem, as it was difficult to do secretly. Most of the evidence was presented by Gaming Control agents who were under cover, playing on the tables, or standing nearby. In the early days of Gaming Control quite a few of the agents were people caught trying to cheat the casinos and were facing jail time. They were given the option to work for the state or go to jail. The premise was that it takes a thief to catch a thief and many of these people were happy to come on board, aware the option could expire, at which point they would be off to the can, never to be allowed in a casino again.

They were pretty effective, too.

31. Swept Under the Rug

Publicity on casino closings was limited. Very little detail was made public, but something had to happen to arouse the state's suspicion. The case of the Royal Nevada closing is a good example of foolish greed. The property on which the hotel sat was owned by local businessman Frank Fishman, who also owned a motel next door to the Dunes Hotel. Frank was in his sixties at the time and was a degenerate Blackjack player, out drinking and gambling almost every night with his present sweetie. His latest was a cocktail waitress from Chicago named Eve Savoy. He even named his motel near the Dunes the Savoy Motel. It was said that Eve "would steal a red-hot stove if she could hold on to it long enough." There were no red-hot stoves available, but she did hold onto Frank long enough to make a lot of money, mostly on the Blackjack tables, of course without his knowledge.

The Royal Nevada was reputedly paying Frank Fishman $25,000 monthly for rent on the property and was cheating him out of it every month, so they were operating rent free. However, that wasn't enough for this particular group; they didn't discriminate when it came to who they cheated.

One night a grizzled, old Blackjack dealer, who everyone knew as "Taffy," got off work and had a little too much to drink. He wandered into the Royal Nevada with his dealer's apron in his back pocket, his paycheck and tips for the night in another. Taffy sat down to play Blackjack and promptly lost it all. Through the haze, he finally realized they were cheating him and he raised holy hell. Taffy was an old war horse and had done a bit of cheating himself so he knew what he saw. They called security and removed him from the casino, which added insult to injury.

Taffy returned an hour later with what was described as a "horse pistol" and started shooting. After destroying the bar mirrors and a few chandeliers, he went looking for the people who cheated him, who, by now, were all on the floor under the tables. The Sheriff's department quickly arrived on the scene, Taffy was out of ammunition so he went quietly. The ensuing newspaper article reported that early in the morning the casino was practically empty so there were no injuries. Nothing ever happened to Taffy, but it was this incident that aroused state suspicions and led to the eventual closing of the Royal Nevada.

As for Frank Fishman, when he was losing he'd get nasty and call the dealers names under his breath. Once in a while he would slip and his voice would get louder than he intended. If you were dealing to him and he muttered under his breath, for example, "asshole," due to his accent it sounded like "hesshole." The dealer would pretend to take it personally, lean across the table and say "What did you call me?" Frank would then apologize and put a $25 chip in the dealer's shirt pocket. This really helped with the tips.

One night at the Dunes Hotel a dealer by the name of Leo Chapian was dealing to him. Frank lost a big hand and called Leo "cocksucker." Leo leaned across the table feigning anger and asked "What did you call me?" Frank was drunk and sheepishly mumbled an apology while reaching out with a $25 chip. Leo leaned back, looked at the chip in Frank's hand and said "Uh-uh, Frank, cocksucker is $50." Frank gave him another chip.

32. Not So Complimentary Laydown

In those earlier days when a new casino opened, most often on the Strip, it was customary for the owners and bosses of some of the established casinos to go in on opening night and make a "complimentary laydown" (meaning to gamble in the new casino purportedly to get them off to a good start). However, should they win, and those guys gambled high, it could result in a bad start.

That was the case with the Silver Slipper. It had been closed and was opening with new owners. That opening night, Bob Rice, Davey "Butch" Goldstein, Major Riddle, and a few other bosses from the Dunes went into "The Slipper" and started shooting Craps. Frankly, these guys didn't need opening night as an excuse to gamble, they played all over town. Bob Rice picked up the dice and proceeded to "shoot the lights out," by making a lot of passes.

When the smoke cleared they had won a substantial amount of money, said to be around $80,000. On their way to cash out they were met by the casino manager and one of the new owners, who asked them if they would take markers (I.O.U.s) for the money until the next day. Their reasoning was that if they parted with that amount of cash it would leave them woefully short of the minimum bankroll required by the state. At the time it was seven times the table limit, per table. If someone else were to win big they wouldn't be able to pay. The guys agreed, The Slipper was able to raise the money, everybody was happy. Naturally the men had to go back to The Slipper to collect their money and predictably they managed to lose some of it back. Not enough however to relieve the financial pressure on the casino.

To tighten their regulation, the Gaming Control Board had begun the practice of going into the casinos on a random basis, confiscating cards and dice from the tables, while games were in progress. The cards and dice would be put in envelopes, signed and sealed by the casino supervisor, then inspected at a later date at gaming headquarters. The cards didn't really mean a lot. Gaming Control could let the casino know if someone was marking them, but the dice had to be perfectly square to a tolerance of 1/10,000th of an inch. Before new dice are introduced into the casino, they are put on a micrometer to make sure they're within tolerance.

On a routine visit, Gaming Control marched into The Slipper about two months after the opening and took the dice, along with a few decks of cards, off the tables. It took them several days to get around to it, but when they inspected the dice, they were found to be "shaved," or purposely altered in tolerance, to give the house a much larger advantage. The word on the street was, one of the new owners of The Slipper had been involved in the close down of the Royal Nevada for cheating, and they had that loss on opening day. Because of that Gaming Control was especially watchful in their case, knowing that they were operating on a shoestring. This resulted in the Silver Slipper being closed down by state gaming authorities. These closings were given very little publicity, just a short mention in the local newspapers, as it could be damaging to the town's image. The man involved in both closings, a Southern gambler named TW Richardson, was subsequently turned down for any future licensing in Nevada. Years later he was to apply for licensing at Bourbon Street, an off-Strip casino down Flamingo Road from the Barbary Coast and was turned down for the last time.

33. Psst!

A casino manager and an owner's worst nightmare is to have someone win a substantial amount of money in his casino, cash out and head to another casino, usually for dinner or a show. Most of the time if the amount was large, the customer would deposit the money in the cashier's cage and be given a deposit slip for the amount. This eliminated the robbery factor and if the slip was lost or stolen, it was worthless. It could only be redeemed by the person to whom it had been issued. However, if a winner presented the slip at another casino, and it was then verified that he didn't owe any of it at the issuing casino, he could get full credit for the amount of the slip, same as cash. If the player lost the whole thing they would send someone down to collect, always in cash, and bring it back to their casino.

This, of course, worked both ways, it usually evened out. If one of your customers took his winnings to another casino, somewhere along the line someone would win in a competitor's place and bring the money to yours. That didn't make it any easier to see the money go out the door. The Blackjack limit on the Strip, except to a few special players, was $200. Then the word got out that the Sands was dealing a $500 limit to anyone. This caused quite a stir on the Strip and had all the other operators contemplating following suit. In a casino, the higher your limit, the greater your liability, and everyone strove to keep the limits as low as possible. While discussion on the limits were taking place, rumors began to filter down that the Sands raised their limit because they were cheating and therefore had no increased liability to speak of. The Las Vegas Strip at that time was the rumor capitol of the world. They spread like wildfire from one place to the next on a nightly basis, so those things were taken with a grain of salt. However, where there's smoke there's usually fire.

Now, that led to a whole different situation. Let's say that you're a casino boss, one of your customers wins a substantial amount of money, puts it in his pocket, and tells you he's going to the Sands to see the show. You *know* that if he gambles there, (and he will), there's little chance he'll win and bring it back to your casino. In those cases, the casino boss would call the customer aside and whisper in his ear. You didn't know exactly what he was saying, but you can bet it was something like "Listen, I wouldn't gamble up there if I were you, etc., etc."

These things caught the attention of Gaming Control, and several months down the road the Sands became the first casino on the Strip to deal Blackjack out of four deck chutes (or "shoes," as they're commonly called). The official reason for this never came to light, but the word on the street was (and it's logical) that was the only way they could keep their license. This pretty much leveled the playing field, and all the other casinos raised their limit to $500 to everyone.

34. A Business Within a Business

There was an enterprising manager on the graveyard shift at the Sands who thought it would be good to go into business for himself. His name was Roy. His shtick was that when a real big player would gamble on his shift he had a mechanic make sure the guy would lose, and then when it was over, they had an agent come in and they would pass off a percentage of what the high roller lost to the agent. For example, if the big player lost $20,000 they would make sure the agent left with say, $5000. It was then split between the shift manager, the floor man and probably 10% each for the mechanic and the agent. This would accomplish two things. One, the casino was still a big winner and their percentage remained high and two, the culprits were able to steal a nice piece of change.

The mechanic was a man by the name of Frank Zemo, who later became the Faro boss at the Stardust. Frank was a handsome man with solid white hair, and a face like a movie star. He was also a classy man whom everybody liked. But most didn't know his aptitude with a deck of cards.

One night, my cousin and I went downtown to see a movie, and instead of the movie we went next door to the Fremont Hotel and gambled with our movie money. We got lucky and won several thousand dollars. Now we were going to do some *real* gambling and headed for the Strip. We went into the Sands, and there was a big player on one of the Blackjack games, betting two hands at $500 a pop, which was the limit. The shift manager was right there, and the tension was palpable. With the low ceilings it seemed like the casino was dark, and this one table was in the spotlight. There was no "reserved" sign on the table so I walked over and bet $300. The dealer was Frank Zemo, and for a moment everything stopped, then out of the side of his mouth he softly said "Geddadahere!"

I started to protest when my cousin grabbed the money and my arm and pulled me away. He said to me "they're whacking this guy out, let's go somewhere else. The evening's results were that we got home at 8AM and had to ask the pit boss for a dollar for the parking attendant. It was shortly after that we'd heard the Sands owners had gotten wind of the situation and fired Roy and his floor man. Roy went off the radar for a while, and I heard that he resurfaced in Reno. Everyone in town was sure that he was out there with Russian Louis.

We couldn't understand how he didn't lose his life, seeing the Mob owned the Sands.

Some players were suspicious of being cheated, and there were those that believed that they were getting a square gamble. For the most part the latter was true. There was always the person that would sit at your game and stare at your hands, never taking their eyes off of the deck. We used to hold our hands at a tilt so the player couldn't see the top card and elevate our arms just to see how far someone's neck could stretch. For the most part the rules were pretty lax. If you were sure that nobody was trying to mark the cards you could lay your hand on the table and flip the cards off with one hand.

35. The Jungle Telegraph

A good example of spreading rumors can be found in a game we would play on a slow night. I would get on the phone and call say, the Riviera. (It could be any hotel) and have the operator page Harry Goodheart over the hotel page system. Harry was the casino manager at the Frontier. We would do this, two or three times over the course of an hour. Then one of us would call someone we knew at the Riviera and tell him that we heard a rumor that Harry was going to take over the Riviera. They would then reply "They've been paging him here all night, it must be true" Then we would sit back and see how long it took for the rumor to work its way up and down the Strip. Usually it took less than three hours before one of us would get a call from somebody at another hotel telling us that they heard we were losing our casino manager. He was going to take over the Riviera casino.

36. The Firemen

There were several ways a dealer could cheat at a Blackjack table, but very few dealers that were capable of doing this. Those dealers were hired for the rare occasion that their services would be needed. In a few cases they would be rewarded with a percentage of what they won for the house. I believe that the going rate was 10%, in cash. Most of the top mechanics, as they were referred to (the term "butchers" was used on occasion) came from Montana or Wyoming, and some from the illegal places in the East. Their methods were quite different.

The mechanics from up north were smooth and took great pride in their work. Quite a few got their experience on trains, dealing to the Chinese laborers who worked for the railroads and had just cashed their paychecks. There, a wrong move could cost you your life, the preferred method being a hatchet in the back of your head. They could then throw you off the train and, even if your body was found, nothing ever came of it. They spent thousands of hours practicing in front of a mirror to learn their trade, and even to the trained eye, it was practically impossible to see them deal a second card. The only way it could be detected was by a light swishing sound as the card came out. That kind of silence didn't exist in a casino, or a moving train for that matter.

The "mechanics" who came from the Eastern part of the country were, for the most part, just the opposite. They would laugh and joke with the players, and appear to be extremely clumsy, to the point they looked like amateurs. Some people even felt a little sorry for them as they were losing the money. After all cheating ceased they were considered substandard, and many lost their jobs. The other dealers had no sympathy for them as they resented the fact that these guys usually worked like everyone else yet received a share of the tips. However, there were many times they would send a high roller and generous tipper to bed early. If you depend on tips for a living, that's hard to watch. In the final analysis, the people who did this had ice water in their veins. The pressure in those situations was enormous, and to do these things when people were looking for it, took cast iron nerves.

37. How It Was Done

For a dealer to deal a second card, he would have to know the top card on the deck. This could be done two ways, one, the cards would have to be marked, which was risky as Gaming Control could take them off the game at any time. The second and most common way was to "peek" at the top card. With the deck in your hand, it was relatively easy and undetectable from the player's viewpoint. There was the "front" peek and the rear, or "hind" peek and they were used depending on the situation.

The next most common move was called "turning the deck." Since all the discards went face up on the bottom of the deck it was easy for the dealer to know what card was on the bottom. If the card was a small one, and the dealer had, say 15 or 16, he would turn the deck over in his hand, thus putting the bottom card on top. After the hand was over he would "break down the deck" (re-shuffle the cards). The way it was done could only be detected by someone who knew what to look for. That practice came to a halt when the Gaming Control Board insisted on discard racks on the tables. A colored plastic card was used to put on the bottom of the deck in place of the face up "burn" card.

There were other ways to improve the edge for the house. In the early '60s the Pioneer club was paid an unannounced visit by Gaming Control agents. They were dealing their games with two decks, (a double deck), and had a few tables with four-deck shoes. The gaming agents took a double deck and the cards out of one of the shoes, went to the Craps, took the dice off one of the games and left the premises after putting them in the required sealed and signed envelopes.

About a week later an article appeared in the local papers stating that there were four 10s or face cards missing from the double deck, and eight missing from the four-deck shoe confiscated by Gaming Control. This gives the house an enormous advantage, well over two times the normal percentage advantage that the house normally enjoyed. The club claimed that it must have been a defective shipment of cards (which was ridiculous; the cards are checked before being put into play). They got off with a citation and were warned that any other violations would cost them their license. No one knows how long they had been getting away with the practice.

38. The Undercut

Last (but hardly least) the "undercut" which was used mostly on the Craps. But if a player was drunk enough, or not the observant type, on rare occasion it could be used on the Blackjack table.

If you've ever gambled I'm sure you have seen the way most dealers pay the bets. They go out with chips in their hand and "size into" the winning bet, snap off the excess chips and go on to the next wager. This is called cutting checks, (checks being the accepted term for chips). There were some Craps dealers that in sizing into a stack of chips would slide into the bet a little high and push four chips off a 5-chip bet for example. The bottom chip would go to the bottom of the chips in the dealer's hand and he would then snap off the chips evenly. It was virtually non-detectable, with the end result that, say, instead of winding up with ten chips, you had eight. Then the player would look at the chips and you could see them wondering if they had bet four or five. There was never a complaint. If the dealer miscalculated and knocked the chips over, it was considered clumsiness, whereas the chips would be restacked and paid properly. This particular move could only be done with wagers of four to six or seven chips. Anything less would be too obvious, and anything more would be too difficult.

This eventually fell by the wayside with the rest of the underhanded practices used by some of the casinos.

39. Do Your Homework

When there were no players at a table the cards were spread face up on the layout. I recall walking into the Birdcage Casino (later to become The Mint, sold to the Horseshoe years later) when the place had just opened, a few of my co-workers and I went to take a look. It was late and they had very little business. I happened to look at the layout to see what their rules were regarding "soft" 17, which is any combination of cards with an ace that can be counted as seven or seventeen, the ace being one or eleven. Some casinos drew on it and some stood pat, and it was stated on the felt layout. I looked at the spread deck and saw that the cards were arranged as follows: 10-10-8-10-10-9-5-A-4-2-3-6-7, repeated four times in the same sequence. If a player were to sit down, the dealer could do a quick false shuffle, and offer the cards to the player to cut. No matter where the cards were cut, if the player played only one hand, he would not win one hand all the way through the deck.

You can try this at home, just don't rearrange the sequence. The game is tough enough without losing the first six or seven hands. There were three tables with that arrangement. We told everyone we knew about it and I'm sure that the practice came to a screeching halt as the word got around.

40. Cleaning Up a Dirty Business

As things began to change in Las Vegas, and more hotels and casinos began to open, the GCB (Gaming Control Board) took a more aggressive stance on enforcement, and although the old gambling bosses complained long and loud, the change was for the better. Gambling in Nevada is what is known as a "privileged Industry." To obtain a license to operate a casino, the scrutiny you are subjected to is mindboggling. They can go clear back to your origins, schools, and in some cases (as with Frank Sinatra and foreign applicants) they can send agents to any country in the world and dig into anything you've ever done or been involved in. This is all at *your* expense.

I've been through the licensing process, and the things they come up with are startling. If they deem you unsuitable you have no recourse. The industry has survived every legal challenge, including the United States Supreme Court, and gaming in Nevada remains to this day a privileged industry. The GCB is the investigative and enforcement agency and the Gaming Commission makes the final decision, taking the Control Board's recommendations into consideration. Incidences of the Commission overruling the Board's recommendations are extremely rare. It even controls the employees, especially in the gaming related areas. Everyone must have a work card, which can be revoked in the event of misconduct. In the case of executive casino employees, they can be called up for licensing as "key employees." The scrutiny is not as severe, but it's still at the casino's expense. If they're turned down, they can still work, but in a lesser capacity. This put the fear of God in the Mob-run casinos and they did everything they could do to avoid scrutiny. That made it tough on the known (and alleged) mechanics who were still working in the industry, albeit strictly on the up and up.

Take the case of one Maynard Hunter, a dealer I worked with at the Stardust for a short time. Maynard not only dealt Blackjack but was an accomplished Roulette dealer as well. He came from somewhere in Montana and worked in several spots around town. He was tall, blond, and had the loose demeanor of a cowboy without a horse. He was also the best Blackjack dealer I've ever seen, and

I've seen 'em all. He had long tapered fingers that were always impeccably manicured, and when he was working he was something to behold. To begin with he could deal a second card right under your nose, after letting you know he was going to do it, and you could not detect it. It was like special effects in a movie. The thing that really made it unusual was that he could do it with either hand!

To break the monotony, he would sometimes deal right-handed one hand and left-handed the next. A few pit bosses thought they were seeing things, and I can't remember one realizing what he was looking at. They "couldn't put their finger on it." Maynard left the Stardust for the Riviera, and worked there for several years, and then inexplicably was let go. He was one of the "alleged" mechanics and he could not find work anywhere in the State. The owners didn't want to have anyone with his abilities working for them, even though there was nothing underhanded going on. The last I heard was that he was selling insurance.

41. Turnabout Is Fair Play

Although it's difficult to find humor in cheating, a funny story can add levity to a shameful situation. For example, my roommate, whose name was Kenny, who was also a dealer, was always looking for a way to cheat at a Blackjack table. One day he told me there was an old dealer at the El Rancho Vegas who looked like it was an effort to stand up, let alone deal and stay alert.

Kenny sent his girlfriend and another woman in to "paint up the deck." That is, mark the cards with what they called "daub," a compound that, on a card, was difficult to detect unless you knew exactly what to look for. Then Kenny would sit down at the table after they left and try to win some money. The girls, both ring-wise hustlers, waited until the old guy got a new deck, and sat down at his table. They bet a buck or two at a time and engaged him in conversation to distract him. It didn't take long to mark every 10 or face card in the deck, at which time they quit, and Kenny sat down and bought in $100.

After playing for a while he was slightly ahead and made a large wager. He was dealt a 6 and a 5, totaling 11 and a good hand for a "double down" where he can double his bet and take one card, face down. If he gets a 10 or a face-card he has 21 and most likely a sure winner. Glancing at the top card on the deck, Kenny saw that it was a face card and he doubled down for almost everything he had. The dealer gave him his card face down and acted on his own hand. The dealer had 17 and when he turned Kenny's' card over it was a four. Kenny almost went into shock. Then the dealer lowered his hand so Kenny could see the top of the deck, and the face card was still there, right on top. Kenny looked up and the old guy just smiled at him.

He knew all along the cards were marked and just waited for his chance, which he got. The "poor old guy" dealt Kenny the second card and Kenny lost his money. Of course, Kenny couldn't accuse the dealer of cheating, so all he could do was get up and leave. This was a classic example of the screwer becoming the screwee.

42. Now the Dice

Cheating on the Craps table is pretty cut and dried. You can't have crooked dice in a game (unless a player puts them in, which is another story altogether) as Gaming Control could come in at any time and confiscate the dice. If they're crooked, they'll probably revoke your license and there goes a multi-million-dollar investment.

The answer is to insert them into the game for a roll or two, and then take them back out. This was usually done by the box-man, the man on the stool that supervises the game and puts the cash buy-ins into the drop box. Generally during a real hot roll when there's pass after pass being made, as the dealers are paying the bets the dice are in the center of the table, directly in front of the box man. Under the pretense of checking the dice, he'll pick them up, look at them, and put them back onto the table. Sometimes they're not the same dice he picked up. The move is sophisticated and, in the heat and excitement of a "hot roll," there's no way anyone could detect it. Even if seen on tape, you would have to watch it a hundred times to even begin to detect it. There were maybe one or two box-men in the whole casino who could do this, always from the illegal casinos in the East. It was a common practice in those places, but in Las Vegas it was done on rare occasion.

At the Flamingo hotel in 1958, a box-man by the name of "Patsy" Rose took the time to show me how he did it. These people had to like you a lot to do this. Getting any information out of these old timers was like pulling teeth. The dice would go in for one or two rolls, bring out a seven or whatever was needed, and then come right back out and into a pocket in their jacket.

Since they sat with their arms folded on the edge of the table, this was not a difficult thing to accomplish. They called their suit coats "Fast Five-Deuce jackets"

43. Wheel of Misfortune

Shady practices were not always condoned by the house. I'm sure you've seen the "Big Six" wheel, sometimes called the Wheel of Fortune. It's a large carnival type wheel covered with real bills of different denominations, or indicators showing the amount of the payoff, like 20 to 1, or 10 to 1, etc. There are commensurate spots on the layout where you can place your wagers. The dealer then spins the wheel and pays whoever bets correctly on where it will stop. Percentage wise it's the strongest game in the casino for the house. It took no talent to deal the game, was way less work than dealing the other games, and the person dealing it was usually "juiced" into the job by one of the owners or a big boss. They also received full salary and a share of the tips, which infuriated the other dealers because the game never made any tips to speak of.

Most of the "Big Six" dealers found that with a few practice spins they could keep the wheel from landing on the large payoffs if someone had a bet on them. They couldn't put it exactly where they wanted, but they could keep it reasonably far away from any large payouts.

This was the talent of "George the Greek" who dealt the Big Six wheel at the Dunes Hotel for years. George was a little guy in his late '50s, who supposedly had some "juice" with the guy who brought in the Detroit junkets. He had a constant scowl on his face, and on breaks would not sit with the other dealers, as he knew how much they resented his presence. The law required all casinos to do an independent audit, along with the in- house accounting, which in those days was highly suspect, to say the least. During one of these audits, it was noticed that the figures on the Big Six-wheel defied logic. They checked and double checked and still came up with the fact that the game had hardly any "fills" for the whole audit period, which was generally six months or a year. A fill is chips or tokens taken to a game when it runs short. All fills come from the cashier's cage and are carefully documented. During an average night it's almost impossible for any game to go without at least two or three fills, not only caused by winners, but from people buying in cash and walking away with chips. This discrepancy was noted in the audit, and of course Gaming Control was made aware of it.

Since the Dunes had a reputation for being Mob controlled (which it was), Gaming Control had undercover agents stake out the wheel on the swing shift just to see if there was something they should know about. It only took a day or so to find out. Seems like somebody bet $5 on the 40 to 1, which pays $200 if the wheel lands on the right slot. George spun the wheel, intending to keep it as far from the 40 to one as possible, but miscalculated, and the wheel was going a little too far as it started to slow down, so George stuck his shoulder against the rim of the wheel and let it rub until he got the desired effect. Gaming watched him do this a few times, got it on tape, and then promptly took George out in handcuffs.

Naturally, George lost his “juice” job, and there wasn’t a teary eye in the place. He’d been doing it for years. The results were much to the delight of the bosses but they really had no idea he was doing it. The game really was penny ante stuff for a major casino, and Nobody paid much attention. George felt that as long as he kept winning he would never lose his job.

44. The Other Side of the Coin

The casinos, on the other hand, were forever unearthing plots to cheat them. These could range from just plain embezzlement or out and out cheating on the tables. If someone came in and tried (or was successful) in cheating the house, it was said to be from the "outside." If a dealer was stealing chips or passing money to an accomplice, it was considered an "inside" situation. This included any collusion between employees, including those working with "agents" which was a term for someone working with the dealer, feigning to be a legitimate customer. If I were to go into every possible way that this was done, this chapter would never end.

45. Auld Lang Syne

New Year's Eve in Las Vegas was the busiest night of the year. The town, which had been almost deserted since Labor Day, filled up well beyond capacity starting a few days before the 31st. There were not that many hotels at that time and the Flamingo had the largest capacity with 500 rooms. That resulted in a dearth of available lodging, and every hotel and small motel were booked solid, including the few in Boulder City 30 miles away.

Bearing in mind that Las Vegas didn't get television until 1953, the newspapers and radio stations appealed to residents to rent out extra rooms, usually by a direct appeal from the mayor. Several days before the holiday "room for rent" signs started to appear in front of some of the homes in the area. As the holiday drew near, tents would start to go up on the courthouse lawn, and on the grassy mall in front of the Union Pacific depot at Main and Fremont Streets, now the location of the Plaza Hotel.

Some people slept in their cars, and some came up from California to party until their money ran out, and then turned around and drove home. There was no freeway, and the highway ran right through the center of such bustling metropolises as Baker, Barstow, Yermo, Victorville and a few other glittering examples of desert living. Each one of these towns had their own police force, as the California Highway Patrol seldom came out that far unless they were called. During the few days of the New Year holiday these departments probably made their budget for the whole year-they were notorious speed traps. That doesn't count the accidents caused by drivers who had been without sleep for two or three days were under the influence, and probably in a highly pissed-off state. Driving home broke and tired didn't do much for a person's frame of mind.

Walking into a casino was like walking into a wall of humanity. You literally had to force your way through the mass of bodies. The noise and smoke would be unacceptable by today's standards. The pit bosses were constantly trying to make room for players at the Craps tables and if you wanted to leave a Blackjack table it was hard to push the stool back far enough so you could get up. This was absolute chaos at its limits. Or a better word, pandemonium.

46. Crime and Punishment

This would describe the Desert Inn casino on New Year's Eve of 1952. At one of the Craps tables there was a hugely obese woman on one end who took up enough room for three people, and since there were only two $5 minimum games in the house, there were several players who wanted to get in but couldn't find a place. The $5 minimum was the high-end table, all the others were $1 and $2 minimums. Both of the $5 games were covered with $100 chips and the pit bosses were moving people aside to get spots for high rollers. They had trouble moving this woman, she was leaning on the rail of the game which caused her to expand even further. The bosses were considering trying to get her to leave, but that just wasn't done in those days.

Walter Lappo, a box-man on that particular game was trying to stuff money into a drop box that was already so full that the paddle used to put the money in the opening on top was sticking up out of the box, it wouldn't go down any further. Then he felt something bump his leg under the table. Sliding back on the stool and looking down he saw a midget under the table, lighting an acetylene torch, obviously to cut into the box, which was made of thin metal.

The torch sprang to life about the time the midget realized he was spotted, and he bolted when Walter started yelling for security, dropping the torch on the carpet, making a terrible smell. The midget shot out from under the table, and the fat lady, seeing this, grabbed her chips and started to fight her way through the crowd. Security, seeing them in a panic, grabbed them both, and hustled them into a room behind the cashier's cage.

The fat lady, knowing what happens to cheaters (especially at the Desert Inn) went to pieces and wet her pants. She stood there crying and sweating in the stuffy room and the midget just shook. Some of the bosses came into the room (my dad was one of them) and demanded to know what the story was. Seems that the midget came in under the fat lady's' dress and stayed there until she found a place at the Craps table (considering the parking situation, a long walk) and then just crawled under the table to cut into the box. The bosses were faced with deciding what to do with the two of them, and her condition, coupled with the close hot atmosphere of the room, made a quick decision imperative.

Finally, Ruby Kolod, the big boss, said, “Let me get this straight. You came in here under her skirt and planned to rob us?” They confessed, and since the casino was busy, and the house was having a good night, he said to the midget, “You’ve been punished enough. But you’ll have to walk out of here under her skirt, the same way you came in, and don’t ever come in here again.” At this point they were escorted out the door and to their car. I don’t know if they realized how lucky they were. I would wager that the midget didn’t feel quite so lucky.

Several months later the drop boxes were redesigned; two layers of thin metal with a layer of concrete in between.

47. The Hotfoot

There was a culprit who used to come into the Desert Inn (and, I'm sure, other casinos) who'd stand behind a player at the Craps who happened to have a whole string of chips on the rail of the game. The rails were designed for that purpose, with three troughs to put the chips in. During an especially exciting moment he would reach in and grab a handful of chips. If he got caught, he would run out the door, and could easily outrun a security guard. The desert was a perfect place to elude a pursuer, and he took advantage of it. Finally, one day someone spotted him standing behind the table, with a security guard close by. When he grabbed the chips, they grabbed him, and the jig was up. They took him into the back room, (where the fat lady had been), and lectured him on the evils of stealing in a casino. Somehow, during the lecture he lost a few teeth, had his nose broken, and God only knows what else.

They, however, weren't through with him. Since he was a known repeat offender, he was put in the security truck and they drove him to a point halfway between Baker, California, and Las Vegas. That would be about 45 miles. It was in the middle of summer, the temperature in the 100's, and the pavement twice as hot, or hotter. After removing his shoes and socks, they put him out of the car, and told him never to come into the Desert Inn again. At which point he had to start walking. There were very few cars on that highway and not a building or a gas station until you reached the outskirts of Las Vegas. I often wondered what happened to him.

I'm sure he avoided the Desert Inn in the future.

48. Counterfeiting

One busy night at the Hilton, a box-man on a dice table was sliding a stack of $25 chips to a dealer when the bottom chip caught on the felt and made it difficult to move the stack. Looking at the chip, he noticed that the paper-insert in the center of the chip (with the denomination on it) was starting to peel. When he scraped it with his fingernail it came off, and underneath was the name of a downtown casino and showing a denomination of 25 Cents. He called it to the bosses' attention, and they started to randomly check other $25 chips around the casino. To their surprise they turned up quite a few of the doctored chips.

Now it was a serious matter. A casino has a specific inventory of its chips, they know how many of each denomination they have, so at any time they can total what's in the cage in reserve, plus the amount in the trays on the tables. Whatever they can't account for is called the "float": chips in play on the tables, in people's pockets, or in the cages of the other casinos, which are redeemed almost daily. Most casinos keep an average of their float over a long period of time, so they have some estimate of what's out there.

When the casino manager had them take an inventory (which was time consuming and unheard of in the middle of a shift) they came up with a huge discrepancy. They had way more $25 chips than they were supposed to. Even in the early 1960s before the casinos started to expand to the size they are today, they could have had, at the very least, an inventory of up to a million dollars in $25 chips. They began to substitute all their uncirculated (new), chips for the ones in the trays, and were faced with the process of checking all the $25 chips, trying not to interrupt the action in the casino. They also notified all the other casinos to put a "hold" on all the Hiltons $25 chips, meaning do not accept them.

It seems that a downtown casino had 25-cent chips that were practically identical to the Hilton's $25 chips, so whoever doctored the chips had the paper inserts copied and pasted over the 25-cents, making them look just like $25. The scam netted a huge amount to the perpetrators, who were never found. I never heard just how much it cost, just rumors that got larger and larger as they flew up and down the Strip.

This led to Gaming Control putting forth a color code for all chips, uniform in all casinos, as other similar incidents occurred. It also was the beginning of the metal inserts in the chips with hidden I.D. that differed from all other chips.

49. A False Sense of Security

Downtown at the Fremont Hotel, a box-man was taken to task by a shift boss, for inaccurately tracking the "Big" on a Craps table the night before. The "Big" is gambling parlance for hundred-dollar bills. The box-man on the game is responsible for keeping track of $100 bills that go into the drop box. It's relatively easy to keep track with marker buttons that are in a rack in front of the chips. They are color coded, and come in $5, $10. $20, $25, $50, $100, $500 and $1000 denominations. This gave the pit managers an idea of how the shift was doing, and was also a tool for keeping track of a cash player's buy-ins.

It seems that the amount tracked by the box-man was higher than the amount of $100 bills that were in the drop box when they took the count in the morning. This was a highly dependable employee, and he never had any major discrepancy in his count. Taking into account that the man who relieved him for his breaks could have erred, they let it pass. Then it happened again, and again.

At this time, the counting room in the Fremont was on the second floor, accessible by a special elevator that opened up into the counting area. When the boxes were removed from the tables, they were put on a cart, which was then taken into the elevator and up to the counting area where they were secured under lock and key until the count team arrived in the morning. This was done by two security guards who resumed their normal duties after they got the boxes secured. After a few more incidents, management was faced with a real mystery. They usually paid attention to the games with heavy action, not bothering with "small potatoes" on other games. To satisfy their nagging suspicions they "salted" the drop box on a game that had a lot of action and a large amount of cash was purposely put in the box during the shift. This means that they took several thousand dollars in large bills and covertly put them in the box at some point during the night. The next morning there was nowhere near what should have been in the box when it was emptied for the count.

Putting two and two together (which wasn't real easy for some of these guys) They had a camera secretly installed in the elevator. This was new technology at that time and was crude compared to the surveillance of today. It was plain old 16-millimeter film, and while the boxes were being taken off the tables, they activated the camera. In the casino office the next morning they played the film, and lo and behold, as soon as the elevator door closed, one of the guards reached in his pocket and removed a key, unlocked the box with the most cash inside, and filled both pockets. The box was then closed, all before the elevator got to the second floor.

It took just a few seconds, and the question was, "Where did they get a key?" The keys to the drop boxes were kept under lock and key, and very few individuals had access. They even had to sign a log before removing the drop box keys. After confronting the guards, they were able to figure it out. The Fremont, as most of the other casinos, was run by the Mob, and these guards were in serious trouble. They owned up to everything. Part of the security duties was to make the rounds of the casino during the shift, and they could see which games had the most cash going into the box. They claimed that they made a wax impression of the key and after several tries, got one that worked. They also said that they just started doing it and hadn't taken a great amount. This, of course is what they all say when they finally get caught.

The truth of the matter is that you never know. It could have been the first few times, or it could have been going on for years. And, the boxes were taken off three times a day, at the end of each shift. Were all the guards doing it? Did they pass the key from shift to shift? These guys wouldn't give up the others, and of course that stopped it. There was no prosecution, even with the film evidence, as the owners didn't want to call any unwanted attention to their counting procedures, which were highly suspect in their own right.

Never heard what happened to the guards. They didn't work in the town again, and some speculated that maybe they retired. Or, worst case scenario, they could be in Lake Mead.

50. Crossroaders

From the 1950s through the 1970s a whole population of cheaters made their living cheating the casinos. Most of this was not in a grand fashion. Most of these cheaters would set a daily limit so as not to arouse suspicion. They would travel from casino to casino, or between Las Vegas and Reno, the only cities with major casinos.

To gamble in one of the small casinos in the little desert outposts in between the two cities was an invitation to disaster. If the little wayside casinos know they'll never see you again your chances of getting out of there with any money are practically nil.

The people who made their living in this fashion were known as "crossroaders" and they employed various means to ply their trade. Everyone had their own "specialty" such as daubing (marking the deck) bending (bending a certain portion of the deck) which they could read easily, and the gutsier pastimes of "hand mucking" which was moving cards in and out of the game or making one large bet and having a Blackjack concealed in the palm of their hand-and getting it on to the table. This took considerable skill and practice and it was done with more frequency than you would imagine.

Again, there were no cameras, just the "eye in the sky" which was a catwalk over one-way mirrors in the ceiling. Most of the time they weren't staffed and not all the casinos had them. Sometimes they would work in groups of two or four and switch cards in certain situations. Quite a few had dealers working with them, merely turning a blind eye for a piece of the action. When the play was over the dealers would go into the restroom on their break and get their share. The cheaters would never not honor the commitment; a dealer as an accomplice was money in the bank.

This would leave the floor man or pit boss as the only means of protection and most of them couldn't find their ass with both hands. These are the ones who would be victimized. To sum it all up, it was a "circle the wagons" mentality on a daily basis. The top of the line was the "cold deck" which would switch the whole deck on the game and someone would come in and make a large bet, win it and leave. This was done by the player who cut the cards, the dealer would be momentarily distracted, such as a fight or a spilled drink and the switch would be made.

A dealer who got "cold decked" most likely would never find another job in the industry.

51. A Lesson Learned

In 1959 during a hectic, noisy night in the Flamingo Hotel casino, I was standing on an empty Blackjack table trying to recover from the last lounge show, which was on a stage about 40 feet from my table. The headliner was Harry James and his big band. The noise was deafening, and would not be permitted today, but at the time there was no OSHA. You could put your mouth inches from a player's ear and scream at the top of your lungs and literally could not hear your own voice. We were submitted to this three times a night, and I'm sure it caused hearing loss in a lot of people.

As I was standing there enjoying the quiet interlude, a woman came into my peripheral vision and said, "If you smile, I'll bet this with you." In her hand was a silver dollar. Agitated, I started to shuffle the cards.

On the other side of the casino, behind me, was a step lounge. It was an alcove with six tiers, each with tables for people to have a drink and look down on the casino. By today's standards it was tiny, but by comparison, everything was smaller in those years.

Chester Simms, the casino manager anointed by Meyer Lansky, would sit on the top level for hours, drinking scotch and watching the action below. By midnight he was usually pretty well oiled. As I set the deck down for the woman to cut, out of nowhere came two big men, bumping into the table and each throwing down $200 in cash, yelling "play the money." I averted my eyes for a split-second and noticed a flash of movement that didn't seem natural. It all happened so fast that instinct told me something wasn't right, and after the cut I started to reshuffle the cards. The two men started to object, and at that moment, Chester Simms stood up in the step lounge and yelled, "Stop those people!"

The two men grabbed their money and ran for the door. The woman, who was wearing a fox stole, started to run around the table, and as she did, her stole caught on one of the chair backs, and the cards flew everywhere. She had switched the decks in the millisecond my eyes were averted and put the deck she removed in her stole. She managed to get out the door, and they headed into the desert across the Strip. (Caesar's Palace was years away). They weren't apprehended.

Chester asked me if I saw the deck come in, and I truthfully answered "No, but I knew something wasn't right, and reshuffled the cards." His words to me were "You know never to take your eyes off of the deck," to which I replied, "Yes sir." He told me that it's a good thing I started to reshuffle, or it would have cost me my job *and* my reputation.

When I started in the business, my father told me two things: "Protect yourself at all times and keep your eyes and ears open and your mouth shut."

Truly words of wisdom.

Little by little, Gaming Control began to demand better supervision, and have undercover agents spread throughout the town. When a cheater was caught by the casino, it usually went very hard for them, many had hands and fingers broken which would rob them of their livelihood. If they were caught by Gaming Control they were photographed and prosecuted, most doing some jail time. Once their faces were known they would have to seek greener pastures, of which there were very few in those days. The casinos had to pay a tax to the state on their winnings, and cheaters had an impact on that revenue.

The practice of cold decking was eliminated when the dealer held the deck in his hand and the customer would insert a plastic "cut card" to facilitate the cutting of the deck. This way the deck never left the dealers hand.

52. The Stardust's Auspicious Opening

The Stardust Hotel opened in the summer of 1958. It was billed as the biggest casino in the world (which it was) and had all of six dice tables, ten Blackjack games and three Roulette wheels. One of the Roulettes was a "double ender" which was one wheel between two tables constructed as one game. This gave them four tables and only three wheels which saved on the gaming taxes. It was the first and only double ender in town.

To round it out there was a Chuck-A-Luck (dice in a cage) game near the front entrance, and horror of horrors, a Keno game. It was the only Keno game on the Strip and everyone was worried that it would "cheapen" the Strip. There were Keno games in all the downtown clubs, but the difference between the Strip and downtown was viewed by everyone as working class compared to the high rent district. To make matters worse (in some people's eyes) the hotel was to have a thousand rooms, supposedly rented out at $10 a night.

The town was abuzz with all sorts of comment, the main, and most persistent one was "They're going to have ten Blackjack games! Where in hell are they going to get enough business to fill 10 games?"

Well, as it turned out, they had no trouble finding the customers, but what they didn't figure on was where were they going to get the dealers? The Craps had been the main game for so many years that they were able to staff the dice games with dealers from the Reno area.

Blackjack was another story. There were no dealer schools in those days, and you had to learn in a casino . . . if you could find a sponsor. Most started as shills in the downtown casinos, and if a boss took a liking to you he would let you "break in" on your own time. Blackjack is the easiest game to deal, and the most difficult to find as a job.

The Stardust owners were faced with a dilemma. How were they going to staff these games? Since there was a connection between the Desert Inn and the Stardust, they set up two Blackjack tables downstairs in the maintenance area for the Desert Inn golf course and made it into a dealer school. They reached out to find personnel—cooks, busboys, cab drivers, waiters—anyone who could stand up and count to 21. I had the pleasure of spending a few sessions as an instructor there, and the outlook wasn't good. Somehow, they were able to put a crew together for opening day, but it looked like the Keystone Kops. The more experienced dealers were put on the night and graveyard shifts, and most of the break-ins were on the day shift. Opening day was a memorable one. They cut the ribbon at 11AM and the place filled immediately.

At about four that afternoon, Frank Portnoy, a pit boss, caught a handmucker trying to slip a Blackjack into a game. After the ensuing chase and hubbub, they decided to change the decks on all ten tables. The fact that a lot of the cards were daubed wasn't a surprise, however, out of the ten decks that were replaced not one contained 52 cards. Still, they made money and never looked back. Some of the dealers who started in that school became top executives in the ensuing years.

53. Loose Lips Sink Scams

A slip of the tongue resulted in the downfall of a crew of card cheats that could have perpetrated the largest scam in Las Vegas history. It all began on the graveyard shift at the Tropicana in the early 1970s.

The graveyard pit manager, Frank Fertitta, had just returned from his days off and noticed a man betting the limit on one of the Blackjack tables. When he asked the outgoing pit manager about it, he was told that this was the first time he had seen the man and didn't know anything about him. All he knew was that he had bought in for $1000. A conscientious pit boss will always approach a new customer who obviously is a substantial player and get his name, offer him dinner or a show, or even a room. Some have a knack for it, most don't bother.

The man was with his wife, an attractive blonde, who came over and took some chips, and went to another game and sat down. Frank approached the man during the shuffle, introduced himself, and the man gave his name as Charles Harrelson, from Houston, Texas. Frank, being from Galveston, engaged in small talk, and asked him where he was staying. Harrelson replied, "We're staying in a little motel down the road." When Frank offered him a complimentary room at the Tropicana, he refused, stating that the "little ole motel" was fine for them.

A while later, Harrelson started to stagger from game to game making large bets, and then moving on to another table. He might wait several minutes before he made a bet and looked inebriated. When he stumbled off to the rest room Frank asked his wife what motel they were at, she replied, "We're not at a motel, we're staying with some friends." Frank, who was as sharp as anyone I had ever met, started to smell a rat. The Harrelsons won a few thousand and called it a night. When they left, several players whom Frank had never seen, got up and drifted out the door or down the hall leading to the rooms. A while later a couple of them walked through the lounge, which was closed and exited the front door.

The next night, they were back, he was stumbling from game to game, making large wagers, and was obviously friendly with several young people who were playing on various tables. This time he won several thousand, as did some of the people he was friendly with, and after he quit for the night (actually around 6AM) they filtered out the door one by one. They returned the next night and followed the same pattern, only this time Frank noticed some familiar faces, and not remembering where he knew them from, realized that they were the same bunch of Texans, only some were in light disguise, glasses, false moustache or goatee, and hairpieces. Now Frank knew for sure that something was amiss, he called Griffin Investigations, who provided a security service for most of the Casinos, made rounds over 24-hour periods, and had a huge data base of casino cheats, including pictures and information. Frank explained what was happening and said that they needed help in identifying these people, and establish for sure what, if anything, was going on.

54. The Book

The Griffin agency was founded by Bob Griffin, an ex-metro police detective, who at one time commanded the Vice Squad. Bob was a tough customer, a legend in Las Vegas law enforcement, and had little trouble lining up all the major casinos as clients. His men all were trained in memory techniques, and went from casino to casino, walking around, and if something or someone was amiss they called it to the attention of the casino bosses. He also had a book with photos of hundreds of casino cheats, along with their associates, and their mode of operation. It was updated constantly, and every major casino had one in the pit. They were pricey, but well worth the money. It was known around town as "the Book."

My first meeting with Bob Griffin was under strange circumstances. I had gotten off work at 3AM and drove down to Musso's, the hangout of choice at the time. Finding the parking lot full, I drove to the alley on the other side of the building. The building was 100 feet from the Sands and sat right on the Strip, with only a narrow sidewalk between it and the street. It was impossible to see any traffic heading north from the alley.

I over-imbibed, and next thing I knew it was 7AM and I was, for lack of a better word, drunk. I decided to head for home. A Desert Inn cocktail waitress lived around the corner from me and asked for a ride. Her name was Close, and she was twice as drunk as I was. To make matters worse when we got into my car she had her panties in one hand and a martini in the other.

Don't ask me about her panties.

I backed out and, since there never was any traffic on the Strip at 7AM, I didn't creep out, and Wham! I ran into something. Looking into the mirror I saw black and white. Now, here I sat, ossified, which was made worse by the sun shining in my eyes, and having just smashed into a sheriff's car. The impact spilled her martini and the car stank of gin on top of everything else.

I told her not to say one word and let me do the talking. The two officers got out of the squad car. Bob Griffin, who was a patrolman at the time, and Lake Headley, who later became a famous private eye and not only wrote books but handled some famous cases.

Griffin came around to my side and asked me to get out of the car and show him my license. I was truthful, and told him, "I'll be glad to show you my license, officer, but I don't think I should get out of the car." When he asked why, I replied, "Because I don't think I can stand up."

I passed my license through the window, he looked at it and said, "Are you related to Frank Soskin at the Desert Inn?" I replied, "Frank is my father." I thought, "So there is a God." He said, "Pull over to the side and we'll go talk this over." I pulled into the lot, and my passenger started screaming, "Dirty lousy goddam cops! You think you're so smart," etc., etc. They dragged her out of the car, handcuffed her and laid her on the back floor of the patrol car. They rolled up the windows (It was already over 100 degrees outside), pulled into the lot next to me, and left her there.

We went in for a cup of coffee. After a few cups of coffee (I had sobered up fast) Bob asked me if I could get home okay, and I said yes. He gave me a ticket for backing out in an improper manner, causing a minor T/C. When I asked what the T/C stood for, he told me it meant Traffic Collision. Of course, I had to pay for the damages. When I asked about Close, they told me they would take her downtown and let her sober up in the pokey.

Down through the years Bob Griffin and I became friends, and once in a while we would meet at a high school track at 4AM and run. I was good for five miles after working all night, and he didn't start to warm up until he got to ten miles. There were times when he would say to people in regard to me, "We ran into each other a long time ago."

Bob Griffin is class act. I imagine he's retired by now. His agency was the number one investigative security office for all the major hotels.

55. John DeLuca

Griffin sent John DeLuca out to the Tropicana to talk to Frank Fertitta about Harrelson and get a look at what was happening. Deluca had come to Las Vegas from Boston in the late '60s and was passing through on his way to Los Angeles where a job was waiting. Las Vegas at that time was a desirable place to live and raise a family, so John and his wife decided to stay. They both got jobs, bought a home, and John wound up working for Griffin, and found his niche.

He was a big bear of a man with a large neck and head, and a scar on his lip that gave him a menacing look. He was fearless, and you did not want to try intimidating him. His memory and instinct made him a valuable asset to the agency.

As it happened, Harrelson's crew was doing its thing when John walked into the Tropicana. Frank familiarized him with the problem, if it was a problem, while they sat in the lounge. Then, Frank went back to work while John observed from the lounge and other areas of the casino.

In a short time, Harrelson cashed out $27,000 in chips and gave it to one of his "friends" to hold. The friend immediately headed for the coffee shop and out the side door. DeLuca followed him out. As the man was getting into his car, he turned and pointed a gun at DeLuca's face, asking, "What do you want? Are you trying to rob me?" John replied "If you're not going to shoot me, put the gun down before I take it away from you, and I *will* shoot you. All I want is some information and ID."

The man presented ID. His name was Kim Wilson and he was a friend of Harrelson's from Texas. Taking down the info and the license plate of the small sports car, John made like he was going back into the casino, but instead went to his nearby car, and followed Wilson.

John had an old beat-up Volkswagen Bug that fit him like a bulletproof vest, and Wilson had no idea he was being followed. He drove to an apartment complex and John went and knocked on the door. He was again greeted by a pistol. In a way, you couldn't blame Wilson, who was carrying $27,000 in cash. John brushed by Wilson and into the apartment where he saw several computers, and stacks of paper with mathematical combinations on them. Wilson acknowledged they were working on a system and breaking no laws. DeLuca headed back to the Tropicana and told Frank what had transpired. The others in the group had left after winning several thousand more. Then it began to sink in. Card counting was coming into its own in Las Vegas, and this seemed like a form of counting that had not previously been seen.

Griffin did some checking on Harrelson and found out that his wife was an ex Blackjack dealer, named Joanne Starr, and Harrelson was not a nice guy. He was sentenced to 15 years for a contract killing in Texas and wound up getting out after five years. He also had been charged with other felonies. Nevada law states that if you are just *suspected* of cheating, you can be detained while the charge is investigated and, if you're clean, they apologize. You have no recourse.

Harrelson did not register as an ex-felon, which was against state law. Now Griffin's people started watching these guys, and clandestinely photographing them. Upon checking with authorities in Texas, they came up with a mixed bag. Some of the people were clean, some involved with small time stuff. Nothing serious.

Putting it all together, Frank surmised that these people were training themselves to count the cards, and when certain situations fell into place they would signal Harrelson, in any number of ways, that the deck was "rich" meaning it was highly in favor of the player. This was done by computer, with the results memorized by the players. Harrelson, feigning intoxication, would stagger over to the game and bet one or two hands at the limit. Just because the odds are in your favor, it doesn't mean you're going to win, but do it enough and you'll wind up ahead.

It was suspected, but not proven (in the Tropicana) that they had also approached a few dealers and offered them a piece of the action if they ignored some of the other things they were doing. Fertitta put it to the test. The next time Harrelson staggered up to the game and made a large bet, Frank told the dealer to reshuffle the cards. They knew it was over, but the Tropicana wasn't the only casino in town.

They transferred their act to the Frontier, which at the time didn't have Griffin's service. Harrelson came into the casino and deposited $10,000 in cash in the cashier's cage, to use as "front money." This way he could take credit at the table until the $10,000 was used up. Then it was the same as the Tropicana, with Harrelson acting like a drunk and staggering from table to table. I happened to be working at the Frontier at the time and had no knowledge of what happened at the Tropicana, and neither did anyone else. I watched them win several times and asked the shift manager for permission to have the dealer reshuffle when Harrelson made a large bet. He refused. Then they quit playing on the night shift and played only during the day.

This time they did it differently. Every night when I came to work Harrelson and his wife were sitting at the same table, with the pit manager standing on one side of the table and the same floor man standing on the other side. They always had a mountain of chips in front of them. It smelled to high heaven. They obviously had the pit manager and the floor man (who had been fired from the Dunes for involvement in a credit scam) working with them. It was a cozy situation. I also noticed the same dealer was always on the game. When I mentioned it to the shift manager, he told me that they always had plenty of money, and that I was crazy. I tried coming to work early to watch from a distance, but they would break it off as soon as I walked into the pit.

A few weeks later I got off work, at 3AM and went to the Tropicana to have a bite with Frank. He related what had happened there, and I realized they were doing the same thing at the Frontier. Without proof I couldn't say anything. One night they popped into the Frontier and started to play, about the time we were due to get off work. I called Frank at the Tropicana, who came down to the Frontier, walked past the table they were on and gave me a slight nod on his way out the door,

Now I had proof. I sat down with Harry Goodheart, the casino manager, and told him in detail what was happening. He called the Griffin agency, and they sent DeLuca over to the Frontier. Harrelson's gig at the Frontier was over. The two pit bosses and the suspect dealer were not fired. Las Vegas, however, remained fertile ground for the Harrelson bunch. Even with photographs, in a busy casino, it's difficult to see through even the smallest disguise. They moved from casino to casino, and if Griffin's guys weren't there at the time, they were in tall clover. With only one or two persons on a shift, covering the whole Strip and some downtown casinos for Griffin, things still looked good for the crew. But nothing good lasts forever, and they were identified and rousted from a few places by DeLuca.

A few blocks from the DeLuca home was an apartment building where a Caesars Palace Blackjack dealer lived. John would see him drive past his house and noticed because he wore a Caesars dealer uniform. One day John got a call from Billy Weinberger, president of Caesars Palace, who asked him to come to Caesars ASAP as they had just been cold decked. They had the dealer and interviewed him and weren't sure he was in on it, so they let him leave the hotel. When John arrived, they told him that the perps had won $27,500, and were able to cash it out before they smelled a rat. Their surveillance on that table, for some reason, was only partial, as if the camera had been moved, maybe by accident. They showed John the dealers file, and from the picture on the file John recognized the dealer who drove by his house. Taking his name and address, John said I'll be back shortly. Driving to the apartment, he went upstairs and banged on the door. When they asked who it was he told them John DeLuca, Statewide Investigations, and you better talk to me or you can deal with Metro and Gaming control. When he opened the door, there were two guys sitting at a table with a pile of cash in front of them. They were dividing up the money. John told the dealer (who was shaking like a leaf) that if he went back to Caesars with him, and returned the money, he could possibly stay out of jail, and maybe someday work in the State again. He also told them that they were not going to have any income for a while and they could keep $2000. For expenses. Back to Caesars he went. The Caesars security chief resented John for his recognition and wanted to press charges. John told the big bosses that the $25,000 was all the dealer had and that he wanted to make restitution. They cut a deal, Caesars didn't press charges, Gaming control revoked his work card and the dealer walked. He did, however, name his accomplices. They were not charged, they had left town.

56. Portrait of an Honest Man

Then DeLuca got a call from Harrelson's friend, Kim Wilson (supposedly) requesting a meeting at a gas station at the corner of Tropicana and Paradise roads. It was a large, well-lit and busy place, but John was still uneasy. He notified the office where he was going, and who he was meeting and, in spite of reservations, he jumped into his little bug and drove to the station. When he arrived, Wilson and Harrelson were waiting. They took him behind the station and pointed out a brand-new Buick Riviera, and told him it was his, and all he had to do was turn away if he happened to enter a casino where they were playing.

John, intending to convey a message, told them he didn't like the color. They told him to go to the Buick agency and they would get him any color he wanted, no problem. John refused and started to leave. Harrelson told him, "We've got a lot of time and money invested in this, and we don't intend to be stopped." John kept walking.

Several days later, John made the rounds downtown, and as he was going through the Golden Nugget, someone came alongside and said, "I'd like to talk to you, let's go out the side door." John knew better than to walk outside alone with a stranger and refused. The guy said, "Okay, let's go out the front door to Fremont Street where it's well lit, and there are a lot of people walking around."

John followed him to the street and asked him what he had to say. The man told John how stupid he was to have turned down the car and asked what it would take to get him off their backs. The man said, "Name your price, we need 18 months to get what we want." John hesitated for a second and the man said, "Do you want it monthly? Tell us how much you want and there will be an envelope every month."

Let's be realistic, for a guy with three young kids this was tempting. John told me he actually thought about it, for a half-second. Knowing that even suspected complicity with these people would prevent him from earning a living, he replied, "Thanks, but I've played it straight all my life, and it's going to stay that way."

Now, this gentleman decided to play hardball. He said, "Listen, for $30,000 we could make you disappear, that's the going rate around here." If someone wished to play hardball and scare somebody, they could find a softer spot than John DeLuca, who told him, "You could hunt around and probably get it done for half of that and save yourself some money." That took some balls, knowing that Harrelson had done time for a hit in Texas, and even claimed at one time to be in on the Kennedy assassination. This was checked and disproved by Texas authorities. Which meant nothing.

57. Bob Righetti

Dick's Pub was a dive a few doors down from the Nugget on Third Street where a lot of cheaters and various culprits hung out. It was a small, dark place with a capacity for maybe 50 persons. Bob Righetti was one of the partners in Griffin Investigations. He was a big man, played semi pro basketball, got an audition with the NBA, and didn't abide any bullshit. He was known to drink a little too much, and that made him more fearless.

Righetti was a Blackjack dealer at the Flamingo in the late '50s. One night he was late for work and, not wanting to waste any time, drove his Thunderbird right up the steps to the casino front door, went in and went to work. When the shift manager saw that he had been drinking, he took him off the game and sent him home. Bob walked out the front door, backed his car down the steps, and headed for the nearest watering hole. I saw it happen and couldn't believe he still had his job.

When Righetti heard about the threat against John's life, he grabbed a sawed-off shotgun and headed for Dick's Pub. He had a snootful and he loved John. Walking into the Pub, he flipped the light switch, and when the lights went on, everyone looked up. He then announced that if anything happened to John DeLuca, everyone in there was a dead man. With that he fired the shotgun into the ceiling, twice, turned the lights back off and left. Griffin kept him out of trouble.

Harrelson and his crew hung out at the Horseshoe, which always made fellow Texans welcome. They knew better than to try anything there, as Benny Binion had little patience with shenanigans in his casino. It wasn't long before the word got out, and Harrelson and his bunch were persona non grata in the Las Vegas Casinos. They really hadn't broken any laws as evidence of cheating was hard to come by, but they were told they weren't welcome in any of the casinos.

58. Change of Occupation

With his scam a dud, Harrelson had to find another way to make a dishonest living. He had met a young man at the Horseshoe by the name of Jamiel "Jimmy" Chagra. Jimmy was from El Paso, where his family had a lot of influence, and reportedly a piece of every racket in town.

Jimmy was a $5 bettor until one day he started showing up with bags full of money, and gambling for high stakes. This caught the attention of the IRS and the federal narcotics people, and he finally got busted on a major narcotics charge. He was to stand trial in the courtroom of Federal Judge John Woods, aka "Maximum John," who always handed out the stiffest possible sentences to narcotics violators. Fearing that he would get sent away for a long time, and consulting with his brother, a prominent El Paso attorney, they agreed that Judge Woods had to be killed. He could possibly be replaced with a judge that could be bribed.

Remembering what Harrelson's real occupation was, Jimmy contacted him, and they agreed on a price of $250,000 for the hit. In 1979 Charles Harrelson gunned down Judge Woods with a rifle. He was convicted and given two life sentences. After an attempted prison escape he was transferred to a maximum-security facility and died there at the age of 69.

His son, actor Woody Harrelson, had solicited famous attorney Alan Dershowitz to try to get an appeal for a new trial. They were unsuccessful. Jimmy Chagra was convicted, among other things, of soliciting the unsuccessful murder attempt against a federal prosecutor. He was never convicted for the killing of Judge John Woods. He did 25 years in prison and died of cancer in Arizona at age 63.

John DeLuca took advantage of his stellar reputation, and opened his own detective agency, Statewide Investigations, where his expertise gained him quite a few high-profile clients.

Several years later Frank Fertitta owned the Palace Station and was on his way to becoming a billionaire.

59. The Firemen

There were several ways a dealer could cheat at a Blackjack table, but very few dealers that were capable of doing this. Those dealers were hired for the rare occasion that their services would be needed. In a few cases they would be rewarded with a percentage of what they won for the house. I believe that the going rate was 10%, in cash. Most of the top mechanics, as they were referred to (the term "butchers" was used on occasion) came from Montana or Wyoming, and some from the illegal places in the East. Their methods were quite different.

The mechanics from up north were smooth and took great pride in their work. Quite a few got their experience on trains, dealing to the Chinese laborers who worked for the railroads and had just cashed their paychecks. There, a wrong move could cost you your life, the preferred method being a hatchet in the back of your head. They could then throw you off the train and, even if your body was found, nothing ever came of it. They spent thousands of hours practicing in front of a mirror to learn their trade, and even to the trained eye, it was practically impossible to see them deal a second card. The only way it could be detected was by a light swishing sound as the card came out. That kind of silence didn't exist in a casino, or a moving train for that matter.

The "mechanics" who came from the Eastern part of the country were, for the most part, just the opposite. They would laugh and joke with the players, and appear to be extremely clumsy, to the point they looked like amateurs. Some people even felt a little sorry for them as they were losing the money. After all cheating ceased they were considered substandard, and many lost their jobs. The other dealers had no sympathy for them as they resented the fact that these guys usually worked like everyone else yet received a share of the tips. However, there were many times they would send a high roller and generous tipper to bed early. If you depend on tips for a living, that's hard to watch. In the final analysis, the people who did this had ice water in their veins. The pressure in those situations was enormous, and to do these things when people were looking for it took cast iron nerves.

60. How It Was Done

For a dealer to deal a second card, he'd have to know the top card on the deck. This could be done by, (a) the cards would have to be marked, (which was risky as Gaming Control could take them off the game at any time), or (b) (and this was the most common way) to "peek" at the top card. With the deck in your hand, it was relatively easy and undetectable from the player's viewpoint. There was the "front" peek or the rear, or "hind" peek and they were used depending on the situation.

The next most common move was called "turning the deck." Since all the discards went face up on the bottom of the deck it was easy for the dealer to know what card was on the bottom. If the card was a small one, and the dealer had, say 15 or 16, he would turn the deck over in his hand, thus putting the bottom card on top. After the hand was over he would "break down the deck" (re-shuffle the cards). The way it was done could only be detected by someone who knew what to look for. That practice came to a halt when the Gaming Control Board insisted on discard racks on the tables. A colored plastic card was used to put on the bottom of the deck in place of the face up "burn" card.

There were other ways to improve the edge for the house. In the early '60s the Pioneer club was paid an unannounced visit by Gaming Control agents. They were dealing their games with two decks, (a double deck), and had a few tables with four-deck shoes. The gaming agents took a double deck and the cards out of one of the shoes, went to the Craps, took the dice off one of the games and left the premises after putting them in the required sealed and signed envelopes.

About a week later an article appeared in the local papers stating that there were four 10s or face cards missing from the double deck, and eight missing from the four-deck shoe confiscated by Gaming Control. This gives the house an enormous advantage, well over two times the normal percentage advantage that the house normally enjoyed. The club claimed that it must have been a defective shipment of cards (which was ridiculous; the cards are checked before being put into play). They got off with a citation and were warned that any other violations would cost them their license. No one knows how long they had been getting away with the practice.

61. Do Your Homework

When there were no players at a table the cards were spread face up on the layout. I recall walking into the Birdcage Casino (later to become The Mint, sold to the Horseshoe years later) when the place had just opened, a few of my co-workers and I went to take a look. It was late and they had very little business. I happened to look at the layout to see what their rules were regarding "soft" 17, which is any combination of cards with an ace that can be counted as seven or seventeen, the ace being one or eleven. Some casinos drew on it and some stood pat, and it was stated on the felt layout. I looked at the spread deck and saw that the cards were arranged as follows: 10-10-8-10-10-9-5-A-4-2-3-6-7, repeated four times in the same sequence. If a player were to sit down, the dealer could do a quick false shuffle, and offer the cards to the player to cut. No matter where the cards were cut, if the player played only one hand, he would not win one hand all the way through the deck.

You can try this at home, just don't rearrange the sequence. The game is tough enough without losing the first six or seven hands. There were three tables with that arrangement. We told everyone we knew about it and I'm sure that the practice came to a screeching halt as the word got around.

62. Cleaning Up a Dirty Business

As things began to change in Las Vegas, and more hotels and casinos began to open, the GCB (Gaming Control Board) took a more aggressive stance on enforcement, and although the old gambling bosses complained long and loud, the change was for the better. Gambling in Nevada is what is known as a "privileged industry." To obtain a license to operate a casino, the scrutiny you are subjected to is mindboggling. They can go clear back to your origins, schools, and in some cases (as with Frank Sinatra and foreign applicants) they can send agents to any country in the world and dig into anything you've ever done or been involved in. This is all at *your expense.*

I've been through the licensing process, and the things they come up with are startling. If they deem you unsuitable you have no recourse. The industry has survived every legal challenge, including the United States Supreme Court, and gaming in Nevada remains to this day a privileged industry.

The GCB is the investigative and enforcement agency and the Gaming Commission makes the final decision, taking the Control Board's recommendations into consideration. Incidences of the Commission overruling the Board's recommendations are extremely rare. It even controls the employees, especially in the gaming related areas. Everyone must have a work card, which can be revoked in the event of misconduct. In the case of executive casino employees, they can be called up for licensing as "key employees." The scrutiny is not as severe, but it's still at the casino's expense. If they're turned down, they can still work, but in a lesser capacity. This put the fear of God in the Mob-run casinos and they did everything they could do to avoid scrutiny. That made it tough on the known (and alleged) mechanics who were still working in the industry, albeit strictly on the up and up.

Take the case of one Maynard Hunter, a dealer I worked with at the Stardust for a short time. Maynard not only dealt Blackjack but was an accomplished Roulette dealer as well. He came from somewhere in Montana and worked in several spots around town. He was tall, blond, and had the loose demeanor of a cowboy without a horse. He was also the best Blackjack dealer I've ever seen, and I've seen 'em all. He had long tapered fingers that were always impeccably manicured, and when he was working he was something to behold. To begin with he could deal a second card right under your nose, after letting you know he was going to do it, and you could not detect it. It was like special effects in a movie. The thing that really made it unusual was that he could do it with either hand!

To break the monotony, he would sometimes deal right-handed one hand and left-handed the next. A few pit bosses thought they were seeing things, and I can't remember one realizing what he was looking at. They "couldn't put their finger on it." Maynard left the Stardust for the Riviera, and worked there for several years, and then inexplicably was let go. He was one of the "alleged" mechanics and he could not find work anywhere in the state. The owners didn't want to have anyone with his abilities working for them, even though there was nothing underhanded going on. The last I heard was that he was selling insurance.

63. Unintended Scare Tactics

During the time I was running the off-Strip casino, hotel and truck stop, we had a large local clientele, and on Fridays and Saturdays we cashed a considerable number of payroll checks along with large checks from truck drivers. Therefore, on Friday mornings we would get an armored car delivery of over a million dollars in cash. One day I had a visit from a Metro Police lieutenant who told me they had gotten a credible tip that there was a group planning a heist on the coming Friday. They were going to come into my office, put a shotgun to my head and march me to the cashier's cage, and demand the shipment before it was taken out of the bags. It was hard to believe, but he said the info was from dependable source, and he wanted to set things up with the SWAT Team. Only myself, my assistant, and the chief of security were to know about it. I agreed and at 4AM Friday morning they moved in and placed a van with dark window tint in front of the casino with a machine gun in the back. In a hotel room overlooking the main entrance they had snipers set up, an unmarked car in the parking lot and had placed a SWAT Sergeant in my office, dressed in military fatigues with an automatic rifle. He was spending the day with me. My office was in a separate building of motel rooms converted to offices, and they had everything covered.

As it happened, two nights previous, a customer came over to the pit boss in the Blackjack and told him that a dealer was giving money away to an accomplice on the table. The dealer was just paying him every hand, win or lose, when the pit boss wasn't looking. The dealer was Vietnamese, and so was the agent taking the money. There had been an influx of Vietnamese coming into Las Vegas and a huge segment of the influx was going to dealer's school. They sometimes had 15 or 20 living together in the same house, and on their nights off they would play on their room- mates tables and rob the casino. They would pick up $100 here and $100 there and move on. Pays the rent and then some. Most of the casinos wouldn't hire them, and I was taking someone's word that she was okay. Her sister worked for us in the cashier's cage and was a good employee. When the pit boss called me, I told him to pull her off the table and fire her. I also left word with the payroll office to give her check to me and tell her she had to see me to get it. I wanted to look her in the eye. That very same Friday morning she came for her check and they sent her to my office. She knocked on the door, and when I opened it she came in and saw the SWAT sergeant with the automatic rifle, and she went ballistic. She thought she was going in front of a firing squad. She was hysterical and ran for the front door without her check. I had to chase her into the parking lot and it took a long time to quiet her down. It's funny now, but at the time it wasn't. I caught hell from the sergeant for exposing myself, as he had to stay out of sight. Nothing ever happened. The police kept a presence there for two days and then left. I never heard another word about it.

64. Unsuccessful Stake-out

In another incident a friend who I had working in the slots came to me and told me he thought my slot manager "was stealing money." I'd known this friend for years and he was totally reliable; sharper than I'd given him credit for. When I asked what made him say that, he told me what he thought was going on. I listened and realized that it was too good *not* to be true.

I thanked him, said I'd look into it, and calmly walked out the door. Then not so calmly, I jumped in my car and headed for Gaming Control. When I explained the situation, they told me they'd have an agent get in touch with me. The next morning, an agent called and asked me to meet him in a hotel bar across the street. I was to bring a check for $1200, and he would provide a receipt. The bar was closed and it was pitch dark. We sat in a far corner and he explained what they were going to do. His name was Mike Cassel, and he was a pure professional. They were going to have at least two agents playing slots and observing almost 24-hours. As long as the slot manager was there, they were watching. Any money left over from the $1200 would be returned to the casino.

There was a large change bank on the casino floor, up against a wall. It contained coin and some cash, and always had the same amount of money in it. When a change girl sold coin for cash, she would run short on coin, and go to the bank and purchase coin for the cash. There was no reason for the bank not to contain the same amount on a consistent basis. This is called an "imprest" bank. The key to the bank was kept in the slot office.

It seems that when the slot manager would perform "maintenance" on the dollar machines, he would take the hopper out of the machine and put it on his bench in the office. The hoppers were always full of $1 tokens. He would then take several hundred of the tokens and put them in racks, usually two or three hundred dollars at a time. Each rack held 100 tokens. He would then take the racks to the change bank and add them to the coin. At that time, the bank was say, $300 *over* what it should be. Now he could return to the bank later and take out $300 in cash and the bank was back in balance. If the coast was clear, he could remove the cash immediately, and put it in a rag that he kept in his pocket. Another possibility was that he could be working with a change girl, who could remove the cash during a coin buy.

When Sid, my friend and employee, spotted the empty racks in the slot office, he put two and two together and came to me. Gaming Control called me on the second day of the stakeout, and told me that they had spotted nothing suspicious, and they needed the agents elsewhere. I begged for one more day, I knew it *had* to be true, it was too good.

They agreed, and the next day, here came Jack (the slot manager) out of the slot office with three racks of dollar tokens and placed them in the change bank. He then turned around and stuffed a rag in his pocket, and the agents grabbed and cuffed him. The shift manager called me in my office and told me that Gaming Control had Jack in the office in handcuffs. I came up to the office, and they took the rag out of his pocket, and it was empty. They jumped too soon, he hadn't time to get the cash out. That precluded any prosecution for embezzlement. They did, however, count down the bank and found it to be $300 over. It was enough to arrest him, but since it was only half a crime they couldn't make it stick. They did however revoke his work card and he didn't work in the industry again, as far as I know.

Before they took him out of the casino, he asked me how I found out about it. I just walked away. Sid got a substantial bonus and a raise, and then died of cancer eight months later. The agent who jumped too soon was named Garrison. His wife was also a Gaming Control agent, and she was a real bitch. It wasn't long afterward that she got caught playing the $5 slots at Caesars Palace with tokens that she'd purportedly taken from the evidence locker at Gaming Control.

Mike Cassel came into our little casino on a routine patrol and pulled a crap dealer off the game who had been caught stealing $25 chips in a downtown casino. They hadn't pulled his work card yet when I hired him. When we had him in my office, Mike asked him why he put the chips in his pocket, and he replied, "I needed the money."

In a strange coincidence, many years later, I was on a ferry from Seattle to Whidbey Island, Washington where I hoped to retire, and my wife and her brother were out on the bow of the boat. It was summer and the ferry was packed with cars and people, I went to the restroom. Coming out, I was looking for my wife and ran right into a man carrying a child. When I looked up to apologize, it was Mike Cassel. Seems his in-laws lived in the area and they were visiting.

Small world. I sincerely hope he had a successful career, he was a consummate professional.

65. Local Color

While walking to the time office at the Tropicana one night in 1965, the guy in front of me tripped and fell into the bushes that lined the walk. I went to help him up and he reeked of alcohol. His name was "Red" Woodward and he was a dice dealer. He somehow made it up the stairs and onto the table with the rest of his crew. However, he was so inebriated that all he could do was hold on to the table lest he fall over backwards. They called the Casino Manager, one Don Speer, and he was furious. He said to Red, "Why did you come to work half drunk?" Red looked at him through blood-shot eyes and replied, "Because I ran out of money."

Lou Kalish was the day shift Blackjack boss at the Tropicana in the '60s. He was not very tall, had blond hair, and spoke with a voice so loud that it seemed he was shouting. He really didn't seem to fit in the swanky Tropicana.

The Tropicana had a Sunday Brunch that was well known on the Strip and usually had a large attendance. One of the better customers at the Tropicana was a gentleman from Canada by the name of Jack Cooper. One Sunday morning he and his wife came down for the brunch and decided to play a few hands on my table first. He was dressed in slacks and a blue blazer with a very expensive tie, and she in a lovely beaded dress. Being mid-day there was no entertainment, and the casino was deathly quiet. Out of nowhere Kalish hollered to his assistant, "Keno Slim" as he (Kalish) was running out of the pit, "Hey Keno, watch this for me, I'm going to take a crap." You could have heard it across the street. For a second everyone was stunned, and Jack Cooper looked up at me and said in a calm voice, "Did you hear the announcement?"

On another occasion Lou got off work and stopped at the cashier's cage. From a distance a customer yelled, "Where are you headed, Lou?" Kalish replied that he was off for the next three days. The man inquired as to what Lou was going to do, and Kalish replied that he was going skiing.

This was the conversation. "Where are you going to ski?" Lou replied "Rice Canyon." The man said, "You mean Bryce Canyon?" Lou replied "No, Rice Canyon" as he headed for the front door. The man yelled after him, “Where’s Rice Canyon?” As he went out the door, Lou replied, “up a Chinaman’s ass” and kept walking. It was really crass. Then, when Lou passed away, it came out that he was a highly decorated Marine Raider during WWII, and all those months of combat were what made him talk so loud.

Speaking of loud talk, there was a dealer and pit boss named Davey Weinstein, who talked so loudly that people thought he was crude and boorish. Davy was an upbeat guy who always had a smile on his face and was always willing to help. We fished together on several occasions, and I thought he was so loud he would scare the fish.

On the night the El Rancho burned down, there were two telephone operators trapped in the area behind the front desk. Davy crawled into the inferno and led them both out on their hands and knees, holding on to him through the thick smoke. He then left when the fire department got there. He wasn’t looking for glory, but as it happened, one of the operators knew him and told the newspapers. They brought out that he had piloted a B-24 Bomber during the war, had been shot down three times, twice rescued by partisans and once had to ditch in the Adriatic Sea. He also was highly-decorated and got his loud voice from screaming over the noise of the bomber’s engines.

No one had any idea of his service.

66. Severance Pay

The Stardust allowed shills and non-gaming employees to play Keno when they were not on duty. An elderly shill, working for $8 a day to supplement his social security, got off work and wrote a 50-cent Keno ticket. He got all eight numbers and collected $12,500. After they paid him off, they fired him.

The Stardust also had a Faro Bank game in the lobby and Poker area. Faro Bank is a dead even gamble, dates back to the old west, and all the old-time gamblers and bosses made it a point to drop in once in a while and play. They called it "Bucking the Tiger." It was the only Faro game in southern Nevada, and there were only five people in the whole town who could deal it. The action generally started around 2AM and with all those old characters and bosses around it was without doubt the best show in town.

The old timers believed that if you got a dealer flustered or mad at you, he would try hard to beat you, and the harder he tried the more he lost. These dealers took a lot of abuse. I went over to the game one night to see if my dad was playing when he got off work, and as I walked to the game I could see everything but the dealers head. Several of these "characters" had gone to the gift shop and bought "Covered Wagon" cigars. They were about a foot long, as big around as a broom handle, and cost 50 cents apiece. This was not quality tobacco. Some said they were made from old army blankets. They would sit there with those cigars about two feet from the dealer and blow the smoke right in his face. Every once in a while, a hand would emerge from the cloud and wave the smoke away.

"Money" Blank would get so mad he would bite the chips in half, until they told him he would be barred from playing if it continued, as he would tape them together and cash them in. One night he "called" a $100 bet. You could do this, but if you lost you had to pay right away before the next hand. Anyway, he lost and blew his nose in the $100 bill before giving it to the dealer, who almost gagged, but dropped it in the box, figuring he would let the count team deal with it.

Money was warned about it, so the next bet he had to pay, he cleared his throat like he was going to spit in it, but the boss told him if he did he was finished forever. It should be noted that losing a "call" bet without the funds to pay it could be detrimental to your health.

These guys would lose a bet and fall out of the chair, faking a heart attack, and when security came with the oxygen they would say they felt better, and get back into the chair. Watching these characters at 6AM with black bags under their eyes and two-day beards was the entertainment bargain of the year.

The game was personal to them and winning made them feel ten feet tall.

67. The Cylinder; An Unsolved Mystery

When it came to being cheated, no casino was exempt. Somewhere along the way everyone got it at one time or another, but some seemed to be targeted more than others.

Take the Las Vegas Hilton International, for example. One night, right after the shift change, a Craps dealer at the Hilton went to pay some bets with $5 chips, and in his hand, along with the chips was a hollow cylinder, made to emulate two $5 chips. It was such a perfect replica that when it sat on the table, it was nearly impossible to detect. At first, they didn't know what to make of it, but it took about three minutes to figure it out. When someone involved with the scam would bet two $5 chips, the dealer would pay them with the cylinder, inside of which were two $25 chips. The cheaters would remove the $25 chips and put the cylinder back onto the table in the form of a bet. When the bet was lost, the cylinder was back in the hands of the dealer, who repeated the process. Nobody paid much attention to a wager of two $5 chips, so there wasn't any scrutiny.

Repeated five or six times, the player would have at least $300, and would then leave the game and another member of the cheaters crew would come in and do the same thing. This cost the hotel thousands of dollars daily. There was no telling how much was taken off the games, and no way of knowing how many people were involved. The only certainty was that the dealer had to be part of the scam. How many dealers were involved? Again, no way of telling. The dealer who called their attention to the cylinder was, of course, not under suspicion.

They found cylinders on some Blackjack tables and Roulette wheels, and the dealers on those games were fired. The cheater was supposed to take the cylinder off the table when the shift changed, unless the oncoming dealer was involved. He didn't. Again, the question was how long was it going on, and how many people were involved? Unless they could make an arrest and get someone to talk, the question remains unanswered.

The scam was too big to ignore, and Gaming Control got involved. After questioning a few of the dealers who were arrested, two names surfaced as the perpetrators of the whole affair. One was Johnny Hicks, son of Marion Hicks, builder and owner of the Thunderbird Hotel, who had died of cancer in the late '50s. Another was a dealer named Bob Murphy, who was a grifter and a thief.

Hicks had a record and was known to law enforcement. Murphy was a personal friend of Judge Tom O'Donnell, a local magistrate who had a reputation of being a ladies' man and even slapped a few around when he was drunk and jealous. This kept Murphy somewhat under the radar.

Then the word got out that Hicks was going to name some names to avoid possible jail time. One night he unlocked the door to his condo, stepped inside, and someone shot him at point blank range with a shotgun. The assassin was never apprehended. Some speculated that it was Murphy. Shortly after, Mr. Murphy knocked on the front door of one Mel Myers, a dealer who supposedly owed someone some money. When the door was opened, Murphy barged in, pistol in hand and started to pistol whip Myers, demanding payment. All this in the presence of Mel's wife. Myers ran to a desk, took out a gun and shot Murphy dead. Of course, it was justifiable homicide, and no charges were filed. Any chance of finding out who else may have been involved in the cylinder scam was now gone.

Mel Myers became a local hero.

68. Caught with His Pants Down

At the Sahara Hotel at 2AM, the oncoming graveyard shift manager was sitting in one of the stalls in the men's room. He'd just finished breakfast and was using the facilities, smoking a cigarette and reading the paper. It was the only quiet place in the casino area, as at 2AM the lounge entertainment was in full swing and the place literally roared. Suddenly the door burst open and the sound of heels echoed off the tile floor. Another sound caught his ears: the sound of chips rattling around.

Gaming chips have a distinctive sound and when they are banging into each other they can make quite a racket, like castanets. Looking under the door of the stall he saw a pair of legs with cowboy boots on, heading for one of the stalls. The rattling noise was coming from the boots. With all the noise in the casino you wouldn't have heard it, but, according to him, in the quiet rest room, it was "like two skeletons fucking on a tin roof."

The individual went into one of the stalls and took off the boots, put the chips in his pocket, (a few fell on the floor, but were recovered quickly), he then headed for the door. Getting up as quickly as sanitation allowed, the boss ran out into the casino to see who it was, but it was too late. Most of the dealers on the night shift had just left. The bosses got together and got the names of all the dealers on the swing shift but couldn't really suspect anyone. In the next few days it was noticed that some of the dealers were wearing cowboy boots, with their pants tucked into the boots. There have always been dealers who were caught wearing "subs" (short for "submarines), sewn into their pants. When the opportunity would present itself, they would slip a few chips into their pants (at the waist) and empty the sub on a break or when they got off. The subs were padded to muffle any sound. Depending on where you worked, should you be caught, you would either be prosecuted for theft, or roughed up and thrown out the door.

The pants in the boots eliminated the need for a sub. Any chips going into the waistband ultimately wound up in the boot. If you didn't get too greedy you had a chance to make some money before you got caught. As a result, the new rules stated that the pants could not be tucked into the boots, and then boots weren't allowed, period. The cowboys wailed long and loud but the rule stood.

69. The Strawberry Patch

"Strawberry patch" in gaming parlance was an expression denoting a casino where the rules and supervision are so lax, that anyone who wanted to steal from the house could do so with impunity. The term was not used loosely, so if you made a comment like that, and it got around, (which it would), you could get a reputation for having a big mouth, and in Las Vegas that was anathema, unless the statement were true.

The Tropicana Hotel was a strawberry patch. Of course, the majority of the employees were honest and dependable, but there were a lot of dishonest things going on. I worked at the Tropicana for several years in the mid '60s and the elite clientele that they catered to made it one of the best jobs in town.

My first night at the "Trop," as it was called, was pretty quiet. The action had all but died out at 2AM, and there were several empty Blackjack tables. I was standing on an empty game and on the next table, the end game in the row of tables, was a dealer by the name of Bobby Friedman. A man walked up and bet two hands at $400 each, with $25 chips. Bobby shuffled the cards and turned and called out, "Money on the layout." which meant there were large wagers being placed. The pit boss, at the podium doing paperwork, looked up and said, "Go ahead," at which point Bobby dealt the cards. The player stood pat on both hands, Bobby turned his cards over, and just went out and paid both the player's hands, which were both losers. The guy grabbed the chips and headed for the door, the whole transaction took a matter of seconds. A few minutes later the pit boss ambled over, glanced at the rack of chips on the game and walked away. As soon as he paid both losing bets, Bobby glanced at me to see if I had noticed what happened. Our eyes met for a second, and I looked away. It wasn't my business, and for all I know, the pit boss was in with the whole affair. Bobby quit a few months later to go into the real estate business.

He had worked at the Trop for several years, and I would surmise that he had done quite well.

70. Benny and Helga

"Helga" was a change girl at the Tropicana. She sat in a tall booth in the middle of the slot area and made change for the slot players. Since the Tropicana didn't have change girls on the casino floor, her booth was the only place in the slot area where a person could get change. If the booth was closed, change had to be bought at the casino cashier's cage.

Helga was from Germany and had a slight accent, which wasn't noticeable as she very rarely spoke to anyone. Her claim to fame was that she had the biggest tits in the place, and it was easy to see that they were "hangers." There was always discussion as to how far they would drop if she took her bra off. General opinion was that they would probably make it to her knees. She was a loner, and I don't recall ever seeing her interact with other employees.

Benny Womack was a slot floor man/manager who worked the same hours as Helga. His job was to maintain the slots, clear jams, etc. and make fills when the machines were short of money. He also paid any jackpots in cash that weren't paid by the machines in coin. Benny was kind of a pasty-faced guy, and pudgy to the point that his pants were way too short, usually ending above his ankles. There were a couple of Swiss waitresses who called them "Hochvasser Hosen" which meant high water pants. The Cubans always said he was "going to catch shrimp."

Benny, like Helga, was a loner, and never even sat with the other employees when he was on a break. Benny's claim to fame was his brother Bobby, who was a sometimes crap dealer, and a motorcycle renegade. Bobby had half his tongue bitten off by a hooker in Tijuana, and it was the talk of the town for a while. But Benny was so nondescript that nobody knew they were brothers.

When jackpot money or "fills" went from the cage to the slots, four signatures were required: the Cage Cashier, Security, Benny and Helga. Security was supposed to go to the machine with the money, and sign the slip; the Cashier would issue the "fill" or "jackpot", and the Security Guard at the cage just signed (and 99 times out of 100 never went to the machine). Benny would take the money to the slot area where Helga would sign, and then to the machine where he would add his signature, all by himself. Standing in the slot area you were practically invisible to the rest of the casino. All the slips were turned into the cage at the end of the shift.

Benny and Helga worked together for nearly ten years, and nobody ever saw them say a word to each other, not even on slow nights, unless it pertained to business. Then they both quit, and the word was out, they had been married all those years. They were moving to Germany where they owned a big home, real estate and a large bowling alley, plus a game arcade, all paid for by The Tropicana. They sold their small home in Las Vegas, and all the furnishings before they left. I know someone (my wife) who bought a couple of Chandeliers from them and told me that everything in the home was expensive, top of the line. There is no telling how much they had stolen in all those years, it had to be a huge amount, and no proof ever existed of the scam.

It was perfect.

71. Mr. Murphy in Action

On another night at the Tropicana, after the players left my game, I walked around to the outside of the table to straighten out the chairs. I glanced over to another game, on which the aforementioned Bob Murphy was dealing, and saw him paying a bet that the player immediately snatched up and put in his pocket. It didn't look quite right, and after I came back around behind the table I turned my head and watched.

The "agent" was playing two hands. He would bet three $5 chips with a $25 chip on top, and Murphy would pay him with four $25 chips. Playing two hands, that amounted to a $200 return on an $80 investment. That's why he snatched the chips so quickly, if you weren't right on top of it you wouldn't see it from the floor. The player was wearing a tan sport coat with patch pockets, and with his back to me the pockets were so full that they looked like saddlebags.

Murphy, without moving his head, cast a sideways glance toward me to see if I was looking, and I just looked away. The Tropicana had just installed cameras over the tables, one of the first hotels on the Strip to do so, and they were installed in holes cut in the ceiling so you could look up and see the whole camera. It caused quite a buzz with the employees, and the casino manager was nice enough to let everybody know that the cameras filmed in black and white, so you couldn't distinguish the color of the chips. There was a little red light on the side of the camera that would come on when the camera was filming, so some of the dealers made a production of straightening their tie or smoothing back their hair when the red light over their game came on.

I got off shift shortly thereafter. Murphy was still on the table. I went to the bar, ordered a drink, then went to the phone and called the Pit Manager, Frank Fertitta, who was a good friend and, like most of us, wasn't a fan of Mr. Murphy. I told him what was going on, told him to nail the SOB and don't mention my name. The pit manager watched several transactions and called the casino manager and told him what he'd observed. The casino manager refused to fire Murphy, period. That of course led to the question, was the casino manager involved with the situation? The Trop was the only place in town that would hire Murphy, but then again, you never know.

72. The Slot Machine That Wasn't There

Pete Goin, Sr., was the slot manager at the Sands Hotel for over nine years. He was a close associate of Ralph Lamb, sheriff of Clark County, one of the most powerful men in the state of Nevada. The Lamb family included United States Senator Floyd Lamb, who once chaired the Senate Finance committee, and was brought down by an FBI sting. He was convicted of accepting bribes, etc., and did jail time. It was said that the Lamb family's influence helped Goin get his job at the Sands.

In 1978, Goin was convicted of embezzling from the Sands, his attorney was Oscar Goodman, famed Mob lawyer, who was to become "Hizzoner," the Mayor of Las Vegas. The amount of the embezzlement was downplayed publicly, claiming it was less than $200,000. The actual figures were in the millions. During a routine independent audit, an accountant noticed a $1 slot machine that had an unusual number of fills and jackpots, and according to the printout figures, never won any money. On further investigation it was discovered that no such machine existed. But what did exist were fills and jackpots on practically a daily basis, each in the amount of one or two thousand dollars.

All the money left the cage in the hands of the slot manager, Pete Goin, and was purportedly taken to the machine (that didn't exist). Large jackpots were hand-paid in cash. This went on for years. I guess if you can't find the machine, just put the money in your pocket. Of course, Summa Corporation (Howard Hughes Company) kept the figures secret, to avoid embarrassment. Goin got a veritable slap on the wrist, thanks to Oscar, and died a few years later.

Pete's son, Pete Goin, Jr., was a Baccarat dealer at the Sands at the time and was worried about losing his job as a result of his father's conviction. He didn't lose his job, but when he discovered that his dad left him a huge amount of cash in various safety deposit boxes, he quit. The amount was reportedly in excess of two million dollars. The exact amount can't be verified.

Pete, Jr. went on a spree. He took several of his friends to Hawaii, all first class, and they partied long and loud. Wine, women, and the designer drugs of the time, all compliments of Pete, Jr. Between gambling and other expensive habits, it took Junior about two years to go through all the money.

He then went back to work, as a Baccarat dealer at the Horseshoe Club in downtown Las Vegas, a long way from the Sands. Not too long after that he was supposedly notified of a safety deposit box that he didn't know about, this one in St. Louis, Missouri, of all places. When he claimed the contents of the box, it was said to hold close to a million dollars. In cash. As soon as he got back to Las Vegas, he quit his job, gathered an entourage, and was off to the races, again. This time it only took him about a year to go through the money. I heard that he found work as a host in one of the casinos in Laughlin, Nevada, on the Colorado River.

A classic Las Vegas "riches to rags" story.

73. The Sneak Joint

Ross Miller was a top executive at the Riviera Hotel. He was an ex bookmaker from Chicago (with ties to the Mob and especially the Teamsters Union), who provided the loan for the purchase of the hotel. He was a big, burly guy with a no-nonsense look about him, and he walked softly and carried a rather large stick.

On a busy Saturday night at the "Riv," Ross was in the casino talking to a friend. He had one arm leaning on a slot machine and had his right arm free to gesture with. At that time, a Craps dealer named Marty "Zee" got off the game for his break and headed for the restroom. He had to walk past Ross to get there and, due to the crowd, he had to pass within a few feet of Mr. Miller. As Marty started to walk by, Ross threw a hard punch to his stomach, causing him to double over and spit out a mouthful of $25 chips. Security was right there and they hustled Marty into the casino office, where he received a "lecture" on the evils of thievery. Then was terminated immediately, along with the words of wisdom.

Several days later an article appeared in the paper stating that Marty, through his attorney, was filing suit against the Riviera, and Ross Miller, for allegedly "roughing him up" prior to termination. They wanted to throw in kidnapping and a few other charges along with assault. They purportedly had photos of the bruises and cuts, and they intended to take it court. The incident got a little notoriety in the press, and then died out.

Nobody knows the outcome, but it was said that Marty, fearful of another lecture, decided to back away. As in all these cases, it's not known how long he'd been stealing, or how much, but within the next few months Marty bought the "Sneak Joint" a popular Las Vegas night spot which he ran successfully for many years.

Ross Miller's son, Robert, graduated from law school and ultimately became assistant district attorney, then district attorney (twice, the only person to have accomplished that), then eventually became a two-term governor of the State of Nevada. He served in that capacity for ten years, having replaced Governor Richard Bryan as interim governor when Bryan was elected to the United States

Senate. Ross was active in the Masons and other local organizations and didn't want his son in the "Racket." The results are evident.

And so it goes.

74. Elementary, But It Worked

Not all dealers are the same. Like everyone else some are tall, some short, some fat, some slim. Since the gaming tables were all the same size, some dealers had trouble reaching out across the felt layout. This was remedied by carpet covered wooden boxes which were under the tables. A short dealer would pull the box out when he went on the game and stand on it and deal. Also, under the tables were pieces of fiberboard, which a dealer could stand on for support if the carpet was too thick and caused back pain.

I worked at the Stardust for a short time in 1958, shortly after it opened. On my first night I reached under a table to get a board to stand on and stuck under the board was a piece of wire with a huge wad of bubblegum on one end. This could have only one purpose: when the table was being cleaned the wire could be put into the opening on the table and put down into the box, and on withdrawal whatever bills were stuck to the bubblegum went into the porter's pocket. There was one of these inventions under almost every board.

Primitive, but it was obviously effective.

75. Creating a Vacuum

Luther was a casino porter at the Flamingo hotel in 1959. He was a quiet man who did his work and never called attention to himself. He had a dignified look about him with grey hair on the sides of his head, and none in the middle. Like the doormen in the high-class apartments in New York, he was excessively polite, with a smile that had a hard look to it, as if to let you know he resented the fact that blacks were not permitted in the hotels. Even the black entertainers had to leave by the back door.

Luther had been at the Flamingo ever since the Bugsy Siegel days, and I don't recall anyone who knew his last name. He and all the other black people in town lived on the "Westside" which was a predominantly black section of town.

The dice pit at the Flamingo had five tables, four back to back and one end table, facing the showroom. The end game was always the first game to be closed as business started to drop off on the night shift. Ultimately there would be one game left open, completely away from the end table. Anyone standing at that end game would have his back to the rest of the casino, and after the last show, the showroom was closed.

Hardly anyone ever walked past that table in the wee hours of the morning, which was when the cleanup would begin. As part of the nightly routine, the felt layouts on the tables would be vacuumed, as they would have cigarette ashes and other debris on them from the evening's festivities. The porters used a loud portable canister vacuum for that purpose. Returning from a day off I was made aware that Luther had been fired. Seems that on a night when there wasn't a player in the place (it was common on the graveyard shift in those days), the shift manager had a hangover, and let it be known he was going into the showroom for a nap. It was dead quiet in there, and the large booths were a comfortable place to stretch out. After his nap he started to walk through the heavy curtains at the entrance to the showroom, and he spotted Luther, who was vacuuming the end Craps table, reach into his porter's jacket and pull out a long thin homemade attachment, and put it on the vacuum. He then inserted it into the drop box and started sucking out the cash. The attachment was too narrow to allow the bills to go into the vacuum, but as they came out of the box, Luther would take them off and put the money in an inside pocket in his coat.

The shift manager got security, and they took Luther into the casino office, relieved him of the cash, and fired him. Luther had been there since the place opened. The shift manager, one Buddy Banner was a classy man, and one of the most capable men in the industry. Buddy had worked with Luther for many years at the Flamingo, back to the Bugsy Siegel era and had no intentions of punishing him. They just took back the money and sent him home without a job. Weeks later, I asked one of the porters if Luther had found a job, and he replied: “Shit, Luther don’t have to work, he owns half the Westside.”

Compared to the wire and bubblegum Luther’s method was a quantum leap in technology.

76. Let's Talk Big Money

Baccarat is the game for high rollers all over the world. It's an offshoot of Chemin De Fer (Bird of Fire) which was first introduced in Las Vegas at the Stardust in 1958. Of all the casino games, Baccarat ("nothing," in French) is the easiest game to play. There are only two ways to wager, either on the "Bank" or the "Players." That's the only decision a person has to make. The rules are set and everything is handled by the three-man crew of dealers. The way the rules are set gives the bank a small advantage over the players, so if you wager on the bank, and win, you pay a 5% commission (vigorish) back to the house. On the main game (now they have "mini" Baccarat tables with only one dealer), the shoe moves from player to player, and as long as the bank wins the shoe stays with the same person. When the players win, the shoe moves on to the next individual. It's the same as a person on a dice game. As long as they keep making "passes" they keep the dice.

Nine is the highest hand in Baccarat, and an eight or nine on the first two cards are automatic winners, like a Blackjack. Face cards count nothing. All the other cards are face value. The person with the shoe deals two cards to the bank (Himself) and two cards to the dealer running the game from the center of the table for the players hand. As a courtesy, the dealer will present the cards to the highest wager for the players, and he gets the honor of turning the cards over and throwing them to the center of the table. The first card out of the shoe belongs to the "players" hand, the second is for the "bank," etc. Scorecards are provided for the customers to keep track of the hands, how many banks in a row, or the number of players. They can then analyze the results and try to find a "pattern" with which they can wager. Frankly, all they tell you is what happened, not what's going to happen. Some people keep collective scorecards from all their trips and feed them into computers, looking for a system. Summing it up, it's mental masturbation, but it's fun, and people love it. Some of the scams that were perpetrated in the Baccarat make cheating on the other games look like penny ante Poker.

Initially, and for many years the game was dealt with cash. Before a game opened they would bring brand new bills from the cage, and they had to be "soaped" before use, as new bills stick together and it's impossible to deal with them. The preferred soap was Dove, and it took four dealers about 20 minutes to soap up to $500,000 in cash. It took a while, but Gaming Control finally realized the consequences of an all cash game. It was impossible to keep track of and forced the hotels to go to chips. Naturally, all the gaming geniuses said that it was the "end" of the game, and that cash was what made people play it. The game never missed a beat. The only effect was that the casinos could no longer do a disappearing act with the cash.

In the early '70s, Caesars Palace had the first Baccarat game in town. And the highest play, by far. As other games opened in major resorts, none could compare to Caesars level of business. Then the word up and down the Strip was that a whole crew, (four dealers and one floor man), got caught stealing and were fired. They would take a few thousand dollars in $100 dollar bills off the table and give it to one of the "shills" to take to the cashier's cage and get $5 and $20 bills, which they supposedly needed on the game. They would put up marker buttons on the table to show that the cash was taken off the game. This was done in case anyone happened to come into the pit while they were taking the money. Supposedly, as procedure indicated, when the shill returned with the smaller bills, they would be put back into the bankroll, and the marker buttons would be removed.

But the shill never got to the cage. She would pocket the money, and after the shift, they would meet and split up the money between the six of them. If they took $10,000 a day, which is a modest estimate, they would get over $1600 apiece. When the opportunity presented itself, one of the dealers would simply take the marker buttons and return them to the rack. All cash, no record, impossible to trace.

Then the shill made a fatal mistake. She started taking her share every day, over to the Aladdin Hotel Baccarat game, and bet $100 bills like they were confetti. They knew she was a shill at Caesars, and she didn't make that kind of money, especially every day. The Baccarat manager at the Aladdin called one of the bosses at Caesars and made him aware of the situation. They staked it out, and it didn't take them long to catch these people in the act. All were fired. The floor man happened to be the Baccarat Manager's son. It was a huge scandal, and the dealers never worked in town again. The Baccarat Manager's son went to work at the Riviera the next day. Figure that out; only in Las Vegas. Nobody knows how long it was going on, or how much they got, but it had to be a substantial amount.

In another cash situation, some Baccarat dealers at the Desert Inn were palming $100 bills, jumping off the game and grabbing Kleenex from a box on a shelf behind them, sneezing or blowing their nose, and dropping the Kleenex, (and the money), into a hole in the shelf under which was a wastebasket. They would do this right in the middle of a game, then sit back down and continue to deal. Periodically the porter would come in and remove the plastic bag from the wastebasket and replace it with a fresh one.

An alert floor man became aware of the situation, and they fired the crew. I don't know what became of the porter, but I'm sure he also did very well.

One particular casino "host" at Caesars, by the name of Ash Resnick, was known to come into the Baccarat with a "customer" and tell the Baccarat boss to give him, say, $50,000. Remember, this was cash, and they would put up marker buttons on the game to designate the $50,000. Back then, they didn't have to sign a marker (a counter check) until the play was over. The "customer" would make a few mediocre bets, then he and the host would walk away with the cash. Nobody tried to stop them, and a few minutes later the host would return to the game and tell the dealers to take the marker buttons down. It wasn't a random occurrence. This particular "host" got half the cash. It was known that he had Mob connections, along with everyone else with any authority in the casino. There was no record of any of these transactions. It wasn't long before Gaming Control required that a marker (in triplicate) be signed as soon as a player was issued credit. It was good while it lasted.

77. Frank Sinatra Throws a Tantrum

On another night in the early '70s, Frank Sinatra was performing at Caesars. After his last show he would come into the Baccarat and start to play. He always had a following, and as soon as he showed up all the games would fill up. He was good for business. Before he started to play, he was to let the Baccarat manager know whether he was shilling, in which case, the play didn't count. If he won, the money would be returned to the rack or if he lost he didn't have to pay. If he declared that he was playing for real with his own money, he was just another customer with a line of credit.

This particular night he came in and told the Baccarat manager he was going to "shill up the games." He took a marker and in a short time he won $50,000. Then he stood up, put the cash in his pockets and started to leave the pit. The Baccarat manager stopped him and told him to give the $50,000 back, as he had declared that he was just going to shill. Sinatra refused, saying that he had declared that he was playing for real. The manager got on the phone and called Sandy Waterman, who was the boss and Mob representative at Caesar's. Sandy walked into the Baccarat, and when Sinatra started to argue, he reached into his coat and drew out a pistol, put it to Sinatra's head, and told him to give back the money. Frank complied and, cursing, walked out of the pit.

Frank Sinatra said he would never play Vegas again, which of course, he did. When he was playing at the Sands, he lost his credit line and asked for more money and was refused. That's when he threw his famous tantrum, and it resulted in Carl Cohen, the casino manager, punching him in the jaw and knocking out a few of his teeth. Some people never learn.

78. Excellent Baccarat Scam

In 1978 there was a group of Chinese people from Canada (Vancouver) going from casino to casino and winning a substantial amount of money. They were mostly elderly women, a few men mixed in, and purportedly couldn't speak English. The leader of the group was a young man who played and did the translating. He was fluent in English, and also was the man who put the groups together.

On many occasions they would be losing as much as $150,000 but would usually wind up getting even and winning thousands. At the time, I was dealing Baccarat at the Sands, and our day shift had yet to see these people, although they had played and won on the other shifts.

Finally, one day they showed up, got their scorecards and started to play. They would make small wagers on both the bank and players, and then they would study the scorecards, stall, converse in Chinese, then they would all make large wagers, always on the players. One of them would have the shoe and make a small bet on the bank. Everyone used to laugh when they did this and would say, "looks like the word is out on the players."

I came in off my break and went on the "pole," which was directing the game and calling out the winners and losers, much like the "stickman" on a Craps table. After each hand the cards would be dropped through an opening in the table into a box or can below. When the shoe ran out, the cards would be reshuffled. After one hand when all the large wagers were on the players, I started to drop the cards in the slot and as I did, I noticed a nick on the edge of the card. Looking closer I saw that there was a small dent on both sides of the card, in the center of the edge. This is the part of the card that's exposed on the face of the shoe, so the card can be pushed out of the shoe. Glancing at the card, I saw that it was a nine. I started to look at the cards after each hand was played and noticed that every eight and nine in the deck had similar nicks, which is easily done by a flick of the thumbnail.

The first card out of the shoe goes to the player's hand, and since eight and nine are the highest hands in the game, this gives the players a substantial edge. The person who had the shoe would merely run his finger along the edge of the card. If he felt the nick, or "crimp" as it was called, he would signal that the first card was an eight or a nine, and everybody would bet substantially on the players. When I came around the table to do my 40 minutes on the dealing side, I told the manager the cards were marked. Some other people could have been in with the cheaters and marked the cards over several hours; there were a lot of ways to accomplish this. Then, when the group came in, everything was ready for them, and all they had to do was sit and play. About 30 minutes later, just before I went on my break, they changed the cards. When I returned, the Chinese were gone, and the boss called me over and said, "We checked the cards, and there was nothing wrong with them." I just smiled and went to work. This told me that the boss was "in" with the play (paid to turn a blind eye) or that if it were exposed, would look incompetent in the eyes of his superiors, and seeing that he *was* incompetent I don't blame him. The fact that these people had won over $100,000 during several different visits could have cost him his job. I knew that the cards were nowhere to be found, probably taken out of the area while I was on my break.

My brother was dealing Baccarat at Caesars Palace, and it was known that these people had been winning a substantial amount of money at that casino. I called him and told him what I had found out, and that he should be the one to expose it at Caesars and get the credit for it. It could be a career enhancer. Several days later an article appeared in the newspaper that the scam had taken place, and some arrests were made. Most of those involved had beat it out of town, and I don't know what happened to the few that were apprehended. Probably nothing. My brother was the one who exposed it, and it didn't enhance his career.

79. Guess What

In an interesting twist to this incident, many years later, I retired and moved to Washington State. One afternoon we were on our way to visit Vancouver, BC, and on our way up interstate 5 we came to a tribal casino, in Bow, Washington, which had a Harrah's sign in front. We stopped and went inside. There I noticed a room off the casino floor, with a large Baccarat table. This was highly unusual in an Indian casino, even one managed by Harrah's, as it's an expensive game to staff and run, costing a lot more than mini Baccarat tables.

I found the Casino Manager (a woman) and introduced myself. We exchanged some shoptalk for a few minutes, and then I mentioned that I had noticed the big Baccarat game and wondered why they would have one. She replied "we have a lot of Asian customers from the Vancouver area who come down on buses a few times a week, and they requested a big Baccarat game, as they didn't like to play big money on a mini Baccarat. So, being Harrah's, we gave them what they wanted." I asked her how they were doing with the game, and she told me, "Not too well right now, but that will change. It seems like we get them in the hole, and they seem to wiggle out and wind up winning." I left it at that. I made a note to come back up on a weekend night and see what was happening on the game, but then decided that I didn't care whether Harrah's was getting screwed or not. About nine months later, we headed up to Vancouver again, and when we got to the casino, the Harrah's sign was no longer there. We went inside, and I noticed that the big Baccarat table was gone. When I asked the shift manager what happened to it, and to Harrah's, she just shrugged her shoulders and walked away. Some people learn lessons the hard way.

80. Short Memory

One Saturday night at the Dunes Hotel I was dealing in a big Roulette game. The place was packed and there were stacks of chips on and around every number. One of the rules on a Roulette wheel in every casino is that when a large wager is put on a number, you call a floor man's attention to it. He then has the option to come over and watch the play. As long as you call it out, you're okay. However, there are times that a bet will be put down a few seconds before the ball falls, and you don't have time to get an acknowledgement. The ball fell, I called out the number (it was 31) and pointed to it, and there on the bottom of a stack of chips of various colors, was a $25-dollar chip. It wasn't directly under the other chips, about 3/4 of the way, causing the chips on the number to tilt a little to the side. I remember feeling numb.

I was sure the chip was put down *after* the ball fell, but I didn't see it come in. It's called past posting, and one of the main ways to cheat a wheel. As a rule, past posters work in teams. One person would reach over the layout as the ball was dropping, purportedly to make a bet. He would be told it's too late, and meanwhile they blocked your view for a second after the ball was in the number, and in comes the chip. Some teams are pretty smooth, if there's any doubt, a dealer will pay the wager, as long as it's not a huge amount.

I was in a bad spot. The payout was $875, and I didn't call anyone's attention to it, and I was sure I'd been had, but not 100% sure. I figured I was in trouble anyway, and getting past-posted wasn't good for my reputation, especially if I got fired for it. So, I decided to take a chance. I asked, "Whose chip is this?" A big, dark-complected guy in a suit standing on the outside of the game said, "It's mine, it's mine." and acted like he was all excited. I flicked the chip back at him and told him "You can bet it on the next roll," and he started to protest, but not too loudly.

I finally told him that I was going to tell the pit boss to call security if he didn't go away. He still argued, so I turned around to call the pit boss over, and he disappeared. A few minutes later, I went on a break and was just sitting down in the dealers' lounge when a porter came in and told me that they wanted to see me in the pit. I got a knot in my stomach because I knew it had to do with the incident. As I was walking to the pit I saw Sid Wyman, one of the big bosses standing there, and just outside the gaming area were two big security guards holding the guy who tried to cheat me. They had him by the arms so he couldn't bolt, and one of the guards had a look on his face that meant he was looking forward to the festivities in the back room. His nickname was "Tiny" and he stood about 6'5" and weighed a good 300 pounds. He made no bones about the fact that he enjoyed hurting "bad guys." The man they were holding was white as a sheet and was sweating profusely.

Tiny was a dumb sonofabitch, and people used to marvel at the fact that such a small brain could propel such a big body. As I came into the pit, Sid Wyman said to me, "I understand that someone tried to past-post you on the wheel a few minutes ago." Obviously, one of the players on the wheel was a guest of Sid's' and ran to tell him about it. I looked directly at the man and for a second my eyes diverted slightly to the left and saw Frank Portnoy, a floor man, and an old timer in the industry. As I looked at him he gave a barely perceptible shake of his head meaning no. I then told Mr. Wyman, "No, this is not the man, it looks a lot like him, but it wasn't him." The guy looked like someone let all the air out of him, his knees wobbled, and his eyes rolled up in relief. They offered apologies and told him he was free to go. He beat it out of there, and I thought Tiny was going to cry, he looked so disappointed.

When everything settled down, Portnoy (whom I had worked with at the Stardust) came up behind me and said, "It's okay, they would have taken him in the back and beat the shit out of him, or worse, and for what? He didn't get away with it, just don't ever forget what he looks like."

Sage advice, as years later I was the wheel boss at the Frontier Hotel, and one night I saw this same guy standing on the outside of one of the wheels with a handful of chips. I walked over to him and said, "Do you remember me?" He looked closely, and said, "No, I don't believe I do," with a smile on his face thinking I was talking to him as a customer. He was a little heavier and his hair a little greyer, but it was the same man. I said to him, "I saved your ass at the

Dunes Hotel several years ago, and now you're paying me back by coming in here to pull the same shit? This time I'm going to call security, have them take your picture, and call the police and Gaming Control if you try to do anything in here."

He then realized who I was and told me he would leave and never come back. As he turned to walk away he glanced at a woman who was sitting on the game and made a slight motion with his head. I saw them walking out the front door together. They were obviously working as a team. She would block the dealers view, and he would slip the chip in. We could have detained him on suspicion, and got some ID and a picture, but I chose not to. I was busy enough, I didn't need the paperwork that was involved in these situations. In the Mob casinos it was different, but this was Summa Corporation (Howard Hughes).

81. Not Your Garden Variety

Then along came the slugs. A slug is a clump of cards whose order has either been memorized or whose sequence has been tracked by computer. There are various ways of doing this. One example would be a person on the outside watching a game and watching the sequence as the dealer picks up the cards and puts them in the discard rack. He could smoke a cigarette and every time he takes a drag he tells the order of the cards to an accomplice with a cell phone. The accomplice then enters it into a computer. The dealer has to be involved, as when he shuffles the cards he purposely doesn't shuffle that particular group of cards, and when a certain sequence appears they would then know what cards are coming out next and bet accordingly.

In Baccarat the cards are "washed" face up on the table and a certain group of cards set aside, and false shuffled. Believe it or not there are individuals that could look at, say, 35 cards and memorize the order they're in. When a certain sequence appears, no matter where in the deck, they know what and where to bet. There were a group of Vietnamese who traveled all over the country, enlisted Vietnamese dealers (and some Caucasians) to work with them. They would promise a dealer as much as $5000 for every false shuffle he makes that results in them winning large wagers.

The casinos (mostly tribal casinos) knew something was going on, because the losses totaled millions, but they didn't know what. They called in the FBI and finally caught the bad guys. They were all sentenced to lengthy jail terms and forced to pay restitution, forfeit bank accounts, etc. One of the cheating dealers at a local Indian Casino was the son of the Mayor of Seattle. He did not go to jail.

82. Junkets

By the late '50s and early '60s the town had started to grow, and the available business was being spread between the hotels. Aside from advertising and promotion, nothing was really done to promote business, although there were a few small conventions, there was no adequate facility for large groups. The Las Vegas Convention Center was completed in 1959, and the city had yet to start booking groups into town. At around 110,000 sq. feet, it couldn't adequately accommodate huge trade shows. And the conventions didn't attract gamblers, so the hotels needed to find ways to tap the huge amounts of money in the major metropolitan areas. Some of the hotels began to "buy" business, which was a new term at the time. Buying business was a euphemism for bringing in groups, buses, etc., and offering free transportation. No other incentives were needed as the rooms, food and entertainment were so cheap, it was the best bargain in the world.

Then an enterprising gentleman (with some unsavory connections) from New York approached the Flamingo Hotel and offered to bring a planeload of gamblers—no dead weight—who had to put up at least $5000 in cash, and he, The New Yorker, would agree to extend credit on his say-so. He would also do the collecting. In return, the hotel had to pay for the plane, all rooms, food and beverage.

His deal with the hotel was most likely on a head count basis; a certain amount per player. The first junket into Las Vegas was brought to the Flamingo in early 1960. It was a charter flight out of New York, and from what I understand the flight was a real party. Thousands of dollars supposedly changed hands in a crap game in the rear of the plane, it was rumored that there were a few hookers along for the ride, provided by the junketeer, and the booze flowed like water.

Anyway, these guys hit the door about 7PM and got right down to business. They had called all the dealers in early and every game in the casino was open. I was on a Blackjack table nearest the door at the time, and one individual stopped at the table and put a small valise on the stool. As he started to open it, I jokingly asked him if he was going to change his underwear, and he said, "My underwear is in my suitcase, and they're taking it to my room. This is my allowance." He opened the valise and it was full of cash: 20's, 50s and hundred-dollar bills. Then he asked me what the limit was. I told him. He said, "Shuffle the cards." I did so and his first bet was $500.

These guys couldn't get enough of wide open legal gaming. Las Vegas was the only place in the world where they could gamble and not look over their shoulder. The junket was a huge success. Beside the cash they brought with them, they all had large credit lines. I don't think they slept for 72 hours, and they were all winning. Every game in the place went sour for the whole time they were there and when it came time for them to go home, collectively, they were winning a substantial amount of money.

They left around 7PM on a Sunday night and the place was practically empty. We all figured that they would start closing down some of the games and we would have a chance to go home early, having worked extra hours to accommodate the business. The junket, plus the normal weekend business, had the hotel and casino personnel stretched to the limits. However, as the action began to wind down, they kept every game in the place open. We stood there in disbelief, looking at each other as if to say, "What the hell's going on?"

We were afraid to ask any questions, the casino manager was drunk, and on the warpath, and the fact that the casino had lost so much money made the dealers expendable. Finally, about midnight, there were only a few players in the place, no more than ten, still, every game was open; we were just standing there. Then, about 1:30 AM, the front door flew open, in rushed the junket that had left earlier and they were not happy.

It seems that the plane developed "engine trouble" about two hours into the flight and had to return to Las Vegas for repairs. The Flamingo was nice enough to offer them rooms and food while the necessary repairs were being made. Of course, to alleviate the boredom, they all hit the tables again, and nobody seemed to notice that all the games were open and waiting for them. The casino's fortunes turned and they managed to win back most of the money they had lost, plus a little extra. Only then were the "repairs" finalized, and they once again headed for the airport. They moaned and groaned, were not just a little suspicious, but nobody wanted to take a chance on a faulty engine. This time it was about 8PM the following evening, and they closed down a bunch of tables as soon as the group departed.

When the news of the lucrative junket at the Flamingo got around town it didn't take long for the other hotels to follow suit. Almost every casino had a "representative" with an office in almost every major city in the country. Their job was to put the junkets together, approve credit and collect for the casinos. At first, they could only approve credit on the information the casino was provided with by their own investigations, but as things progressed, that changed. It wasn't long before the golden goose began to lose a little of its luster. It started with the wives (What else?).

Seems that some of the single guys mentioned the female companionship that was provided on the flight, and the wives got wind of it. Now, in quite a few cases the wives insisted on being with the group. After all, they loved Las Vegas too. Some of them were players in their own right, and although the slots were still not a major factor in the casino revenue, they managed to hold up their end of the action, although not to the extent that their husbands did. Many times, a husband would join his wife at the Blackjack table and bet $5 chips to the tune of $10 or $20 a hand, and as soon as his spouse got involved in the game he would go over to the Craps, take five or ten thousand in credit and bet $100 chips by the handful. I never heard a wife question the color of the chips, although the men would play with one eye on the crap game and the other on their wives.

This then, made it more expensive for the casino to bring in the junket as the cost of food and beverage doubled. Some wives would order a case (or two) of champagne sent to the room, pour it into the bath tub, mix in a little hot water, and take a champagne bath, probably just to say they did it. The men-only junkets ordered bottles of liquor to their rooms, and even a case or two, and took it home with them. The bellmen even remarked how much liquor went out the door when the groups departed, yet it was still a profitable situation for the casino. However, the profits began to erode, if ever so slightly.

The only restaurants in the hotels were what the term "coffee shop" describes, although the food was excellent and inexpensive. All the hotels also offered a buffet, which was called "The Chuck Wagon" to keep with the western motif. These were amazing. They offered every kind of seafood imaginable—shrimp, lobster, crab, clams, oysters etc.—along with prime rib, turkey, hams, huge assortments of fruits and vegetables, and endless desserts. The price of the chuck wagons was $1. That's right, all this was available for a buck, in every Strip hotel. The showrooms were no cover, no minimum, you could see the finest entertainment in the world for the price of a coke. The only requirement was that if you attended the first show (there were two a night) you had to eat dinner. The most expensive dinner on the menu was a New York Steak dinner for $5.50. The Desert Inn showroom seated 350, with a partition that could be removed to add additional tables. The Flamingo could accommodate 500. The Stardust had the largest capacity, but not by much. The main restaurant in the Desert Inn was the Cactus Room, with the Patio Room adjacent, for outdoor dining. The discriminating customers from the East weren't happy with the fact that this was the only available dining in a town known for luxury. The Stardust had a seafood restaurant, but it wasn't what you would call gourmet. The Sands served great Chinese food in the coffee shop.

The only gourmet restaurant opened in Las Vegas was in 1950, it was called LaRue's, was large, fancy, and lasted barely a year. It fell victim to a fire of "suspicious" origin and burned to the ground. It wasn't long after that the Sands was built on the foundation. You had to go down two steps to get into LaRue's, and down the same two steps to get into the Sands casino a few years later.

83. The First Gourmet Restaurant in a Hotel

This led to the opening of the first gourmet room on the Las Vegas Strip, the Candlelight Room in the Flamingo Hotel. The Maître D' was Nat Hart, a famous chef and gourmet, who was the Maître D' of the Flamingo showroom. The Candlelight Room was small and ritzy. the food supposedly rivaling the best restaurants anywhere. It was also comparatively expensive, and most of the patrons were complimentary guests of the casino. This was what was called a “comp room.” Not many were willing to spend money on an expensive meal with everything else that was available at the time for a lot less. It was a big success and before long people from other hotel junkets were going to the Flamingo for a gourmet dinner.

This, in turn, led to the proliferation of gourmet rooms in most of the hotels, but it all started with the Candlelight Room. It brought quite a bit of lucrative business into the Flamingo while the other hotels were following suit. The fact that the Flamingo had been purchased by the owners of the Fontainebleau and Eden Roc in Miami Beach, and were familiar with gourmet amenities, didn’t hurt the situation. The Candlelight Room started Las Vegas on the way to becoming a gourmet paradise.

With the junket business increasing on the Strip, some hotels reached out to other countries, such as Mexico, and the Pacific Rim. Macau had gambling, but compared to Las Vegas it was a shoddy situation, and it wasn’t until 20 years later that it began to compete with Las Vegas for the business of the players who were becoming wealthy as a result of the international economy. Before Baccarat, the few customers from South of the Border were mostly Roulette and Blackjack players. Some were what we called high rollers, but they were a rarity. Enter Baccarat, and everything changed; all the hotels reached out for their business.

84. Nothing But the Best

By the late ‘70s, the hotels were getting old and the bugs and mice moved in. In 1978, a high roller got up from our Baccarat table to have dinner in the Regency room, the gourmet restaurant. When he returned I asked him how his dinner had been. He replied, “When we ordered, a cockroach ran across the top of the table, and I called for the Maître D' and told him what happened.” The Maître D' told him, “Don’t worry, these are gourmet cockroaches.”

On New Year’s Eve there wasn’t an empty room in town and a Mexican millionaire told the chief host Bucky Harris that his wife had seen a mouse run across the floor of their room, and she refused to stay. I overheard the phone conversation from just a few feet away. The hotel manager told Bucky that there were *no* rooms anywhere. Bucky replied, “Can’t we do something for him? Can we send him a cat?”

85. Bienvenido

There was a constant influx of junkets from Mexico, and they were a large segment of the Baccarat business. They represented two segments of the Mexican population. The European transplants whose families fled Europe prior to world war two, and had names like Kershenovich, Liebowitz, Kluter, Klein, Greenberg, etc., and the native Mexicans with the traditional Spanish names. They were tough to deal with. Some were honorable, most couldn't be trusted. Baccarat was the national game of Mexico, and the casinos were the enemy. Period. Among those who had lines of credit were industrialists, business moguls, and those blessed with old money, brought from Europe and multiplied a thousand times. They, however, paled in comparison to the credit lines extended to high-ranking law enforcement officials. One of the largest credit lines was extended to the Police Chief of Mexico City. Chiefs of police forces from resort areas weren't far behind. The lines extended to lesser police dignitaries were commensurately smaller, but still substantial.

Dealing with a foreign country and the language barrier made for a tough situation in regard to checking credit and collections. This was left to the "junketeers," who created additional problems. A wealthy Mexican businessman got off a cruise ship in Los Angeles, instead of going home, he came directly to Las Vegas without going through the Sands Hotel's Mexican representative. He had a $30,000 credit line and they immediately put him in a suite. When he came down to play, he asked for a marker, and was told that he still owed $30,000 from a junket trip, three months before. He replied, "I paid that marker to Jose (Jose Breault, the Mexican representative) two weeks after we got home." Seems that Jose was collecting the money from the players and depositing it in a Mexican bank under his name. The interest rates in Mexico at that time were substantially higher than those in the US, and not subject to scrutiny. He would leave the money for two or three months, draw the interest, then pay the casino. It was like having a savings account of at least $300,000 to over $500,000 drawing interest compounded, probably through a special deal with the bank. He of course, approved the man for another $30,000 and wired the money to the Sands. Whatever he told his customers, nobody knows. These guys knew every angle in the book.

86. Innocent Mistake

I recall an incident that happened in the Baccarat at the Sands. It was a slow afternoon, and a man who was with the Junket from Mexico sat down at our game and asked for a $5000 marker. We gave him the chips, he signed the marker and in a matter of ten minutes won several thousand dollars. He then pushed $5,000 in chips to the center of the table and announced that he wanted to buy his marker back. The markers were kept in an accordion file on a small podium near the computer. As a rule, one of the shills would act as a pit clerk and handle the paperwork. Because it wasn't busy at the time, all the girls were on the games. The floor man, whose name was Bud Milner walked over to the file, took out a marker and, walking over to the customer, looked the marker over, and handed it to him. The player looked at the marker, did a quick double take, and proceeded to tear it up. But this wasn't a normal ripping up of a marker. He tore it into little pieces, and tore the little pieces into littler pieces, and then started on the littler pieces. I was working with a couple of dealers that had been around a while and were pretty savvy. When the gentleman put the teeny pieces in the ash tray and started to swish them around with a lit cigarette, the other two dealers on the game and I looked at each other, and we knew what happened.

The player got up and left and, within ten minutes, another Mexican came in and asked for a $10,000 marker. Bud went over to the computer, came back to the game and told him that his credit line of $50,000 was all used up. He couldn't get any more money. This man said, "That's not true, I paid my marker." After Bud told him that the computer showed him owing $50,000. The man replied, "The computer is in error, if I owe the money, show me the marker." Let me add that in any dispute of this nature, when all the possibilities are exhausted, the final proof is the signed marker. No marker, no obligation. When Bud went to get the marker, of course it wasn't there. He had given it to the man who was paying his $5,000 marker. We could see it coming. It was even two different names.

Now, Bud was in deep doo-doo. He called the shift manager, who called the casino manager and the junket representative, and they all came into the Baccarat pit. They huddled in a corner a few feet from me, and I heard Bud tell the casino manager that the girl handed him the marker that he gave to the player. I turned around and said, "That's bullshit, Bud. There wasn't a girl over there, I saw you get the marker yourself" I thought he was going to pass out. At that point I could have cared less. I'd known the casino manager for years, and, wasn't afraid to speak up. Here was a guy trying to blame a girl with a couple of kids, and possibly cause her to lose her job, for his own stupid mistake. If it would have come down to her word against his, she would have lost. In the end the casino had to eat the $50,000. Bud didn't lose his job, why, I'll never know. This is the character of a large portion of the casino workers in those days.

The Sands was a Howard Hughes hotel at the time of the incident.

87. The Main Attraction under the Big Top

When I worked in the Baccarat at Circus Circus, we had a large Mexican clientele, junkets for the most part. Some would bring cash, most took credit. When they would get lucky and win, they would try to cash out without paying their markers and put the cash in a safety deposit box provided by the cashier's cage. This was, of course, confidential territory, nobody could get into their box but them, or so they thought. The casino manager had a key and when the group was in town, he checked their boxes every night. They could have $20,000 in cash in a box, and want to leave town owing the hotel, taking that cash with them, claiming they were broke.

The casino manager finally told the junket rep to tell his people that we keep track of their cash-outs, and know they have "some" cash, and if they didn't pay, he was going to call the police. When they heard the word "police" they couldn't pay fast enough. Although they threatened to take their business elsewhere, nobody bolted.

Here's why. The Baccarat game at Circus Circus was a phenomenon. If ever there was a casino that shouldn't have a Baccarat game it was the "Circus." It was a really nice area but located on the midway that circled the gaming area, next to the shooting gallery, and the Skee Ball. On the other side was the basketball shoot. Coupled with the constant Circus noises it was an unlikely situation. But the Mexican business kept it going in great fashion. The high rolling Mexicans from Caesars Palace or some of the other places used to come in when they were in town, though you would think that they wouldn't be caught dead in Circus Circus. The reason? Patootie. We had eight shills (four on each shift) and they were all attractive. After they were hired they would be told "We have some customers that want female companionship when they're here, and if you're willing, we pay $50. If *they* pay, you can get whatever the traffic will bear. You'll never have to go with anyone you don't care to, and it is not a prerequisite to keeping your job. It's your choice."

I was amazed that all but one accepted the proposition. Some of these women were married with families. I doubt their husbands were aware. Of course, everything was strictly confidential. Whenever they were in town, no matter where they were staying, these Mexican high rollers would send their wives to the malls with open credit, and head for Circus Circus. They knew they had to gamble to receive these "services," and when they sat down at the game, they immediately began looking the ladies over. They were like the proverbial bull in the China shop. Circus had recently built two towers of rooms and suites, and the suites were always available for these liaisons. It was never discussed outside the Baccarat area, and there was never a problem. Along with alcohol, "patootie" was the biggest ally of a gambling house. Together, they were a lethal combination.

88. Jay Sarno; Genius and Lecher

Jay Sarno was the owner (with hidden partners) of Circus Circus. He was also the founder of Caesars Palace. He lived in a suite upstairs. A couple times a week he would come into the Baccarat and look over the girls, make small conversation and leave. Inevitably the phone would ring a few minutes later and one of the girls would get up and leave. They were never gone very long. Jay was suspected to be a pervert of sorts, but no charges were ever filed. There was one girl, supposedly a waitress, across the street at the Riviera, that he wanted in the worst way, and she would have nothing to do with him. That is, until he offered her any concession on the midway. She chose the shooting gallery. It was all legal; papers were drawn up making her the concessionaire, for a couple of bucks a month, with an ironclad lease. This was pretty lucrative for a few minutes of her time, and she only had to do it twice, supposedly.

Kenny Rogers was playing the lounge in the Riviera across the Strip from the Circus, and he was dating the lady that owned the shooting gallery. Every morning at 2AM he would come into the place, empty the coin boxes, convert them to cash at the cashier's cage, come into the Baccarat and play $5 a hand. If he was the only player we would sometimes close the game early, and he would complain. But, the next night he would be back. He was a pretty nice guy. We referred to him as "Count De Nichols." Who knew how famous he was destined to become?

89. No Spikka Da English

The really high players were mostly from Asia, China, Malaysia, Japan, etc. Whenever anyone appeared with a suitcase full of cash, it was from these areas. The Arabs gambled high, but mostly on credit. The Desert Inn had a representative on Taiwan, who also had some heavyweights (high players) from mainland China. They (supposedly) spoke little or no English, and all the interpreting was done through the junketeer. He could say anything he wanted and nobody would know the difference. The casino tried to find a Baccarat dealer who spoke Chinese, but there were so many different dialects they gave up on the idea. They had soft tip pens available as all the markers were signed in Chinese. For all they knew a player could take a $5000 (or larger) marker and sign "Screw you." where the name was supposed to be.

On more than one occasion when the casino questioned why a customer hadn't paid his marker the junketeer would say "Oh, he die". My brother saw one of these "corpses" in a group about nine months after his demise, and when he brought it to the Baccarat managers attention, the manager said, "Can't be, he's dead." To top it all off, when it came time to pay, the really big players wanted a discount on what they owed, they asked for 5%. When the casino balked, it was agreed that a 2% discount over a certain amount was part of the deal.

This was a Summa Corp. hotel (Howard Hughes). I don't think any of the other casinos agreed to blanket discounts, however they probably negotiated on an individual basis. Quote from an old gaming boss, "Everybody wants to play, nobody wants to pay."

As time wore on, the junkets were becoming less and less profitable for the casinos, With the exception of some from out of the country. Most of the American customers were broke, or on their way to being so. Remember that, if a person has a credit line of $20,000, which he should be able to pay, he probably has the same line with four or five other casinos, which brings his available credit to over $100,000. This could cause problems. Finally, the hotels all plugged into "central credit" so they could find out who owes what and where, and for how long. It was a great innovation.

The end result for the junkets from the big U.S. cities came down to the fact that the loan sharks (known as "shylocks," or "shys") made more money than the casinos, who had to pay airfare and rooms, food and beverage, which was becoming more and more expensive. On a frequent basis, the junketeer would call a shylock right from the gaming area and see if he wanted to approve someone for more credit if their line was used up. The loan sharks would guarantee the money, and the poor sucker was up against 2 to 5% interest ("juice," or "vig") *weekly*. If you didn't pay, you had a real problem. Lots of people were ruined this way.

90. The Quick Fix Is In

In 1958 a group from Las Vegas opened a casino in the Rosarito Beach Hotel in Rosarito, Mexico. A couple of the guys who went down to open it were employed at the Riviera Hotel in Las Vegas. One, a fella by the name of Kemp told me that they had a solid "fix' in with the local police and politicians and they were "in like Flynn."

The Rosarito Beach Hotel was the playground for a lot of Hollywood stars, and it was, at the time, the "place to be" in Mexico. The same cocktail waitress that I dated at the Stardust told me that one of the floor men told her to come down to Rosarito and he would arrange for someone to pass some money off to us, probably at a gaming table. Being a charter member of the Red-Hot Stove club, she jumped at the chance, so she, my roommate and I drove down to Rosarito and checked into the hotel.

The hotel was magnificent, the grounds and view of the ocean were not to be believed. We spent a few hours at the pool, and I was in a lounge chair next to the actor Jack Palance who was quite amiable. We had dinner and walked through a tunnel-like hall toward the casino. The hall was solid mosaic tile, floor, ceiling and walls. This made the acoustics such that we could hear the dice rattling down the table before we got to the gaming area.

When we walked into the casino the floor man we were supposed to be colluding with, pulled his nose when he saw us, which meant that everything was off. If he had pulled on his ear that would mean it's a "go." That's a universal signal in casinos in situations like these.

So, there we were, all dressed up and nowhere to go. The next morning, we headed back towards San Diego, stopped in Tijuana and bought a lot of liquor, which cost about half of its cost in the US. We also bought several large piggy banks that resembled bulls to take to friends. When we crossed the border, we stopped at customs and they asked if we were bringing anything back from Mexico. I told him that we had bought some booze and the souvenir bulls. When they inventoried the liquor, they told us that we had to pay duty on it, and it would have wound up costing us twice as much as buying it in California. They said we had two choices, throw it in the large cans at the back of the customs building or pay the duty. We drove around the back and made a production of throwing the piggy banks into the trash and kept the liquor, then drove off.

At the time there was no freeway to Los Angeles or anywhere else from San Diego, we were driving up highway 101. About ten miles up the road I heard a siren and there was a car behind me with the lights flashing, behind the car was a whole line of motorcycles all with flashing lights. They surrounded us, placed us under arrest, and we headed back down to customs. They had gone back to get their booze, (I'm sure they were going to keep it for themselves) and found the piggy banks. Now, they told us the fine was $2400 for the driver (me) and $1200 for each passenger. You could buy a Cadillac for $6000. We just sat there for two hours, and they told us that if we didn't have the money we're headed for the hoosegow. They had us scared to death. Finally, they told us we could leave, and gave us a lecture. I hope they enjoyed the liquor. I'm sure they would have pocketed any fine we paid, too.

When we got back to Las Vegas we heard that the Federales raided the casino in Rosarito the day we left and locked up everybody involved in the casino. They also confiscated their cars, boats and jewelry. Seems like their "fix" got nervous, pocketed their "down payment" and notified the Federales.

Now, in those times nobody cared about a bunch of "dirty gamblers" that got jailed in Mexico, this includes the government. So, there they sat, for almost a year, until some of the families got through to one of the congressmen, who, although taking his good old time, got them released. They were walked across the border, and met by families and friends, no official welcome. They also returned without their cars, boats and personal items. Just the clothes on their backs. Their expensive gamblers' wardrobes were being worn by their "fix" and his friends.

91. George Capri; Family Man

George Capri was a host at the Flamingo hotel. He and his brother Billy owned the Flamingo Capri motel, on the Strip about 500 yards north of the Flamingo Hotel. They were separated by a huge dry wash that ran clear down into the valley. In later years a huge rainstorm in the mountains caused a flash flood which wiped out the Caesars Palace parking lot and sent quite a few cars down the wash, under the Strip, and into the desert. My brother's Cadillac was found six miles away.

George and Billy didn't look like brothers. George was tall, with white hair which was always perfectly coiffed. He had a perennial deep tan and dressed impeccably. Billy, on the other hand was short, always dressed in khaki pants, white tennis shoes and a loose polo shirt. He always had a smile on his face, and a little sunburn on the end of his nose.

George was a classy man with a quiet demeanor who was pleasant to everybody, whether you were a dealer, porter or busboy. On more than one occasion he would come through the casino carrying a suitcase, and if I had no players on my game he would stop and inquire about the fishing. I asked him if he was taking a trip, and he would say he was going to New York to visit family. He did this quite often, and being young, and in the business for just a few years, I thought that here was a man that truly loved his family to the point where he would travel a great distance to spend time with them.

On December 16th, 1960, two airliners collided over New York City. Large chunks of fiery wreckage and body parts fell to the ground in Brooklyn and on Staten Island. Besides the 127 passengers and crew, five people on the ground were killed and many more injured. The flaming wreckage was strewn over several miles. George Capri was on one of the planes. The ensuing news covering the incident (mostly in the news magazines) had brief mention of large sums of money that were found scattered in the area-some as far as eight miles away. Bills of different denominations were found on balconies, rooftops and on the streets, although the snow was deep enough to cover a lot of currency.

In my naiveté I didn't realize that the "family" he was referring to was the New York crime syndicate, and he wasn't carrying clean underwear in that suitcase. Then, of course the word around town was that he was the "bag-man" and the amount of money he was carrying grew larger by the day.

92. More Local Color

Wally Sanders was a funny little guy. He was short, with a pear-shaped body and a little red nose. He was shy and quiet, and always looked like he was apologizing for his presence. Wally's generosity far exceeded his good looks. He always had a $20 bill for anyone that looked hungry or down on his luck and if you were lucky enough to have him at your wedding or some such occasion, there was always a crisp $100 bill that he would stick in your pocket and run away, sometimes before you had a chance to thank him.

Wally lived alone, was never married, and could be found at the Faro game at the Stardust with a four-day beard and bloodshot eyes held up by bags underneath. Nobody knew what he did for a living. He was a gofer for some of the "Boys" on occasion, hustled some hot goods once in a while and, being from Cleveland, probably got a monthly check from the Ohio State disability fund, which was huge because of the unions. Everybody I knew from Cleveland got one of these checks, thanks to the lawyers and doctors who colluded with each other on the "examinations." I don't know how far up the ladder the corruption went, but I imagine it went quite a ways, and the lawyers and doctors involved got wealthy and then some.

When illegal gambling opened in Florida in the '40s, Wally happened to be "around." There was a bar where quite a few casino employees gathered after the casino closed for the night; everyone sat around and relaxed before going home.

One early morning, Wally came in and sat at the end of the bar and ordered a drink. Several of the guys were at the bar and one of them bought Wally's drink. When the bartender took the money off the bar to pay for it, Wally saw he overcharged the guy. Not being sure, he watched and saw the bartender not only overcharge, but when he wiped the bar with the rag, a few dollars would come off with the rag. These casino guys were good tippers, steady customers and never paid much attention to what they had on the bar. When the money would get low, they would just add to it and keep drinking. Wally motioned the bartender over and said, "I saw what you've been doing, and I don't care what you do to anyone else, but we don't deserve to have that happen to us. Cut it out." The bartender, a big man, looked at Wally and told him to mind his own business.

Wally ordered another drink and, when the bartender put the drink on the bar, he found himself with a snub-nosed 38 pistol up against his neck under his jaw. Wally said "I told you these guys are my friends." Cocking the gun, he added, "Do it again and you'll find out if I mean what I say."

I'm told that the bartender never abused the privilege of serving these gentlemen again. When the guys asked Wally what that was all about, he told them what was going on. They still came in on nights the casino was open and spent their money.

Me, I'd have found another watering hole.

On another occasion, the 12-year-old son of a good friend of Wally's got a job putting circulars under the windshield wipers of cars parked in downtown Miami. They owed the kid $20, and when he went for his money they refused to pay him, accusing him of throwing the circulars in the bay. When the kid told them that some of the other guys did it, but he didn't, they chased him out of their office. Wally found out about it, and the next day he gave the kid a check for $20, from the advertising company.

Word had it that he gave the advertising people the same lecture that he gave the bartender.

93. The Court Jester

Wally was also the perpetrator of some of the funniest pranks that ever happened in Las Vegas. One night he came into the Desert Inn lounge, where I was in a booth with my dad and a few guys having a drink after work. He sat down and nudged me and showed me an apparatus the likes of which I had never seen. It was a bent piece of wire coat hanger, with a couple of rubber bands and a metal washer. I said, "What is it?" and he replied, "Watch."

He then wound up the washer, placed it on the seat of the booth and sat on it. Then he rose up off the seat, and it sounded just like someone was breaking wind (or farting, if you will) and it was loud. When he lowered himself back down, it stopped. It got everyone's attention, and he explained that you can do it repeatedly until the rubber bands unwound all the way. The sound was perfect every time and the volume depended on the fabric you were sitting on. In a vinyl booth or on a Blackjack stool it was like a 21-gun salute. Even with the noise from the group on the stage, it turned a few heads. We were in the booths that backed up to the casino and were no more than 15 feet from the Blackjack tables. Wally said, "Watch."

He walked out of the lounge and up to a Blackjack table right in front of our booth. There were two elderly women playing a few bucks on the table, and the dealer was an older guy with his glasses on the end of his nose. Wally sat down in the first seat and slipped his "invention" underneath him. He bet a dollar and the dealer dealt the cards.

Remember, the lounge music was deafening, and everything that happened was in pantomime; you couldn't hear a thing. After the hand was dealt, Wally, being short, scratched for another card, and in doing so he raised up off the stool several inches. The dealer's eyes widened and he leaned back like there was a Cobra on the table. The two women had their backs to us and you could see them flinch. The dealer looked at Wally like he didn't believe what he just heard, and Wally looked at him with a perfectly bland face. The two ladies regarded Wally out of the corner of their eyes. Then the next hand was dealt, Wally looked at his cards, put them under his bet indicating he didn't want another card, and rose off the seat and *stayed* up. The dealer looked frantic, he'd probably been dealing 100 years and never had anything like this happen. The two women took their money, went out of their way not to look at Wally, and beat it off the table. Wally then walked back to our booth.

I can't remember ever having laughed so hard. We were hysterical. When Wally got back to the booth he showed me how to manufacture this gadget. I'm sure it didn't appear in popular mechanics, nor were there any patents pending.

A couple of weeks later he went into the Stardust Coffee Shop around 4AM and it was practically empty. The coffee shop had two rows of booths in the center of the floor. All the booths were for four people, and two booths sat side by side in the row, separated by a low, thin wood partition, definitely not for privacy. The only people there were two couples in one of the booths. Wally sat in the adjoining booth and ordered a cup of coffee. He had some Keno tickets in his hand, and when the game was over he made like he wanted to check the board on the wall to see if he had won. The board he was facing was out of order so he had to use the one on the wall behind him We were alerted to the fact that he was going to use his "apparatus" so we stood at the entrance to the room. When he raised himself to look behind him, this thing let go, and it was deafening.

One of the women in the booth alongside was not demure. She jumped out of the booth and yelled, "Jesus Christ!" One of the men said, "Oh my God!" and they all ran up to the hostess to see if there was anything she could do. Wally got scared, dropped a few bucks on the table and went into the lobby and sat down at the Faro Game. He was better than any floor show.

Wally's next escapade occurred several months later, on a busy Saturday night. I had stopped at the Desert Inn to have a bite with my father after work, it was 3AM and the place was packed. The Skillet Room was the place to be after hours for a late snack, and it sat at the end of the lounge and casino bar. When it was crowded some of the tables on the floor between the bar and the booths were just a few feet from the backs of the bar stools.

So, in comes Wally. He pulls up a chair, sits down and orders a steak with two eggs. After some small talk, he looks around, reaches inside his shirt and comes out with a huge plastic penis, well over a foot long, ivory-colored with a large pink tip. It looks almost real. This is in the '60s and pornography is still illegal. Getting caught with dirty movies or something like this could get you in trouble.

Contrary to popular belief, Las Vegas outwardly was tame compared to the rest of the country, including the Bible Belt. There was one Strip joint, in North Las Vegas, as far away from the Hotels/Casinos as they could get, and not only did the girls travel to work on broomsticks, but they had to cover up everything. That was it. You could see more flesh at the Stardust or the Tropicana.

Across the State line in California they had clubs that made the Las Vegas attractions look like a scene from Mary Poppins. Also, the technology was different in those days, especially when it came to these appurtenances. This was hard plastic, and it took some effort to bend it.

So back to Wally. Sitting at the bar is Rosie, the cigarette girl, having a nightcap. Rosie is in her 40's, blond, and has the look that lets you know she'd been around the block a time or two (or three). Being from the East Coast she spoke a cross between Philly speak and Brooklynese. Plenty of "youse, dese and dems." The stool next to her was just vacated, and Wally said "watch this" (again.)

Wally then stuffs this object down into his pants, where it ends just above the knee, and is noticeable. He climbs up on the stool next to Rosie, takes a sip of her water and tells her his knee itches, and would she scratch it. She reaches down to scratch his knee and says, "What the hell is that?" Wally tells her, "It's my joint."

He then tells her that every time he looks at her it gets that way, and he can't help it. (We heard this from him later. Although we weren't 20 feet away, we couldn't hear the conversation.) She then replies, "Geddadahere, you probably don't have more than two inches." With this, Wally reaches down, and being under the bar overhang, unzips his fly and starts to pull this thing out. Well, it takes great effort to bend it enough to clear his fly, and when it's freed it springs straight up.

As it happens, there are two couples sitting at a table just a few feet from the bar, and one of the women has seen this monster spring free (at eye level) and she lets out a shriek you can have heard in Reno. This attracts a lot of attention, and several other women join in. The husbands are highly irate, and Wally tries desperately to get this thing back in his pants as it is supposed to be for Rosie's eyes only. Of course, the thing won't bend enough and Wally, out of options and in a panic, holds it up in his hand and runs for the back door, with security on the way. When he goes past us he looks like a relay runner in the Olympics getting ready to pass the baton. With all the commotion, we laugh so hard we almost throw up. My dad has to go outside and keep security from calling the cops. Wally is afraid to come back in, so he never gets his steak.

94. After All, What Are Friends For?

Louis Strauss, AKA "Russian Louis," was a Mobster. He hung around The Los Angeles area, and was frequently seen in Las Vegas. He purportedly tried to shake down Benny Binion of Horseshoe Club fame who was a Las Vegas legend. Benny was the survivor of a vicious Texas gang war that cost a lot of lives, and then moved his family to Las Vegas. He bought the Eldorado Club, and later renamed it the Horseshoe. When the limit all over town was $200, Benny advertised that if you bring cash, you can bet as much as you have the balls for, and your first bet was your limit for that session. He took bets close to a million dollars. It made great press and made the Horseshoe Club famous for a square gamble and an old west atmosphere. If you were going to shake anyone down, you could find an easier target than Benny Binion.

Anyhow, Russian Louis disappeared in 1953. Some California Mobsters claimed they were responsible, having set him up and strangled him. The method they claimed was, after setting up a meeting with his "best friend," the best friend grabbed him in a bear hug, and two other "friends" slipped a rope around his neck and pulled in opposite directions.

This is hard on the neck.

Others say he was part of the Desert Inn golf course, and there were those who say he's "somewhere" out in the Desert. Which led to a lot of clichés. When someone disappeared, it would be said that "He's out there with Russian Louie," or if you wanted to convey a threat, you could say, "I'll put you out there with Russian Louie." So, with all the versions of his demise, the only thing one can assume *was* his demise. Where he wound up was immaterial.

That brings to mind the time I was told that *I* could possibly be rubbing shoulders with Russian Louie. I was dealing Blackjack at the Dunes Hotel at the time, dealing to a gentleman who happened to be a pharmacist from San Diego. He was personable, and was winning several thousand dollars, which was probably why he was so personable. His wife kept coming over and taking money to play the dollar slots, which made them excellent customers. It so happens that the Dunes was going through one of those periods that happens in all casinos, a lengthy losing streak. It's something that happens to every casino, unless you're cheating, which by this time was ancient history. Mostly.

As I was dealing to this man, playing two hands at $200 per, we were suddenly enveloped in a thick cloud of cigar smoke. I glanced down and standing right next to me was Charles "Kewpie" Rich, one of the Dunes owners from St. Louis. Charles Rich was barely five feet tall, and had thick lips, and two eyes that were in a perpetual squint. He also was bald as a cueball, and his head looked like somebody polished it. He was the living embodiment of a Kewpie Doll in a suit, hence the nickname "Kewpie."

He was smoking a huge cigar, purposely blowing the smoke in our faces from a distance of no more than six inches and was staring at the customer. When the customer finally said to him, "What's the matter with you? He replied, "I know youse guys are doing something to me," which in gaming parlance means we were cheating him. Then he looked right in my face and said "I know you're doing something, you cocksucker, and when I find out what it is I'm going to put you in the desert with Russian Louie."

I was more embarrassed than scared, but the smoke damn near choked me to death. The customer remarked that he "didn't need this shit" and took his chips and cashed out. He and his wife passed by on their way out the door, and he looked at me and just shook his head. That was the only time I had seen Kewpie in the pit area.

95. We've Got to Stop Meeting Like This

Bob Sims was a piano player, and a good one. He could play jazz one moment and go right into Rachmaninoff the next. He holds the record for the longest lounge engagement in Las Vegas history, playing the lounge at the Flamingo Hotel for over eight years. Bob looked like anything but a piano player, he stood over six feet tall and weighed at least 230 pounds. He had hands like hams and fingers like sausages and looked more like a football player than a musician.

But Bob was an easygoing guy with a shy smile and a heart of gold. On occasion we would leave the hotel after his 2AM set and head for Lake Mead to fish for a few hours before going home. When his gig at the Flamingo was over he transferred his act to the Frontier Hotel where he played in the main casino lounge, and also the lounge in the gourmet steakhouse. I was a floor man at the Frontier at the time.

Bob's wife was the head "goddess" at Caesars Palace. While all the hotels had cocktail waitresses, Caesar's had "goddesses." A lot of people in town would dispute the "goddess" classification, but Caesar's maintained they had the best. Bob's wife had the job of making sure the girls were impeccably made up and their uniforms were clean and perfect. They even had a big article in the Las Vegas Sunday Paper with pictures of her performing her duties.

It was at the Frontier Hotel that Bob went the way of all flesh. He began an affair with a hefty blond cocktail waitress named Phyllis Lawless. She wasn't exactly a "goddess," but was an attractive girl. Bob drove an old van to work, and his wife drove their Cadillac.

On occasion Bob and his paramour would sneak out to the van after work, or even on a long break for a "quickie." Bob would drive the van all the way to the back fence of the Frontier parking lot, where it would sit in the shadows, and he and Phyllis would do the nasty. The parking lot was huge, actually several acres, and the distance from the employees parking to the fence was at least a quarter of a mile. I don't know how long this went on, but one night there was a notice that the Bob Sims Trio wouldn't be performing until the following week.

Several days later I was on my way to the restaurant for dinner and here came Bob walking down the hall. He was limping, his arm was in a sling (not a cast) he had a black eye and a gash over his nose and eyebrow. I thought that maybe he was in an accident as Bob would never get into a fight and jeopardize his hands. He told me what happened and we looked at each other and burst out laughing.

Seems like Bob got off at 2AM and he and Phyllis headed out to the van. Bob's wife left work early and hurried down to the Frontier to see if she could catch up with him and go for a bite to eat. She drove around the back to the parking lot to see if he was still there and spotted the van against the fence. Driving over to the van she started to get out of the car and having her windows open heard what was going on. From what Bob says the van was jumping up and down on squeaky springs and his wife was no dummy.

She got back in the car and backed all the way to the employee parking area, put the car in drive, and floored it. She hit the back of the van at what Bob said was 100 mph, which of course was a huge exaggeration, but I guess it felt like it. The way he described it was that he was about to gain entrance to the temple of love when the impact did it for him. He and Phyllis slammed into the back of the front seat, and Bob barely had time to say, "It's my wife." when Phyllis in a panic screamed, "Oh my God, here she comes again." The two of them held on for dear life as they survived two more collisions. The fence around the lot was heavy chain link and every time they got rear ended the van would fly into the fence and bounce back. Then she drove away, the front of the Cadillac in ruins, and the van a few feet shorter than it was before the incident.

Bob and his sweetie were pretty badly banged up, and it was a few weeks before Phyllis got up enough nerve to come back to work, being scared to death. Bob got a motel room and had to sneak home for clean clothes while wifey was at work. It was too bad. Bob and his wife were both nice people, and up to the time that he fell victim to "the muff," they had a good marriage.

It was shortly thereafter that Bob was transferred to the Sands.

96. Happy Birthday, Harry

Harry Goodheart was the casino manager at the Sands Hotel. He'd been a manager at the Beverly Hills Country Club in Newport, Kentucky, owned by the Cleveland "outfit."

The Beverly Hills was known for its food and world class entertainment, which rivaled anything Las Vegas had to offer. It also had one of the biggest illegal casinos in the country. The boys from Cleveland were established and doing quite well in Las Vegas. But, tired of the pressure from local politicians they couldn't do business with, they sold the whole shebang. It operated for several years as the Beverly Hills Supper Club then burned to the ground with one of the biggest losses of life (165) in any fire in US history.

Harry, his wife and two sons moved to Las Vegas in the early '60s, where Harry went to work as a pit manager at the Desert Inn. When the Hughes Corporation bought the Desert Inn, and gobbled up several other casinos, Harry became the casino manager at the Frontier Hotel. He then moved to the Sands, where he ran the casino for the rest of his career. He was an extremely capable casino operator, fair with his employees, and was a staunch family man. If he had any skeletons in his closet he kept them well hidden.

Harry was a small man, barely five feet tall, wore black horned rim glasses and, for a person of his small stature, had a strong voice. Being so short, he was referred to by his employees as the "eye in the rug," as opposed to the usual "eye in the sky."

Harry had one shortcoming; he was a "screamer." When he got upset his normally strong voice got much stronger, and tuned up an octave or so, so when he let go, he terrified everyone in sight.

This came to evidence one busy weekend night at the Sands, where I was employed at the time as a Baccarat dealer. It had not been a good week for the Sands. The Casino had been mired in a losing streak, just a few days earlier Gaming Control had caught several floor persons and a couple of dealers operating a credit scam. Some of these employees were people, or relatives of people that Harry had known for years. On top of that, someone had approved $25,000 in phony travelers checks on a Mexican bank, and a

$50,000 marker in the Baccarat had disappeared. The Craps tables and the Blackjacks were losing.

And it was Harry's birthday.

I happened to be on a Baccarat table that looked out into the area between the Craps and Blackjack pits so I had a clear view of Harry standing with two ashen-faced shift managers whom he was blaming for most of his ills. He was about 40 feet away, so I couldn't hear every word, but it was evident that things weren't going well for these shift managers.

The Bob Sims trio was playing in the lounge, the winners on the dice tables were screaming on every roll, and the Mexicans in the Baccarat were riding a winning shoe, and the noise was deafening. It was the beginning of a perfect storm.

Suddenly, an obese woman appeared in a pink Scheherazade outfit, with baubles and bangles galore, and accompanied by a big fat guy in a gorilla suit playing an accordion. She started dancing around Harry and singing "Happy Birthday" accompanied by the guy in the gorilla suit. The outfit she was wearing was midriff style, so her big fat belly button was right in Harry's nose, and every time her boobs would separate from her stomach you caught a glance of Harry's horn-rimmed glasses, then the glasses would disappear. Bob Sims picked up on the celebration, and with a maniacal look on his face stood up at the piano and started playing "Happy Birthday" as loud as he could. It was like a scene from Dante's Inferno set in an insane asylum. Above this cacophony, you could hear Harry's voice screaming "WHAT THE FUCK IS THIS? WHAT THE FUCK IS THIS?!" over and over.

The two shift managers were shaking like a couple of dogs passing peach seeds, and finally Harry screamed at the woman, "Who sent you?" followed by "Someone get Security." The fat lady took the hint and headed for the door, followed by the gorilla and the accordion as Goodheart yelled, "Stop those people, I want to know who sent them?"

The "entertainers" made a clean getaway and Harry vowed to find out who booked the surprise, and supposedly spent the next day moving heaven and earth to catch the perps. However, he began to cool off and I don't think anything really came of it. Eastern Onion was the name of the company that provided this type of service, and they wouldn't say who booked it as it was paid in cash. It was supposed to be all in fun.

But the timing was a little off.

97. The Biggest Prick in Town

Sailor was the biggest prick in town. A dubious distinction. However, to achieve that status in a town full of big pricks takes some doing. I never knew him by any other name but Sailor, and neither did anyone I was acquainted with. Sailor was a hustler, never was known to have a job, and could be seen in just about any casino. He was a big man, well above six feet and an easy 240 lbs.

Word got around that he had made a big score, upwards of $50,000, in some big Poker games and on the Baccarat. Where, I can't say. One night in the '60s I was working the swing (night) shift at the Dunes. As I went in the pit to go to work, I heard a lot of commotion in the Baccarat, and was told that Sailor was in the process of losing big bucks at the Baccarat table. He was not happy from the sound of things, as in the best of circumstances he was a miserable SOB.

About two hours later I was standing on an empty Blackjack table when word filtered down that Sailor had lost everything he had, save for a few hundred in chips. As he was headed for the door, he stopped at my table and slammed two handfuls of chips down on two separate hands. I went to straighten out the bets, and he growled, "Don't touch my money." Sal Parisey was the floor man, and he nodded, it was OK. I shuffled the deck and set it out for Sailor to cut, and he swiped at it with his hand, knocking cards all over the table and on to the floor. Then he snarled "now shuffle them again, *dealer*." We picked up the cards, I reshuffled and put the cards out to cut. Sailor, knowing if he did it again we wouldn't deal to him, cut the cards while staring at me with a murderous look. I dealt the hands out and turned up a king for myself. When I looked under at my hole card, it was an ace. Party over. I hesitated for a second then turned over my hand. It's not a nice thing to do, (hesitate), as it's really a lack of etiquette and is taken as a needle.

Sailor and I reached for the chips at the same time. I was able to get some of them, but he held on to a handful. Sal was about to call for security when Sailor wound up and threw the chips right into my face, as hard as he could. Those chips are heavy, have a lead base, and the edges are sharp. The pain was excruciating, and I lost it. I went right across the top of the table. As I did, Sal grabbed me by the back of my pants and held on. Here I was, one knee in the chip rack, one leg hanging down, both hands flat on the table, and my bleeding face sticking straight out with no way of defending myself.

I remember thinking, “This guy is about punch my face in” when he ran between the tables, grabbed a heavy crystal ashtray and hit Sal in the head with it. Why he didn’t hit me, I’ll never know. But Sal went down and the blood was everywhere. His whole head was split open and he eventually took quite a few stitches. Sailor then ran down the middle of the pit and out the front door. The whole episode only took a couple of minutes, if that.

They took Sal to the security office and, when the commotion died down, some of the bosses and owners met in the dice pit. It was a high-level conference, as these things just didn’t happen. Then Jackie Mandel got on the phone and you could hear him tell someone to “break his (Sailor’s) arms and legs, and if he dies, don’t worry about it.”

That’s the only time I ever heard anybody put out a contract, where it could be heard by anyone standing close by. But the bosses were livid. Things calmed down. About two hours later a man came running in the front door, wearing a tuxedo, with a frantic look on his face. He ran into the dice pit and started talking to Jackie Mandel. I found out later that the man was a captain in the lounge at the Riviera, Sailor was married to his daughter, and she was pregnant. He was begging them not to follow up on the “directive,” and offered to give Sal enough to cover his wages if he wasn’t able to work for a few days.

I really don’t know what transpired after that, but a few months later Sailor was found dead in Los Angeles, supposedly in an alley behind the Beverly Wilshire Hotel. No cause of death was mentioned and people went on about their business. For some reason it took quite a while for the news to get around. They probably used his real name in the small newspaper article, and nobody knew it was Sailor. I don’t think the title of the “Biggest Prick in Las Vegas” was bestowed on anyone else.

So many candidates made it a difficult choice.

98. So-and-So Sent Me

Came the ‘70s, Sal Parisey was now a floor man at the Frontier hotel. He was a hustler of sorts, always out to make a buck, and dabbled in “hot” jewelry on occasion. He tried to get in on the loan sharking racket on his own, but someone had a “discussion” with him on the perils of trying to get involved with a business that belongs to somebody else, and he decided against it.

One afternoon a man walked into the Frontier and asked for Sal. When Sal came over the man said, “So-and-so from Indianapolis told me to look you up, is there a place where we can talk in private?” Sal took him over to a corner in between the slot machines. The man glanced around over his shoulder, reached into his jacket pocket and came out with a booklet type of case. He handed it to Sal and said, “What do you think of these? Sal opened the packet and there was a collection of diamonds. The guy told Sal that they had a lot of “heat on them” and he had to get rid of them in a hurry.

Taking out his jewelers’ loupe, Sal looked them over, and saw that not only were they genuine, but worth a lot of money. He asked what the man wanted for them and was told, “They’re worth at least $50,000, and I’ll take $15,000. I have a partner in this caper.” They went back and forth, and after the man threatened to forget about it they agreed on $10,000. The man then warned him that he (Sal) should not try to fence them for at least 18 months, as they were just too hot.

Sal told him that he didn’t have that kind of cash with him, and he would have to get the money out of his safety deposit box. They agreed to meet back at the Frontier at 4PM Sal went to the bank on his lunch break and got the cash. At 4PM the man arrived, they met in the slot area and the man said, “I can’t stay more than a minute, do you have the money?” and glanced furtively over his shoulder several times. Sal handed him the money, he counted it, and reminded Sal to hang on to the diamonds for at least 18 months. With that, he offered his hand, they shook, he handed Sal the packet of gems, Sal looked to make sure they were all there, and the man headed out the door.

Several hours later, Benjamin "Money" Blank came to work, and he was also in the jewelry hustling business on the side. He screwed so many people it was a wonder he was walking around. Sal couldn't wait to show "Money" the fabulous deal he'd made. When he produced the gems, Money's eyes opened wide, not believing Sal could be so fortunate. He then pulled out his own jeweler's loupe and examined the goods. After a thorough examination he looked at Sal and said, "These are phony, I wouldn't give you five bucks for them."

Came the dawn. Sal turned white as a sheet, grabbed his loupe and looked for himself. Sure enough, they were phony. His first move was to run out the door, thinking maybe the guy hung around for six hours after screwing him. Then in a panic he called so-and-so from Indianapolis and found out that he didn't know what Sal was talking about (maybe).

Sal didn't have a reputation for being excessively brilliant, and this proved it. He fell for the oldest scam in the book. He never checked the stones the second time around. Money made him feel better by telling him, "How could you be so fucking dumb?"

I don't think Sal ever recovered from that. A couple of years later He was caught in a scam of sorts and was unceremoniously marched out of the Frontier. He'd been involved in the same type of scam at the Dunes years earlier and suffered the same fate. To make it all worse, his son committed suicide by hanging himself. He was a dealer at the Frontier.

99. Here Come Da Judge

Harry Claiborne was a Las Vegas attorney appointed to the Federal Bench in 1974 by President Jimmy Carter. Harry was one of the "good ol' boys" in Las Vegas, and there were those who swore by his legal acumen. In 1986 Harry was impeached by the Senate. Prior to that he was indicted on bribery, fraud and tax evasion charges. He was convicted of tax evasion and did 17 months in prison. He purportedly survived an attempt on his life in a parking garage. After finishing his prison sentence, he was reinstated to the Nevada Bar by the Nevada Supreme Court. Only in Nevada.

Harry, married four times, had a weakness for cocktail waitresses. His third wife was a Dunes beauty by the name of Lynne O'Day. Lynne was a tall attractive blonde who made sure that none of her suitors were short of funds or reputation. The term used was that "She never followed any empty wagons."

Lynne was a cocktail waitress at the Dunes when Mel Golden became the casino manager. Lynne and Mel immediately became an item, much to Mel's wife's chagrin. Mel was about 5' 5" tall and Lynne towered over him, together they looked like the old Mutt and Jeff cartoons. A joke around the hotel said that someone had to "put him up to it." When Mel lost his job, he lost his sweetie with it.

It wasn't much later that Judge Harry Claiborne was bitten by the love bug. He fell for Lynne and they became an item. A high rolling Oklahoma oilman by the name of Miles Jackson spent several days at the Dunes, and he too was smitten by Lynne. Using the excuse that she was good luck, he requested to have her sit with him when he gambled and he gambled all day and into the night. When he came down to play Blackjack, they would have a couple of girls cover for her and Lynne would change into her street clothes and sit with Miles and "bring him luck." This was permitted because the bosses knew that as long as she was with him he wouldn't go to another casino. She made a substantial amount of money gambling with him, and never tipped the dealers, which had everybody really pissed.

I remember dealing to them one day and as I looked up here was Judge Claiborne peeking between two slot machines like a jealous schoolboy. He would duck if she glanced in that direction, and then resume his spying. He did it for most of the day. Not what you would expect from a federal judge. Old and sick, Harry Claiborne took his own life in 2004.

100. The Wheels of Justice

Judge Walter Richards was a municipal judge. Richards enjoyed his nights out. No judge or law enforcement official in Las Vegas ever had to pay for food or drink. Everywhere they went it was "on the house" On more than one occasion in the wee hours of the morning I would see one or two security guards helping Judge Richards through the casino to the front door, with his legs flopping about like a marionette. I asked if they put him in a cab, and they told me the valet brought his car and parked it right by the front door. They would pour him into his car, and he would drive home, and the next morning (I would assume with a vicious hangover) he would sit in judgment of drunken drivers and other culprits.

When I got called for jury duty and brought this up, they excused me permanently.

My parents, Frank and Frieda Soskin, with the actor, Edward G. Robinson at the D.I.

My dad, casino manager Frank Soskin (rolling the dice) with the Ritz Brothers who were headlining the D.I. in the early '50s. The dealer on the right, Ben Riggio, went on to become a well-known casino executive.

My dad, Frank Soskin, as Desert Inn Casino Manager, 1951. Though my dad was never connected with the Mob, his picture once hung in Las Vegas's Mob Museum

Preparing a crap table during opening week at the D.I. in 1950. My father is next to the security guard. The man on the right, Abe Goldberg, was later to become a well-known shift manager at the Sands. The man to my father's left is Benjamin "Money" Blank. Note the wooden rails on the table. The first padded rails were put on the blackjack tables at the Desert Inn sometime in the early '50s. The primary reason wasn't comfort, but to make it harder for a cheater to move cards in and out of the game, which was the D.I.'s intention all along. When the reaction from the customers was favorable, they put them on all the tables. The other strip casinos quickly followed suit. The padding was an upholstered plywood cap fitted to the table and removable for cleaning underneath. There were always chips, silver dollars and sometimes cards underneath when the cap was lifted, much to the delight of the porters. If they found a card or two, the bosses screamed bloody murder.

Frank and Frieda Soskin (on the right) with State Senator Eileen Brookman and Governor Mike O'Callaghan at a state dinner in Las Vegas. Both Brookman and O'Callaghan have Las Vegas schools named after them.

R. to L.; Frank Soskin, Casino Manager, Desert Inn, Harry Goodheart, Casino Manager, Frontier and Frank Sinatra at a party during the Hughes Invitational golf tournament.

Freedman at the Desert Inn, 1950. He was shortly to become the Roulette boss at the Riviera. Note the low ceiling, which was the norm for all the strip hotels at the time. The smoke was thick as a result.

Singer/actor Vic Damone with an 8lb. Rainbow Trout on the Colorado River. He wasn't aware I was in the picture wearing his hat. Since I taught him how to fish, he wasn't too upset about me as a co-star. I'm sure that somewhere along the line I might have been edited out. Taken from my boat by my fishing companion.

Second-Generation Gaming Boss Mike Soskin

By SUZAN DIBELLA
Today Editor

A steady, purring stream of interstate traffic hums along I-15 past the Tropicana exit as the Strip glitters less than a mile away, beckoning to a Friday night crowd pouring in from L.A.

Just west of that exit, the King 8 Inn motel, truck stop and gambling hall waits placidly for its share of the business, which, according to Casino Manager Mike Soskin, has been — and continues to be — enough.

"We aren't competing with anyone," Soskin, 46, says matter-of-factly, acknowledging the limitations of the 6,000-square-foot, eight-table truck stop gambling hall. "We just can't compete with the giants on the Strip or out at Sam's Town. We have what we have."

Soskin, a second-generation Nevada casino boss who has worked in six major Strip resorts in the last 26 years, isn't afraid to call a spade a spade.

"It's all right to call the King 8 a 'truck stop casino.' That's what it is. We have a neighborhood casino here. We enjoy a fair amount of local business, and we have some tour groups coming through. And Jimmy (Jim Thacker, Soskin's assistant and long-time friend) and I have a following from our days on the Strip. We recognize that those customers probably want to do their gambling on the Strip, but we get a representative amount of business from them. Some even stay with us."

An 18-wheeler diesel engine bellows outside Soskin's open window as the talks about the casino industry, a reminder of the unique parameters of his professional undertaking. It is admittedly a far cry from the smooth glamour of the Strip.

"THE DIFFERENCE was like night and day," he says of his move to the King 8. "I had to scale myself down. It took some time. It was really just a matter of perspective. I had been counting in the tens of thousands and suddenly I was counting dollars."

Yet, working for a smaller organization has its advantages, he says. Soskin, who came in on the ground floor when King 8 Inn owner John Rothman bought the establishment in January 1979, had never actually run a full casino before. Some last minute legal technicalities in the purchase caused a somewhat harried takeover of the casino, Soskin remembers, recounting the events.

"Jim (Thacker) and I went to the bank the day we were due to open and got $300,000 in cash and silver. When we loaded it into his Blazer truck to the ceiling, the tires almost went flat," he says smiling. "So we got some air in the tires with the security we had hired, got our food and beverage truck and went in a caravan down the highway."

"We didn't say a word to one another. We knew what we had to do," he says, recalling the determination and the challenge. "We took over at 12:01 a.m. Jan. 1, 1979 and didn't finish checking everything in until 9 a.m. the next morning. I was back at 4 p.m. that day." For the next six months, he says, either

GAMING VETERAN — King 8 Inn Casino Manager Mike Soskin has worked in six major Strip resorts — and in every facet of gaming — in his 26 years in the business.

"The day I was old enough to shuffle, I went to work" says Soskin, a second-generation casino boss. [Today Photos By Herb Herpolsheimer]

he or Thacker covered the casino 24 hours a day.

Since then, Soskin notes, the King 8 has

eight-acre parking lot next to the 300-room motel. Plans for a truckers' recreation room — complete with sauna

101. How Not to Run a Casino

Major Arteburn Riddle was the second owner of the Dunes hotel in the mid '50s. The hotel had foundered a year after opening, and Major Riddle and his partner Jake Gottlieb, along with a small investment from a local entertainment agent, purchased the hotel with the backing of the Teamsters Pension Fund. Major Riddle made his fortune in the trucking business in Chicago and by coincidence his partner, Jake Gottlieb, was also a trucking magnate in Chicago. They both had strong Mob ties.

It was said that Major Riddle (his first name was Major, it was not a military title) would hire a truck driver, and sell him a truck, with the driver making the payments to Riddle. When the truck was nearly paid off, Riddle would fire the driver, and when the unemployed driver missed a few payments, repossess the truck. He would then hire another driver and sell him the same truck. All with the blessing of the Teamsters Union.

He brought his business practices to Las Vegas.

The three partners all had one thing in common, none of them had ever run a casino. Major Riddle was a tall, gaunt figure with a beak of a nose, and he walked with a slight stoop, giving him a hawk like appearance. He was referred to as Major Riddle, "the Maj," "Riddle" and several other names which I'd rather not repeat. He was a nasty individual who made it tough on all his employees. He was paranoid to the point that if anyone were to win in the casino, he felt that he was cheated. He would accuse the dealers and the pit boss of being in cahoots with the winner, and the atmosphere in the place was not what you wanted in a casino.

Major Riddle, a high roller, would win, say $25,000, return to the Dunes and if some customer had $500 in chips in front of him, would run into the pit and demand to know how the person got the chips. He would then stand behind the table and glower at the customer and suffer and mumble every time the poor guy won a bet.

One night he won $25,000 at the Sands. The next night he went back and lost several thousand dollars, then grabbed the dice off of the table and put them in his pocket, announcing that he was going to have them checked. That's the same as accusing the Sands of cheating, something that just wasn't done in Las Vegas. The Sands told him to take his business somewhere else.

It got to the point where the pit bosses had so much pressure on them that if a dealer was losing they would go to a dealer standing on an empty game and send him to the losing table, putting the dealer he just took off on the empty game. Customers noticed the switch and it wasn't unusual for that dealer to lose maybe four or five hands, and they would send *another* dealer to the table, or change the cards more than once.

It's known that if a person wins in a certain casino, when he returns to Las Vegas, he will always go to the casino where he was a winner. This is true 99% of the time. It was not that way with the Dunes. In all casinos the bosses swallow hard and make it look like they're glad the person won. Anyone winning at the Dunes left there with a bad taste in their mouth. As a result, the business was falling off at a rapid pace.

I can vividly recall one Dunes incident that was one of the most disgusting things I'd seen in any casino. One day an elderly man and his wife came into the casino when it was practically empty. They had first timers written all over them. They stopped at my table ordered a drink and told me they were on their way to California, decided to spend a few days in Las Vegas, and maybe see a movie star. They won about $30, gave me a couple of bucks and started to walk away.

The pit boss, Cleo Simon, called them over and said, "Play another hand and I'll deal to you." As if having a boss deal to you was a real treat. They looked at each other, shrugged, and each bet what looked to be about $8. Cleo dealt the cards, and when it came time to act on his own hand he fumbled around and dealt a second card to himself, thus attempting to cheat them out of their money. I had been dealing less than a year at the time, and even as naïve as I was it was obvious what he was doing. They lost one of the bets, picked up the other one and left, looking at each other as if to say, "What was all that about?" Simon tried to call them back again, but they headed out the door. All this for around $18? Cleo then walked over to the wastebasket by the podium and vomited. That was my first experience at the Dunes.

Over the years I worked there four different times. Major Riddle also played in high stakes Poker games, and he was known as the biggest sucker in town, losing over $300,000 to one group in the span of two days. Everyone knew that they cheated him with the classic “three-pluck-one” set-up. The three other guys in the game were partners and in a situation like that it’s not hard to manipulate the betting. It was said that the winners had to pay a “street tax” to Tony Spilotro, a Mob enforcer from Chicago.

When it looked like the Dunes might go under again, there were several different entities interested in taking over, the Sands included, but they concluded it would be a drain on the profits from their own highly successful casino. Finally, a group made up of St. Louis and Chicago (of course) investors came in, including Sid Wyman, Charles “Kewpie” Rich, and his stepson, George Duckworth. They had the backing of the Teamsters and the Mob, and they knew what they were doing. The main stipulation to the deal was that Major Riddle stay out of the casino. He had no say in policy.

102. Attaining Celebrity Status

The men's room in the Dunes was a tight fit. It was narrow, had five urinals and about as many stalls and sinks. They put a shoeshine stand across from the urinals, which made it even narrower. When the stand was in use, it was a tight fit.

One day, I was on a break and was getting a shoe shine when in walked Major Riddle, splendidly dressed in a cream-colored suit with white and brown wing tip shoes. Right behind him staggered a drunk that could hardly stand up. The "Maj" stood at a urinal and the drunk took the one right next to him, rested his arm on the plumbing at the top of the urinal, and put his head on his arm, all the while fumbling with his fly. Their backs were to me, and I was just a few feet away. Then I noticed a stream of urine coming sideways from where the drunk was standing, splash on the floor, and then on to Major Riddles white wingtips, where it began to rise, up the cream-colored pants leg, and then proceeded up the suit coat. It got all the way to the elbow before the "Maj" noticed it. By the time he figured out what was happening he was pretty well soaked. The look on his face was priceless. He recoiled and backed away quickly, pissing on his own shoes. Not knowing whether the guy was a good customer, he said nothing and beat it out of there. I'm sure he went upstairs to his suite to change. When my shine was done, I went into the coffee shop and told some of the dealers what I had just witnessed.

Within the next half-hour I had attained celebrity status. Everyone in the place knew about it. I was the man of the hour. For the rest of the day everyone asked me what I saw and howled with laughter. A cocktail waitress leaned across the table to serve a drink and whispered in my ear, "Did you really see someone piss on Major Riddle?"

To most, it was a classic example of poetic justice.

Another claim to fame for Major Riddle was that he was the first to keep a percentage, or "per" on each individual dealer, which was an absolute impossibility. However, they put the dealers on a game and noted whether the game won or lost for that day. Depending on the amount of business a dealer would only spend 40 minutes at the most on the table every hour. The relief dealer could lose a bunch while the guy was on his break. If a high roller got on a game (sometimes they would close the table to everyone else) and won a large amount of money, there goes the dealers "percentage." Of course, it wasn't possible to do it accurately, but that gave them an excuse to fire a dealer, and they fired a few, telling them their "per" was low. Not that they really needed a reason in those days.

I saw dealers get fired for talking to a boss's "girlfriend" on a break, or even for wearing pants without pleats. When continental clothes first appeared on the scene in 1957, two guys opened a store on 3rd street downtown, where they specialized in continental apparel, which was catching on in all the major cities. This consisted of "stove pipe" slacks, and narrow jackets. The stove pipe pants were very narrow and had no pleats. The bosses in the casinos were all "macho" in those days and to them, anyone who wore clothes like that was a "fruit."

In most places if you showed up for work wearing those pants, they would either send you home to change or fire you on the spot. When the Mob ran the casinos, they didn't need a reason to terminate anyone at any time. Most of the termination slips said "change of personnel."

Major Riddle wasn't the last to keep a percentage on the Blackjack dealers, they tried it at the Tropicana in the mid '60s, and never would say how they intended to do it. It only lasted a few months. That would have changed nothing at the Tropicana; they were barking up the wrong tree.

The place had more leaks than the Titanic.

103. The Lowest of the Low

When a dealer got fired for stealing from the casino, in time he could probably find another job. If the casino didn't prosecute, or involve Gaming Control, and his prospective employer didn't call his previous employer it would just be forgotten. A lot of casino bosses in those days wouldn't say anything bad about the people they fired. They always figured that if you couldn't protect yourself, you deserved whatever you got. The only exception being if you were asked by a personal friend, and even then, they were hesitant. Strangely enough, the only thing that *would* keep you from finding work is if you got caught stealing tips. Stealing from your fellow workers was as low as a person could stoop, and the word was all over town in a hurry. In this instance, if a person were to call and inquire why he was terminated from his previous job, they were told the truth immediately. If that were the case, they might as well leave town. Nobody would touch them with a ten-foot pole.

I worked at the Stardust for six months after it opened and moved on to the Flamingo. I was dating a cocktail waitress from the Stardust who told me that she had been colluding with a dealer to steal tips for almost 3 months. The tip box was in a drawer in one of the podiums in the pit, and in the drawer below it, were the cigarettes. If a customer asked for a pack of cigarettes, the waitress would get them from the drawer and take them to the player. Whenever this dealer got off the game with tips in his pocket, he would go to the drawer where the tip box was and she would go to the cigarette drawer. She would hold her tray under his open drawer and he would put the chips on her tray. They would then split the take at an agreed location. His name was Phil Rosen, and he had been with the Desert Inn and Stardust people for years. I was furious, they had actually been stealing from me while I worked there. I called a friend who was still working there and told him what was going on, and he refused to believe it. A short time later Phil got caught and fired. A few months later he came to the Flamingo and asked me to introduce him to a pit boss who might be able to help him get a job. When I flatly refused he said "you don't believe all the things they're saying about me stealing tips, do you.?

He didn’t know that I was dating the waitress he was colluding with. He never worked in Las Vegas again.

104. Trusted Employees

The Palm Springs Spa was the newest and nicest hotel in Palm Springs. They had an annual golf tournament that attracted national attention and the town filled up. Every year the big bosses from the Dunes would rent the two biggest suites in the hotel and travel down for the tournament. They did this for several years. As it happened, with the help of Gaming Control, they unearthed a credit scam that involved a few dealers, several pit bosses, and a couple of high rolling customers.

It was a classic credit scam. For example, a player would take $5000 in chips at the table, and the floor man would give him a marker to sign for $500. The dealer involved would sign the slip and drop it in the box. When the next dealer would come in, who was not involved, the player would pay off the $500, tear up the marker, and walk to the cashier with $4500. The money was split between everybody involved. Nobody knows how long it was going on, but it was obviously lucrative while it lasted. They fired everybody involved and it was big news all over town. A few months later the Dunes owners called to reserve the suites for the tournament and were told that the suites were already rented. They pissed and moaned but the hotel had to honor the reservations, so the bosses had to settle for individual rooms which they were lucky to get. On the first night of the tournament the bosses left their rooms to go to dinner, and as they walked down the hall the door to one of the suites opened and out walked some of the guys that they had fired for stealing a few months earlier. Call it an awkward moment. The perps had rented both suites. They were lucky that there wasn't some sort of retaliation.

105. The Audition from Hell

My first time at the Dunes Hotel was a notable experience. I had "broken in" (learned to deal Blackjack) at the Thunderbird. After about three weeks, my benefactor George Rosen, the shift manager, came to me and said, "You're ready to work. I don't have a spot for you right now, but my friend Mel Golden is the casino manager at the Dunes and he's coming down tonight to watch you work. If he likes what he sees he will put you to work at the Dunes until I can open a spot for you."

Remember that the day shift at the Thunderbird had a total of 12 dealers, as did most of the major casinos. This included the four-man dice crew. After working a lot of hours for three weeks with no pay, I was ready to go to work. If the dealers had a good tip day, they would give me a few bucks, but it wasn't much.

At around 6PM, Mel Golden showed up and stood in front of my game and watched me deal. As it happened, we were busy, and on my game was an Oriental gentleman who was betting two hands at the limit which was $200, and he was a generous tipper. As a result, my shirt pocket was full to the brim with silver dollars and chips. The hotel had decided to try a different type of card that very day, and the new cards were plastic, the same narrow Poker card they used in the card rooms. None of them were flat, and they were very slippery, as they rubbed them in talcum powder to keep them from sticking together.

Someone sat down at the game and bought in with a $20 bill. As I put the money in the drop box, the cards squirted out of the back of my hand and went all over the floor, some under the table. George walked over to me and said, "Go ahead and pick them up." I got down on my hands and knees to retrieve the cards and all the tips fell out of my pocket.

I wanted to die.

Here I was, supposedly auditioning, and I was under the table, trying to pick up cards and a pocket full of chips and silver dollars. When I finally stood up again, Mel was gone and, I thought, so were my chances. When I got off the game George told me to report to work at the Dunes the next night at 7PM I worked there for about three weeks, and one night, Mel came over to me and said, "You start at the Thunderbird tomorrow morning at ten o'clock. I'll bring your check down in a few days."

There were no applications to fill out and no paperwork. You just went to work.

My first Sunday morning at the Thunderbird, I went in to start my shift and relieved the graveyard shift dealer who was going home. I wasn't told that when they went to change the drop box on the table, there was a malfunction of the lock, and they took the box back to the cage to repair it.

I put the paddle in the money slot on the table and we started to get busy. I was putting money into the slot, and without a box it was going straight through to the floor. After about 15 minutes when the shift change settled down, George came over to me and said "If you see a porter call him over and have him sweep this mess up."

I looked down and saw a large pile of bills on the floor. It's a good thing the porter didn't notice, he'd have pocketed the money before it hit the floor. It looked like the counting room in most of the hotels that the Mob was involved in. Shortly after that, metal sleeves were bolted to the tables in all the casinos and the boxes fitted inside the sleeves.

No more money on the floor.

Three years later I was working at the Flamingo and had just finished learning how to deal Roulette. It was not an easy apprenticeship. Contrary to Blackjack, it takes quite a while and a lot of practice to master Roulette.

To top it off, the senior wheel dealer at the Flamingo was a fellow named Ray Ryan. Ray and his brothers were part of a large clique of Irish wheel dealers that went clear back to the speakeasys and the illegal casinos in the South and East. Some worked in Cuba. There were the three Ryan brothers O'Leary: Feeney, Brady, Houlihan, etc. They were a happy go lucky bunch, and the bullshit that flowed from them was unequalled in the industry. However, they took pride in their work, and getting any help or information from them was impossible. They looked down on newcomers, especially young ones, and although they were friendly they were a tight-mouthed bunch.

Leo O'Leary, a charter member of the clique, was a disbarred Chicago attorney. He would never tell us why he was disbarred, but would say he wound up in a more honorable profession. Leo had a huge stomach and would eat huge meals and if the waitress asked him if he wanted anything to drink, he would order a Tab, a one calorie diet drink, and laugh out loud. His stomach was so big that Roulette chips that were missing from the game would reappear when he went on a break.

They were under his stomach and he couldn't see them.

106. No Threat to Monopoly

Heading back to work after a break we spotted Joe Byrne and his companion "Kelly" walking to the elevators. Joe was reputed to be a higher up in Revlon Cosmetics, and was in his late 80's. For some reason he wore a tight shower cap on his head which looked like a condom. He was a tall, gaunt man, and the condom made him look like a cadaver.

Kelly, on the other hand, was an attractive Asian girl in her late 20s. She was supposed to be a nurse, or something of that nature, and of course the rumors as to their relationship were a topic of discussion. Leo remarked that they were going up to their room to play a game of "flops." This was a new one to me, and I inquired as to the nature of "flops." According to Leo, Joe would lay on the bed face up and naked. Kelly would lift his penis straight up and then let go. They would then bet on which side it would flop to. Leo, though he no longer had a license to practice law, always claimed he still had an MBA. When we asked what MBA stood for he replied "Master Bullshit Artist."

He wore the title well.

107. Cracking the Emerald Ceiling

The casino manager at the Flamingo took a liking to me and wanted me to learn Roulette in the event he decided to promote me to floor man. He asked Ray Ryan to teach me the wheel and Ray flatly refused.

Now, Ray was in his sixties, with stringy white hair, a pot belly, and a demeanor that seemed to indicate that he was in constant pain. Chester (the casino manager) took Ray up into the step lounge where they had a drink and conversed for quite a while. They had worked together in Florida and Cuba and their relationship went back a lot of years. When the conversation concluded, Ray came down and went back to work. I was told to talk to him on my next break. When I went over to where he was standing on an empty Roulette table, he said to me, and I quote, "Alright, you mongrel sonofabitch, I'm going to teach you how to deal this game. Show up tomorrow night 30 minutes early and have all the multiples of 17 memorized from 1 thru 20. I'm going to ask you questions and you have to answer automatically without having to calculate. If you hem or haw one time, I'm not going to fuck with you." In Roulette, a "split" between two numbers pays 17 to 1, and when the game is heavy, you don't have time to calculate.

Down through the years, this helped me immensely. For the next several months I spent my breaks enjoying his tutelage, although not having a break to get off your feet was tiring. He was happy with my progress and we got along great. Then came New Year's Eve, and they added a third Roulette wheel to the floor. In the days before Baccarat, Roulette was the game of choice for players from Europe, South America and Mexico, and they loved to bet mountains of small denomination chips instead of a few larger ones. The additional wheel was my game for fourteen hours. Remember in 1959 you could play ten-cent Roulette chips on the Strip, and because it was New Year's we had one game that was designated for 25-cent chips. My game was one of the dime games.

The players, who were all drunk, would buy all the chips, and then bet them all on the next roll. You could hardly see over them We had a chip "mucker" named George Germaine, who had an in with the casino manager, and his job was to help the dealer pick up the chips on the busy games. When a dealer sweeps the losing chips off of the layout, the piles of different colored chips were called the "muck," hence the term "chip mucker" (or "racker").

108. The Human Firehose

George Germaine was in his late 50s and stood an easy 6-foot-3. He was a throat cancer survivor and had no larynx, so all he could do to talk was force a whisper. When he talked, he spit a fine spray of saliva, or whatever, and you wished you had a raincoat, or at least an umbrella. If you wore glasses, you had to clean them when the conversation was over.

My game was the busiest, so George was helping me out. Once the winning bets were paid, all the chips had to be picked up, sorted and stacked before you start the next roll, so I was glad he was there. Then the casino manager came into the pit and called George and the pit manager over and explained what he wanted. There were two brothers, doctors who owned a clinic in Broken Bow, Nebraska, and they used to come to the Flamingo once or twice a year, get drunk and gamble for reasonably high stakes. One of them had a $20,000 credit line, which in those days was huge. They couldn't make it to Las Vegas for the New Year because they were at a party somewhere near their home, inebriated, and wanted to play Roulette. So, they played over the phone. The Casino Manager took the bets over the phone, and had to relay them to George, because the phone cord wasn't long enough to reach the table. There were no cordless phones in those days. George, in turn, would pass it on to me, and I would place the bets. The pit manager kept track of how much they won or lost. Now, picture this: Las Vegas, New Year's Eve, pandemonium everywhere, everybody drunk, and Harry James and his big band in the lounge, less than 50 feet away, and the noise so loud you couldn't hear your own voice. George is trying to scream into my ear with the bets, and it's like getting sprayed with a hose.

I had spittle dripping off my ear and my shirt, and the side of my head. I was soaked. When I went for my break, I came back with a dry bar towel on my shoulder, which helped my shirt, but I couldn't cover my ear. Finally, after almost two hours, they quit, having lost almost the whole $20,000, over the telephone, no less. I don't think I could have been that trusting no matter how much I had to drink. When I finally got home. I showered and fell into bed.

I had another 14 hours ahead of me.

109. Long Way to the Top

In a lot of stories about Las Vegas successes and failures, humble beginnings rarely receive mention. I would imagine that the "historians" or gaming, insider wannabes, don't really know about the stories behind the people and institutions they write so gleefully about.

Carl Wesley Thomas was a high school teacher in West Virginia in the early '50s. West Virginia was an impoverished state, and things weren't going to get any better in the near future, so Carl and his family (two young children) packed up and moved to Las Vegas, which to most people at that time was practically mythical.

Carl got a job as a laborer at the Nevada test site, and it didn't take him long to realize that sweating in the hot sun wasn't for him. He decided he wanted to deal. At the time the Stardust was nearing completion and was training dealers, in short supply, in preparation for the opening.

One night, Carl walked into the Desert Inn and asked for the boss. As it happened, Moe Dalitz, (the *Big* Boss) happened to be heading for the front door. Carl approached him, introduced himself, and said he wanted to become a dealer. Moe, I'm sure, was amused that this kid had the balls to approach him and referred him to one of the pit bosses helping out in the dealers' school. According to Carl, he told the pit boss that Moe Dalitz told him to talk to him (the pit boss) in regards to learning to deal. You could not get a stronger recommendation.

The next day he reported to the dealers' school in the maintenance area of the Desert Inn golf course. I was helping out a few mornings a week at the school, and from the beginning it was evident that Carl was the prize prospect of the whole class. He picked it up in half the time it took the others and went to work at the Stardust on opening day. After a year at the Stardust, Carl went to work at the Riviera, which was a step up for a dealer. The Stardust was what was known as a "boiler factory" meaning a lot of work and no money. It was the worst dealing job on the Strip. He was dealing Blackjack and attending the university where he got a degree in political science.

Carl also joined the Masons and, in becoming a Shriner, met Ross Miller, who was the big boss and Mob overseer at the Riviera. Ross was impressed with Carl's intelligence (there was nobody else with a college degree in the whole place) and took Carl under his wing. Ross was an official in the Shrine, and Carl wrote his speeches for him. Soon Carl was promoted to pit manager, and Ross began to introduce him to some of the important people in the Teamsters Union. Carl and Allen Dorfman, the liaison between the Mob and the Las Vegas Casinos, became fast friends. They even took their sons on a rafting trip through the Grand Canyon. Allen, a lawyer, helped regulate the huge teamster pension fund and knew everything that was going on between the Mob and the teamsters. The Mob was always looking for fresh faces who could pose a positive image, and what better than an ex schoolteacher with a ton of intelligence and a clean background.

Carl rose swiftly through the ranks and soon became the Casino manager at Circus Circus, and also ran the Slots of Fun casino which belonged to Ross Miller and was located right next door. At one time Carl was running Argent Corporation, which was Mob controlled, and consisted of the Hacienda, Stardust, Marina and Fremont hotels. Carl was a dynamo and had a charisma about him that made him immensely popular around town. He hobnobbed with business leaders, politicians and bankers, and probably could have had a future in politics.

He made everyone he met feel important and he never forgot where he came from.

110. The Billion Dollar Idea

With a nose for business, Carl Thomas made successful investments and did quite well financially. There was a Mini Price motel right off the freeway exit at Sahara Avenue and, for being off the beaten path, it had quite a bit of traffic. The motel had no restaurant and Carl approached the owner with the idea of putting a hot dog stand and sandwich bar in the lobby, along with a couple of slot machines. This graduated up to ten slots and then they added a Blackjack table. Carl had no problem getting licensed and realized that the town was expanding at a rapid pace and there wasn't any place that catered strictly to locals. He negotiated a long-term lease with the owner of the motel, which included all the property that the motel was on and the surrounding raw land. The lease was ridiculously cheap (most likely an offer he couldn't refuse).

Carl got financing for an expansion and made plans to put a full-service casino adjacent to the motel that would cater to local business. Carl's closest friend, Frank Fertitta, Jr., went to work for Carl and helped with the planning.

Frank was from Galveston, Texas. He got to Las Vegas about the same time Carl arrived. Frank's first job was as a bellman at the Tropicana Hotel. Franks uncle, Lorenzo Grilet, was a shift manager at the Stardust and, after Frank learned to deal, he put him to work at the Stardust. After a short time, Frank was dealing at the Tropicana, the best dealing job in town.

I met Frank in 1964 when I also began at the Tropicana. He was the sharpest man I ever met in the business, a cut above everyone else and a quiet, respectful individual. Carl and Frank had a lot in common, young kids and an urge to get ahead. While at the Stardust they brought their lunch in brown bags and volunteered for any overtime they could get. Years later I would remind Frank of the time he said to me in a conversation in his home, "How would you like to have three kids and a $520 a month house payment?" He replied, "It was $540."

111. Beginning of the End

Several years later, in the middle of the Bingo Palace expansion, the bombshell hit. The FBI had wiretapped the homes of several Kansas City and Chicago Mob leaders. They had Carl on tape, in the basement rec room of Nick Civella, the Kansas City Mob boss, explaining how to set up the skim in the Tropicana Hotel. They had just finished the expansion of "The Casino," added a bingo parlor, and changed the name to the "Bingo Palace."

A grand jury indicted all those involved, including Carl, in 1981. The news sped through town. It was headlines in both newspapers and suddenly Carl was in big trouble. His name was on the loan for the expansion of the Bingo Palace. Were he to lose his license, a certainty, they would close the place, and Carl would be forced into bankruptcy. All the Gaming Control Board had to do was have a special meeting with the Gaming Commission, and they could shut down the Bingo Palace.

Carl went to the most influential banker in town, supposedly one Parry Thomas, and arranged for Frank to get a loan for a million dollars and buy Carl out of the Bingo Palace. The loan was processed quickly, and the papers were signed. Carl was out, the Gaming Commission was furious, and Frank was the sole owner of the Bingo Palace. The deal was strictly legal, and although the Control Board tried to find a reason to deny Frank a license, they couldn't. This and the previous Stardust slot-skimming scam was the beginning of the end for the Mob in Las Vegas.

112. Frank Fertitta

Carl and his Mob associates were facing certain jail time. Allen Dorfman was gunned down after leaving a Chicago restaurant with his wife. She wasn't harmed. Joe Agosto, in charge of the Tropicana skim, died of a "heart attack" the day before standing trial in Kansas City. There was no autopsy. Marty Buccieri, a Mob relative and Caesars Palace floor man was found dead in his car with three bullets in his head. A wealthy San Diego woman, Tamara Rand, who knew too much, and claimed to have been bilked out of an investment in Argent Corporation, was found shot to death in her kitchen one week before the trial. Carl was sentenced to 15 years in prison but agreed to turn state's evidence and the sentence was reduced to five years. He was released after serving two.

He bought a ranch in Oregon and tried to maintain a low profile. He and Frank never saw each other again. Carl was persona non grata in Las Vegas, and there was too much at stake. Carl died in 1993 at age 60. He was driving on a road near his ranch in a 1992 Suburban, and he mysteriously went off the road and rolled. He was thrown from the car and crushed. He was supposed to testify before the Missouri Gaming Commission as to his purported connection with Frank Fertitta.

The Fertittas were seeking a gaming license in Missouri. There was a ton of speculation and rumor in regard to the accident. There were no witnesses and Carl had a few ounces of cocaine in his pocket. Some say it was Mob revenge and some speculated that Frank had something to do with it, which was ludicrous. Some said the cocaine was planted. So, with Carl and the others dead, Frank was on his way to becoming a billionaire.

The road wasn't easy. The Justice Department and the FBI were investigating him for racketeering and Mob association, and the Gaming Control Board was also trying to prove that he had Mob connections because of his friendship with Carl Thomas. One member of the Board, an ex-cop by the name of Gerald Cunningham, was obsessed with the investigation and moved heaven and earth trying to bring Frank down. Anyone coming up for licensing who had ever worked with or for Frank was put through the grinder and threatened with denial unless they could help him prove that Frank was "dirty" (Cunningham's own words). Even people who held small managerial positions were threatened with being called up for licensing as "key personnel" which was a ploy to intimidate an individual. The Control Board didn't need a reason to deny you the right to work. They could say you went to Kindergarten with Al Capone.

When I came up for licensing to share in casino profits at a small off Strip hotel/casino, they made me miserable. The scrutiny was beyond common sense, and Cunningham said to me more than once, "I know Fertitta's dirty, and I want you to tell me what you know about him. You had several big jobs (not so big) he hired you for at the Tropicana and Circus Circus. Why would he seek you out?" My reply was always the same: "Maybe he liked my work." A Control Board agent who was working on my investigation asked me if Frank Fertitta was my "Godfather." She also told my wife that she was the token female and "token" nigger" working at Gaming Control. The agent was later terminated and went to work for the city of North Las Vegas. Not long after, she was arrested for embezzlement. Nothing personal, but I hope she's still in jail. Her name was Lorraine Lindsay.

Years later Jeff Silver, then chairman of the Control Board, admitted that I was "abused," but mostly it was about Frank's relationship with Carl Thomas. Carl and Frank knew they would never see each other again and a lot of Carl's friends had jobs at the Bingo Palace. When Carl would come into town, these guys would pal around with him. One was the casino manager Don Gordon, who was Carl's cousin and the rest were shift managers, the chief of security, Harry MacBride, who was also Carl's unofficial bodyguard. Frank warned them to quit fraternizing with Carl, it could cause a lot of grief, but they didn't listen.

Frank fired them all and MacBride, who thought that Carl was a God, didn't take it well. He went to the justice department and told them that he saw Frank in the counting room of the Fremont Hotel while the skimming was going on. When Carl was running Argent Corporation he made Frank General manager of the Fremont Hotel and Casino. That's where Carl stayed until the Chicago Mob overruled the Kansas City outfit and appointed Frank Rosenthal as the overseer for Argent. MacBride, who was an oaf and a disgruntled employee, gave a deposition under oath that Frank lied about being in the counting room.

One night, while Frank was at the Fremont, I stopped in and had dinner with him. He told me that he attempted to observe the count and was locked out of the counting room. As general manager he felt he had the right to do what he wanted. When he complained to Carl he was told to forget about it and just do his job. Carl obviously didn't want him anywhere near the counting room. The deposition caused an uproar, and Frank's attorneys had their work cut out for them. Of course, the "investigative reporters" had a field day with it. However, nothing came of it and Frank remained under investigation for five long years. He had big plans but could do nothing but sit until he knew that he was cleared.

In the interim he expanded the Bingo Palace and renamed it the Palace Station with a Railroad theme. The name was a result of a contest sponsored by the Bingo Palace to find a name for the new casino. The prize was substantial and they had a lot of entries. Due to Frank's business acumen and a keen understanding of the gaming industry, the place was a huge success. Frank became wealthy while he waited for the investigations to conclude. While he was languishing at the Palace Station, he began buying up every property in Las Vegas that was zoned Hotel/Casino. Finally, the Justice department acknowledged that they couldn't prove he was guilty of anything and gave him a clean bill, the Gaming Control Board concurring. He immediately started construction of the Boulder Station and took the company public. At one time they were the biggest publicly traded gaming company in the U.S.

All this started with a hot dog stand and a couple of slot machines.

Frank gave back to the community in a big way. His philanthropy was legend. There was a school named after Victoria, his wife, and they financed buildings for the university. When Frank's old high school (a Catholic school) in Galveston was run down and about to close for lack of backing, it suddenly was remodeled and provided with the latest in educational tools, plus an endowment to make sure it continued to operate.

It was said that the contributor was "anonymous," but it was obvious who it was. His contributions to the church earned him an engraved plaque from the Pope. No one will ever know about the people he helped or the agencies he contributed to. Frank was a humble man and he never forgot where he came from. On the other side of his good fortune, Frank was plagued with heart disease at an early age. It was hereditary and bypass surgery was beginning to come into its own. The best place for the surgery was in Houston where all the cutting-edge technology was being practiced. He flew to Houston and underwent surgery. Several of us locally gave blood for the event. The operation was a success, but weeks later Frank got a call from the hospital and was told that he, and quite a few others, had been transfused with blood tainted with the Hepatitis C virus. There was nothing that could be done. Basically, the disease eats away at your heart, slowly, but incurably.

Frank traveled all over the world to seek medical advice but nobody seemed able to help. There were times when he was bedridden for months as a result of the disease. We would talk about it on occasion, but I never heard him complain. One thing it did was make a different person out of him. He always said he was "blessed" with his good fortune and became very religious. He went to church almost every day for the remaining years of his life. Prior to that, Frank was far from being a saint. Living in Las Vegas wasn't conducive to saintly living. Frank purchased the last piece of private beachfront in Southern California and built a huge home overlooking the Pacific Ocean. He traveled all over the world in his private jet but told me he was happiest at the "beach" with friends and family.

Here's something the Control Board's Gerald Cunningham didn't know.

In 1977, Frank called me and told me that Carl was going to take over the casino in the Tropicana hotel. Frank was going to be a shift manager and Baccarat manager rolled into one. He asked me to join the management team as the night shift Baccarat manager. I gave notice at the Dunes, and on a Sunday night we marched in and took over the casino. What we didn't know was that Carl was sent into the Tropicana by the Kansas City crime boss Nick Civella. Carl was going to direct the skim and see that the money was sent back East.

I had heard rumors that Carl could be "connected" but never gave it any thought and didn't want to. The real boss at the Tropicana was Joe Agosto, a highly trusted Mobster who also was "Director of the Folies Bergere," the showroom revue, and answered only to Civella and Chicago Mob boss Joey Aiuppa. His association with the show gave him his cover. He always wore black and spoke with a strong Italian accent, "jus' like inna movies."

There were other factions involved in the casino and there were objections to us being there. After a meeting between Civella and Aiuppa, it was decided that Chicago was going to call the shots, and we were out after only three months. Now all of us were unemployed and many of us had families to support. Carl felt badly and footed the bill for all of us to go to Puerto Vallarta, Mexico for five days of sun and fishing. While there, he had a meeting and told us that the issue was still undecided, and that he wanted to keep the "team" together, in case he had to go back into the Tropicana. We were going to get paid while we waited for the outcome. Our checks came from the Folies Bergere and were marked "special payroll." The checks were signed by Joe Agosto. That's when I realized what the situation was, and was glad that I just had a job, and not a major position. I knew the implications.

Anyway, the second day in Sunny Mexico I came down with "Montezuma's Revenge," called my wife and told here I was coming home early, and headed back to Las Vegas, where I spent the next four weeks on the pot. As it happened, things didn't change and everyone had to look for work, as the checks were only going to keep coming for another month.

A year later, Carl was headed back to the Tropicana at the behest of Civella and Aiuppa, and Frank had a heart attack and bypass surgery. While he was home recuperating, the FBI and Gaming Control were zeroing in on Carl and all the other Mob-connected individuals. That's when the FBI got Carl on tape setting up the skim in Civella's house in Kansas City. The bombshell blew the roof off the town. It was the end of Mob involvement in Las Vegas.

113. Lucky Heart Attack

The man who replaced Frank wound up in jail along with Carl and several others, and none were able to work in the industry again. A few years later, when I was up for licensing, Cunningham threatened me every way he could so I'd tell him what I knew about Frank's Mob involvement. I truthfully told him that I had no knowledge of anything of the sort. He didn't buy it. Then I realized that the only thing that could keep me from being licensed was the "special payroll." Frank was on it, too, and although we did nothing illegal, just a check signed by Joe Agosto would associate us with organized crime and make us persona non grata in Nevada. In distress I met Frank at the Palace Station and said, "What about the special payroll?" It was the first time I had used the words in years. Frank replied, "It's gone, there's no trace of it." I didn't question it and it was never mentioned again.

Had that come to light, there wouldn't have been Station Casinos, and all the Philanthropy and other financial empires that emanated from it.

114. Party Number One

Frank's kids threw a surprise anniversary party for their mom and dad's 30th anniversary. They booked the Inglenook Winery for the night up in the Napa Valley wine country. Frank loved the area and the family decided to fly up and have dinner. The invitees were flown in a chartered jet, with full beverage service. When we landed at the Napa airport we were taken by bus to the winery. The winery was a huge mansion type building. In the entranceway was a chamber orchestra playing as we entered. Inside were two tables (each had to be 50 feet long) loaded with every type of seafood and appetizers, etc. The family flew to Napa in the family plane and when they arrived the lights in the dining hall were dimmed. As they walked in, the lights went on and everybody, of course, hollered "SURPRISE!" After a sit-down dinner and dancing we climbed aboard the buses and headed for the airport.

We were back in Las Vegas by 1AM

115. Frank Fertitta's Cruise of the Century

The Fertitta's 50th anniversary made "Lifestyles of the Rich and Famous" look like hard times. All the wealthy Las Vegas society patrons were invited to a fundraiser for a national charity. Part of the fundraiser was the auctioning of cruises on Sea Dream Cruise Lines. Sea Dream Cruises are on board yachts that can handle about 110 people. As the most expensive cruise line, with a crew of 112 (more than one crew member for each guest), you can imagine what the service was like.

The ships have a large swimming pool, four bars, one large restaurant area (most meals on board are served outside in the Caribbean), a social area complete with a stage, that seats 120, plus a spa, a small casino, (one Blackjack table), and a fitness center. The staterooms are spacious and come with full liquor cabinets.

With their 50th anniversary coming up, The Fertittas still hadn't decided how to celebrate. Before any bidding started, Frank said, "I know what I want to do for our anniversary." With that he booked the whole cruise ship for a five-day Caribbean cruise.

In our mail one day there was what looked like an ad for a cruise line with a picture of a young couple on the front. Before I threw it away my wife said, "That looks like Frank and Vickie when they were young." Sure enough, it was an invitation to a private Sea Dream Caribbean cruise for the Fertitta's 50th anniversary. My wife and I and another couple from Los Angeles, were the only people invited not living in Las Vegas. The other couple was Frank's Insurance agent and his wife, the actress Julie Haggerty from the movie "Airplane."

Frank's secretary had made arrangements for us at the Red Rock hotel and casino. There, we were sent to the VIP check in, where the concierge introduced us to our "butler." We were told we had comp privileges of $1000 a day. The butler took us up to our accommodations. When we entered, I was floored. After 45-odd years in the casino business it took a lot to impress me, but this was unbelievable. The suite, at least 4000 square feet, had two bedrooms separated by a huge dining and living area, with a pool table and a full wet bar, a fully stocked kitchen. The master bedroom contained a huge enclosed Jacuzzi. I explained to the butler that we were not high rollers, that we were friends of the Fertitta family and we certainly didn't need a butler.

After two days of Red Rock luxury we were limousined to the Hughes terminal at McCarran airport, where all the charter and private flights originated. The family stewardess and two other hostesses served us. In Houston, we picked up the other invitees, family, elderly friends of Frank's parents, friends (including two nuns who had taught at Frank's Catholic school, and we were off to Puerto Rico on a chartered airliner loaded with all the seafood, pastries and liquor you could imagine.

That evening, we deplaned in San Juan and boarded two buses immediately surrounded by a platoon of motorcycle policeman, with a police cruiser in front and at the rear. We flew through the streets of San Juan with lights flashing and sirens blaring, causing vehicles to pull over and let us pass. Arriving at the ship, Frank and Vickie were at the top of the gangplank to greet us personally.

In the morning I noticed a "Do Not Disturb" sign on every door. Everyone was seasick.

That evening we dined on either live Maine lobster, flown in for the occasion, or steaks of Kobe beef, convening after at the social area, now a nightclub with a bar and three tiers of comfortable chairs and tables. On stage came George Wallace, the comic who'd just headlined at the Flamingo. Frank had jetted him into San Juan where he was helicoptered to St. Barths. After his show he socialized with us then was jetted back to Las Vegas.

Next evening, we dined aboard the ship again, entertained by Michael Cavanaugh, of Broadway, films, and "Dueling Pianos" fame. Then on to Virgin Gorda where we were ferried to the Bitter End yacht club, as seen in Robin Leach's "Lifestyles of the Rich and Famous." After dinner, Frank and Vickie repeated their vows on the beach in a lovely ceremony and were presented with a huge plaque with a personal engraving and anniversary wishes from the Pope.

I looked at everyone together. I saw a priest, two nuns, the widow of an old friend, the family's private physician, relatives and old family friends, quite a few who were scraping by on social security and small pensions. I said to Frank, "Do you realize what a dream come true this is to all these people?" He replied, "I could have had a huge bash in Las Vegas or anywhere, and have politicians, celebrities, and wealthy business moguls from all over the world, but it would have been an expensive party, nothing else. Everyone on this trip means something to us; they've been in our lives for years, back when we were all scratching out a living. You're all important to us." "I can't tell you how much pleasure we're getting from this."

After dinner, tenders took us to a remote beach where we walked very carefully down a dark, winding path, passing a sign indicating we were in a state park or nature reserve. At a large clearing, a circle of lights came on, and right there in front of us was a huge sound stage and dance floor. Out came Michael McDonald with his band. Everyone drank and danced the night away, a night that ended with a massive fireworks display. We arrived in San Juan the following morning.

Heading home, the crew of the Sea Dream told us they'd never seen anything like this.

Two years later, Frank passed away. I talked to him about six weeks before he died, after Stanford Medical Center had told him there was nothing more they could do for him. He said, "I'm 70 years old, and I've been blessed with a wonderful life." I'm ready to go if that's the way it has to be."

A lot of wealthy people have short memories. Frank's was long. He never forgot where he came from or the friends he met along the way.

116. The Famous Stardust Slot Skim

The Stardust slot skim was discovered in 1976, about the time the Bingo Palace was being built. The slots had become such a large part of the gaming revenue in Nevada that the Control Board was sensitive to any hint of wrongdoing. Gone were the days when they counted coin with small machines, instead the coins were put on a conveyor belt in the buckets from under the machines and were weighed on specially calibrated scales.

The results were tracked by computer and reported to the Gaming Control Board. The slot manager was Jay Vandermark, one of the slot geniuses in the industry, and supposedly did a little slot cheating on his own at one time. He diddled with the scales so that they would weigh ten percent less than the actual amount in the bucket, and they skimmed the difference. There was a switch installed on the scales that would put them back in calibration if necessary. The daily skim was huge, as the daily gross slot take in places as big as the Stardust usually ran between $200,000 and $300,000 a day.

This was before jackpots, fills of coin, payroll and maintenance. The extra coin was put on carts and installed in a bank behind the main change booth. Whenever the change girls ran short of coin and long on cash, they would go to this bank and buy more coin with the cash. By the end of the day most of the coin was converted to cash and the cash was out the door, on its way to be divided amongst the Mob factions in Chicago, New York, Cleveland and Kansas City. The day after the raid, Jay Vandermark left for a long, well needed vacation.

Gaming Control was not happy. They (and the FBI) wanted to talk to him. His son said he was in Mexico and would return shortly. He was never seen again. Shortly after, his son was found dead in their home with a crushed skull. The murder was never solved and Jay never surfaced (literally). Some say he's living the good life in Mexico and some say he's rooming with Russian Louis.

I think everyone has a good idea what happened to him.

117. Lefty

Frank “Lefty” Rosenthal was the big boss at the Stardust and the Mob’s representative in the operation. He was featured in the movie “Casino.” His character was played by Robert DeNiro. He was portrayed as some sort of casino expert when, in truth, that wasn’t so. He was disliked by his peers, and his talents (except as a bookmaker) were not what he made them out to be. Unlike other Mob representatives who went out of their way to keep a low profile, he couldn’t keep his mouth shut and was constantly in the spotlight, making the boys in the east uncomfortable. He was a legend in his own mind.

Lefty’s only claim to fame was that he fired a bunch of older dealers at the Stardust and replaced them with young, attractive women who, for the most part, couldn’t deal worth a shit. It made all the papers and left a bad taste in everybody’s mouth. Jobs were hard to find at the time and most of these men, though highly qualified, couldn’t find work. They eventually filed a class action suit against the Stardust, and Rosenthal and, although it took years to work its way through the courts, the dealers prevailed. By the time they received any compensation some of them had died.

Rosenthal married a showgirl by the name of Geri Marmor. Her first job in Las Vegas was serving cocktails in the Stardust Coffee shop. The year was 1958. On her first night, she and I met for a drink at the New Yorker Bar and Grill downtown near the Golden Nugget. Geri was no angel, but she was a nice girl, although she took a few wrong turns down through the years. We had a few drinks together and, because I had my paycheck in my pocket, I bid her goodnight and headed for the Golden Nugget, where I lost it (my paycheck) on the crap table. Geri and I remained friends for years and years, and she married Rosenthal in 1968.

I was amazed at Sharon Stone’s portrayal of her in the movie; her facial expressions and mannerisms were uncanny. Geri, after a fight with Rosenthal, was frightened and fled to Los Angeles. Some said that the police provided an escort. Several weeks later she was found dead in front of the motel she was living in, purportedly from a drug overdose.

I'm sure it was an overdose, but it wasn't self-administered. Geri knew too much, and she was given a "hot shot," which is a lethal dose of drugs forcibly injected. When someone has a history of occasional drug abuse, it's difficult to prove. They didn't even attempt to prove it, and the consensus was that her husband knew about it. She had taken a large amount of cash and jewelry when she left Las Vegas, and he wasn't happy about it. It was rumored that Lefty paid $50,000 for a private autopsy, which proved nothing. I imagine he wanted to protect his "image." In spite of her transgressions, Geri was a good mother to their two children and never would have taken the chance to leave her kids without a mother.

118. A Bad Break

About a month later, Lefty Rosenthal went to Tony Roma's restaurant to pick up some ribs. When he went to start his Cadillac, there was a fiery explosion and, according to Rosenthal, he was fortunate enough to exit the car and roll on the ground. He was a mess. Most of his clothes were burned off, his hair was badly singed, he was bloody and had a wild look in his eye. The TV stations were on it almost as fast as the police and the ambulance.

As they were preparing to load him into the ambulance, a TV news lady leaned in and shoved a microphone in his face. She said, "Mr. Rosenthal, do you have any idea as to who might have placed the bomb in your car?" He replied, "I can assure you that it wasn't the Boy Scouts of America."

Everybody had a good chuckle over it, in spite of the fact that they were disappointed that the attempt failed. He was not well-liked. The Control Board revoked his license and put him in the "Black Book of Excluded Persons" which meant he was not permitted to enter a Las Vegas casino ever again. He had a home in Miami that looked like a fortress, with high walls and floodlights all around the perimeter. He never lived a day without worrying that the Mob was going to catch up with him. I can't believe that they didn't, no matter how long it took.

119. The Unluckiest Man in the World

In the early 1980s I had an interest and ran the gaming in a small hotel casino, and truck stop complex just off the Strip. We got a lot of local business along with the tourists and truckers and cashed a large amount of payroll checks.

Donna was a cashier in our casino cage, and although she was both personable and dependable, she had a problem with shortages. In a casino cage, if a cashier comes up short in her drawer at the end of the shift, she doesn't have to make up the shortage, as opposed to a change girl on the floor. On Fridays we could cash between one and two million dollars in payroll checks. The lines at the windows were long and the work for the cashiers was tedious and grueling. I tried cashing checks in the cage just to familiarize myself to what it entailed for about 40 minutes one busy Friday, and it was everything I could do to keep a clear mind. It was more intense than dealing in a big casino game. In doing so I gained a lot of respect for those individuals who spent hours nose-to-nose to our clientele, (who were not all, shall we say, refined). Donna had a problem with shortages. She tried hard, but kept coming up with some large shortages. Although they were honest mistakes, it was just something we couldn't tolerate, so we had to let her go.

Over a year later, a couple of new places opened and, being much larger operations than ours, had a higher pay scale, causing us to lose several cage cashiers. Our controller came to me one day and said we were painfully short of help, with no prospects at the time. As the overtime aspects were being discussed, she said to me, "Donna is not working right now and is looking for employment. Do you want to give her another chance?

I agreed, we were in a desperate situation, and Donna was, after all, familiar with our operation. We put her on the late shift where it was usually slower and hoped she would stay out of trouble. At 12:01AM on a slow night Donna opened her window and began her shift. It was her first night back. Less than three minutes later I took a call in the casino from the cashier cage, and Donna said, "Sir, there's a man at my window trying to pass a bad check." When I asked her how she knew the check was bad she replied "It's written on a cement company in Yermo, California (near Victorville), and my grandfather owned that company, it has his signature on it and he's been dead over two years."

I had Security detain the man and call the police who had the bunko squad there in a very short time. It turns out he had recently been paroled from prison for forgery, etc., and going through the trunk of his car they found forgery materials, checks, etc., plus a handgun. Being an ex-felon in possession of a weapon automatically qualified him for more jail time, besides the bad check and other paraphernalia. His next stint was going to be a long one.

Now, to sum this up, here's a guy recently paroled, gets in his car and drives to Las Vegas, pulls off the Strip and randomly picks a small place to try to pass a bad check. He picks our establishment, goes to Donna's window, on her first night back, and he was her first customer. There were two other windows open at the time. She was the only person in Las Vegas who could know the check was bad. Now he was headed back to prison. If *that* doesn't make him the unluckiest man in the world at that time, what does? Donna's shortage problem continued, and we had to let her go again.

It just wasn't her cup of tea.

120. Las Vegas; a Union Town

Pat K. was a cocktail waitress in the lounge at the Stardust. She was considerably older than her sister waitresses. On top of that she was slightly bowlegged and a little on the hefty side. People wondered how she could keep the job, competing with the pretty young girls (some underage) who vied for these positions.

Word filtered out that some of the mobsters who had interests in these casinos had, shall we say, unusual sexual proclivities in which most girls wouldn't participate, job or no job. It was said that Pat shared their tastes for the quirky, and this was the reason she was still working. She was also known to turn a trick on occasion with the right individual, or at the request of the bosses.

In spite of her habits, she was a nice person, with a pleasant personality, and a heart of gold. Many years later, I was working as a pit boss at the Frontier Hotel, I looked up and saw her standing there. She had aged, and put on weight, but still had that pleasant smile. I said, "Pat, my God, I haven't seen you in in sixteen years, how have you been?" We made small talk and I asked her what she was doing. She told me she was working at the Safeway market in Henderson. When I asked what she did there she told me that she was a "meat wrapper."

She added, "Same business, but now I belong to the union."

121. Here Come the Girls

The Stardust Hotel opened with the first European revue in Las Vegas, rather than big name entertainment. Not only was it a new wrinkle, but in the long run it saved the casino a great deal of money, as they wouldn't have to get involved in a bidding war with other casinos for high priced entertainers.

The revue was the "Lido De Paris," which had been the toast of Paris for years. It had several acts, but most important it had near nude topless dancers and showgirls, a first for the Las Vegas Strip.

Several months before the hotel was due to open, the Lido personnel arrived in Las Vegas preceded by much fanfare and publicity. They arrived by plane from Los Angeles, after crossing the Atlantic on TWA. They were met by local dignitaries, the press, photographers by the dozen, and most of the young single guys in Las Vegas, (who had to stay behind the fence). The girls were from France, England, the Netherlands, with a handful of Scandinavians tossed in. The planes pulled up to the gates and they rolled out the steps so they could deplane.

When the door of the plane opened, they began to filter out with small bags and big sunglasses and smiles. They had to go down the stairs and walk across the tarmac to the gates, so everybody got a good look. To everyone's amazement, they looked just like any other girls, albeit a bit taller. Some of them had men with them, who happened to be their boyfriends, who got to fly free with the show. Some were speaking in their native languages, the largest part being French. The local studs now had a choice of chorus girls (each hotel had a chorus line which did a number to start the show, one prior to the headliner coming on, and the finale).

There were the Texas Copa Girls at the Sands, the June Taylor Dancers at the Dunes, The Donn Arden dancers at the Desert Inn and the rest were just generic chorus lines. All pretty girls. After the last show they were required to "mingle" in the lounge for one hour. This kept the customers interested, and they were in there, pitching every night. The girls were required to stay only an hour, and they didn't have to do anything they didn't want to do. Most of them gave up the chance to make some money when they were invited to gamble with some of the casino patrons, and just beat it out the door. Some, of course, stayed. The Lido girls were *not* required to mingle. The show was a huge success and ran for a lot of years.

I was a dealer in the Stardust at the time, and the girls would come through the casino to get backstage prior to the show. We got to know quite a few of them, and they would often stop and make small talk if we weren't busy. They had a lot of sayings that we were hearing for the first time. One being that when they were going to walk away, they would say, "Ta-ta, dearie, keep your pecker up." Which was, "Keep your chin up" in our English. When they would say that we would howl with laughter. When someone told them what "pecker" referred to in the states, they would say, "Keep that up, too."

122. A Cure for Baldness

One night two British girls came in the front door, obviously involved in some kind of spat, as you could hear them arguing the minute they came in. When they got alongside my table, one stopped cold and the other kept walking. The girl who stopped then called out to the other one "Up your mucket, dearie," which was a new expression to me. Thinking I may be on to something, I questioned one of the wardrobe girls as to the term "mucket." The definition floored me. Seems as though the Europeans, who were a bit negligent in the hygiene department (the wardrobe personnel said the dressing room resembled a high school locker room after the big game) had to play by different rules in the U. S. of A. They couldn't have hair under their arms, and due to the skimpiness of the outfits they wore they had to keep their pubic hair tightly trimmed. Most just shaved the whole thing. This wasn't long after the movie "Anna" with Silvana Mangano, had been censored in this country because she had hairy armpits.

Anyway, a lot of the girls had their paramours from Europe with them, and European men liked their women hairy. This, I guess, posed a libido problem in some relationships, and the solution was a mucket, which quite simply was a hairpiece for one's private parts.

Seeing that the Tropicana was bringing in the "Folies Bergere," also from Paris, a local businessman took advantage of the situation. He owned the Stage Door costume shop just across Sahara avenue from the Sahara Hotel, and that was where one could purchase a mucket. They came in colors and sizes (don't ask me how they attached) and were not cheap. Hence the expression "Up your mucket, dearie." You won't find too many people who can tell you what a mucket is (or was).

I guess they were easy to make as they all parted down the middle.

123. Politically Incorrect

Clara Barron checked into the Desert Inn one sunny day in June, 1957. She took two adjoining rooms (the hotel had a total of 300), unpacked her baggage, and went down to the cashier's cage. She announced that she wanted to make arrangements to have all her mail and correspondence forwarded from her home in Beverly Hills to the Desert Inn. This included dividend checks, bank statements and all financial documents, along with personal mail. The big bosses were notified that her stay was open ended, she had no checkout date.

When they questioned her in regard to a credit limit, and a possible free room arrangement, she told them that she intended to stay until almost all of her assets were depleted. This was a bit unusual, even for early Las Vegas, and when asked why, she replied that she despised her son-in-law, her daughter married him against her (Clara's) wishes, and when she died she didn't want him to benefit in any way from her considerable fortune. When, upon further investigation, it was determined that her assets were indeed considerable, she became the queen of the Desert Inn. She sat and played Blackjack a minimum of 12 hours a day, wagering between \$25 and \$100. Remember, the limit was \$200 and that made Clara a huge asset to the casino.

Clara was slender, in her mid 60s, and wore her grey hair swept back into a tight bun. She wore a cardigan sweater day and night, and the only time she was away from the Blackjack table was when she was sleeping or eating. I never knew her to go anywhere else to gamble. She would force a smile (grimace?) when you would say hello, but generally looked like a woman on a mission and in a permanent snit. The first few weeks of her stay she didn't seem to mind losing, although this is against human nature, especially in a casino. It didn't take long before she was just like everyone else, easygoing when she was winning, and irritable and nasty when on a losing streak. She would chide the dealers and get a bit testy with the other customers, a practice which is not tolerated in any gambling establishment. For Clara, however, they stretched their patience, biting their tongues again and again to keep from offending her.

In the 1950s, before the economy became global, it was rare to see an Asian, or any foreigner in the Las Vegas casinos; this was about to change in a hurry. One morning I heard that Clara had played until 5AM, and lost quite a bit of money, and was in rare form when she retired for the night. She had just come down to play when I went to work and she came to my table. She never was excessively meticulous about her appearance, but this morning she looked like 90 miles of bad road. I just nodded and said good morning, which elicited a grunt and a nasty stare. She was slamming the cards down, complained about the coffee, and was generally in a really bad mood.

A short time later an Asian gentleman, dressed in an expensive suit, came over to the table, said good morning in perfect English and laid five $100 bills on the table to purchase chips. Being Asian he stood out, and the $100 bills really attracted attention. The pit boss greeted him and offered a cocktail or coffee. Clara stared at him with a contemptuous look on her kisser and announced out loud, to no one in particular, "Looks like things are awful good in the laundry business." The man just glanced up at her for a split second and made his wagers. It was an embarrassing situation, but it passed.

When I got off the game the shift manager told me that if she does it again they were going to read her the riot act, even if it meant losing her business. Clara stayed at the DI for nine months, and was practically a fixture, when she finally determined that she couldn't lose enough to overcome her income, so she ultimately checked out and went back to Beverly Hills. Her losses were estimated to be in the vicinity of a million dollars. The exact figure (and they had an exact figure) was never revealed.

124. The Drive-In King

Stan Burke was credited with starting the Drive-In craze in California. He owned several "Stan's Drive-Ins" in the Los Angeles area, and the rest of the nation followed. He was also a Blackjack aficionado and more than a little eccentric. He was a tall stocky fellow with a gray crew cut and played and stayed at the Flamingo. When he would come up to your game, you would say, "Good evening, Mr. Burke," and in some cases he would say (with a grin), "It's Stan, please call me Stan." like he was your best friend. Then you knew that he had been winning. If things went sour for him, and you walked up to where he was playing and said, "Stan, how are you doing?" he would lift his finger and say, "It's Mr. Burke, please address me as Mr. Burke."

One night, on a losing streak, he lost his whole credit line. After he lost the last bet, he stood behind the table with a drink in his hand. Andy Verchick, the dealer, stood and stared straight ahead. Stan (Mr. Burke) wasn't too happy and it was an awkward situation. Then "Mr. Burke" reached over and dumped the drink on Andy's head. Andy was a big tough guy and, to his credit, he didn't move a muscle, just stood there and stared ahead. Mr. Burke walked off.

The attendant in the ladies' room dried Andy's shirt with a hair dryer.

125. Marion Hicks' Nephews

Marion Hicks was the owner of the Thunderbird, which opened in 1948, the third hotel on the Strip, and the first with the swimming pool in the rear of the hotel. He, like most of the other owners had "partners" from the East, notably the Boston area. Marion was diagnosed with incurable cancer in 1956 and spent very little time at the hotel. He preferred to spend his last days on his yacht.

He had two nephews, Marty and Billy, whom he chose to "represent" his interests. This, of course included assisting in the count at the end of each shift. Billy, the oldest, worked the night shift, was capable, efficient and took his job seriously. He was heavyset, with a pleasant moon-shaped face and was a sharp dresser.

Marty was a horse of a different color. He lived in a room on the second floor but spent most of his time at the bar. He usually wore a suit, open shirt collar, and his lanky hair usually was in a state of disarray, as was he. During the day there was very little business in the casino, and he would sit at the bar, turn around and face the gaming tables and drink himself into a semi-stupor. It was said that he also used some other stuff, which in those days was highly unusual. Once in a while he would jump off the bar stool and shoot the dice at the crap table with his own money. If he lost, he would get back on the stool, and take a crack at every single woman who came into the place. When they took the boxes off and into the count room at the end of the shift, Marty would go into the counting room with the count team, and it seems he always came out with money. Regulations were lax in those days and a lot of places used the "deuce" system when taking the count. A "deuce" is a small cocktail table for two persons, generally not much more than 12 inches in diameter. The "deuce" system is when they have one of these small tables in the counting room, and after opening a box they would hold it up in the air and shake the bills out. They would count whatever landed on the table. Your guess is as good as mine as to what happened to the bills that landed on the floor. This is kind of an industry joke; however, it was pretty close to the truth. Marty would then have enough for the evening's festivities.

He had that look that personified the word "pervert."

126. The Gold Pen

Early one afternoon a woman walked into the casino, took a brief look and turned around to leave. There were only four or five people in the whole place, and Marty was in his "office" at the bar. She was blond, in her 40s, well-built, and looked like she had been around the block a few times, but that didn't faze Marty. He called her over and offered to buy her a drink or dinner, or whatever she wanted, and that got her up on the stool.

As the afternoon progressed and the alcohol flowed they got chummy. Marty couldn't keep his hands off her and she would give him the old high thigh squeeze on occasion, and the stage was set. About 3 o'clock they headed for his room. Came time for the count (7PM) and no Marty. They called his room, got no answer, then sent "Muscles," the casino gofer, up to knock on his door.

Muscles was short and pudgy, and wore the same suit every day, a threadbare double breasted that could have been brown at one time, but was now a light orange, with a bowtie. He hung around and ran errands for the bosses, or anyone who would slip him a few bucks, and he always got a meal on the house. Nobody knew his name—it was just Muscles or "Mus."

So, Muscles banged on Marty's door and still no answer. They checked out front, and his car was in the usual place, so they sent Security up with a pass key. They wanted to get the count over with so they could go home. Well, there was a flurry of activity, the elevator door flew open and one of the guards ran out into the parking lot, while the other took George Rosen (the shift manager) aside and whispered in his ear, and they both headed for the elevator.

Marty didn't make the count, and everything was hush-hush for a while But, in true Las Vegas form, the word got out. They had opened Marty's door and he was passed out, nude on the bed, lying on his stomach, with his gold (engraved) pen inserted in his rectum with a note impaled on the pen. His watch, money and anything of value was gone. The note read simply, "Thanks for a great time."

After that, every time he made a flourish of pulling out his gold pen to sign a check, everyone made a face.

127. Shorty

Carl Van Dyke was a dice dealer at the Thunderbird Hotel. He was a happy-go-lucky guy in his mid 30s and stood 6-4. He, like a high percentage of the casino help, was a "rounder," a person who made the rounds of the bars and casinos almost every night and, as a result, had nothing to his name but his car and whatever he had in his pocket.

The Thunderbird was getting ready to close for remodeling, business was slow, so they started laying off casino employees. The place had a strip of lawn that separated it from the Strip, on which sat the big sign, and was in the center of a circular driveway, leading up to the main entrance. I drove into the driveway on my way to work one morning, and noticed a small pup tent, in the shade of the sign, with two feet sticking out the door of the tent. When I got into the casino I mentioned it, and found out that it was Carl, who had been laid off and, living in a weekly motel, couldn't pay his rent, so they evicted him.

He'd get up in the morning, come into the casino with a towel and his shaving kit, and clean up in the restroom. Then he'd come out to the casino bar, get down on his knees and ask them to buy "Shorty" a drink. He was able to mooch a few meals, but that only lasted a few days before they evicted him from the front lawn. Never found out what happened to Carl. Some said he went to Reno, some said that he went back east where his father was a famous brain surgeon. Seems like everyone in the racket had a brother or father who was a famous surgeon or attorney.

This was never verified.

128. Levinsky; I'm Punchy, What's Your Excuse?

Kingfish Levinsky was a heavyweight boxer who fought through the late '30s and early '40s. He fought all the top fighters of his day and beat very few of them. His claim to fame was winning a four round exhibition bout with Jack Dempsey, the old and over-the-hill ex-heavyweight champion, who was considering a comeback. After the fight Dempsey decided against the comeback and Kingfish got bouts with some of the top heavyweights of the day.

He got murdered.

Joe Louis knocked him out in the first round. Max Baer almost killed him. He soaked up a lot of leather. His first pro fight was with some old war horse who had never won a fight. He knocked Kingfish around the ring and took the decision. His sister, Lena, aka "Leapin' Lena," was his manager and she didn't care who she put him in the ring with. As a result, he wound up seriously punch drunk. He did make some money that Lena managed (and spent), so he wound up in the tie business, first in Miami and then in Las Vegas. They would drive to Los Angeles and buy a bunch of the old "hand painted" ties that you could buy on any street corner for a buck. The ties had pictures of a horse's head, a dog, a duck taking flight, some even had the logos of the Las Vegas hotels. Once in a while you actually saw someone wearing one, but it was rare. Then they would drive back to Las Vegas and Kingfish would sell them for $5. Or more if he cornered some poor tourist.

Levinsky was a big man over six feet tall and well over 250 pounds. With his square head and jaw, and sagging pot belly, he looked like the quintessential Neanderthal. He always needed a shave and his hygiene was not good. As a matter of fact, he smelled like a thousand locker rooms, if you got close enough (probably about 10 feet) he could make your eyes water. This was good for his business, as you would buy anything, just to get him away from you.

He was married four times, and all of his exes had nothing good to say about his hygiene. I was going to work one morning at the Thunderbird hotel, and Lena's Cadillac convertible pulled up to the front door. The door flew open and Kingfish leaped out and started running in place for a good minute, then reached in and grabbed his suitcase and literally ran into the casino. It was over 100 degrees outside, and by the time he got inside he was good and ripe. I stalled before I went in, trying to avoid him, and thought I was successful. I went on a table that had several players on it, and a minute later I felt two arms come over my shoulders, and I almost passed out. It was Kingfish. He told me he would wait for me in the lobby, he had a great tie for me. When the players looked at him he said, "I'm punchy, what's *your* excuse?" Most everyone of the casino employees would buy a tie (there were about 14 of us) and when Kingfish would leave, we would throw them in the trash receptacle in front of the cashier's cage. Hours later, near the end of the day, Kingfish would come in, go directly to the trash can, take the ties out and sell them to the night shift.

In a way, it was sad to see, but Las Vegas had a lot of stories like that.

129. Another Sad Scene

I can recall working the night shift at the Flamingo, and every night there were about ten old men who would straggle in the front door, go to the cashier's cage, sign the "shill payroll" and be given $8 in cash. They looked and walked like the down and out and homeless. Everyone would shuffle and look down at the floor, as if ashamed to have someone see their face. They would take their $8, go over to the chuck wagon buffet, and load up for a buck. Then they would shuffle back out the door. When I asked who they were, I was told they were old, broke dealers and people the casino manager knew from the past, who were down and out.

The image remains with me to this day.

130. The Million Dollar Miscalculation

John Dixon was the graveyard shift manager at the Frontier Hotel. John was a cocky kind of guy. He walked with a bit of swagger and was more than a little short with the help. He was a veteran gamer with a lot of years in the racket, and had held several management positions. He was also an archaeologist. Every moment of his off time was spent in the desert, close to Las Vegas and as far away as Arizona and New Mexico. He had a collection of artifacts that equaled or surpassed that of any museum–all encased in glass-covered display cases at his home. He was known as the ultimate authority on prehistoric desert-dwellers and lectured at several universities. He authored several texts that were used in some college classrooms around the country. I had been in his home and got a firsthand look at his marvelous collection, which was later donated to the University of Nevada. Along with that, he had a Japanese wife, and was fluent in Japanese. John was adept in almost everything he did, except in a gambling house. His expertise and people skills were sorely lacking, and although I liked him and knew him well, I wondered how the hell he got the position he was in.

One night, before I went home from my job as a pit boss at the Frontier, a little man walked up to a Blackjack table in my area. He was quite short, with a dark, swarthy complexion and a large smile. He reached into his pocket and brought out a handful of $100 bills and bought in for $3000, a substantial amount for 1971.

He proceeded to bet the limit ($500) on two hands and lost the money in short order. He motioned me over, and I went to the outside of the table to keep our conversation private. He reached into the side pocket of his sport jacket and brought out a book of travelers checks in $1000 denominations. Glancing down into his pocket, I could see that his pocket was stuffed with similar booklets, as was the pocket on the other side. A rough estimate on my part was that if they were all the same denomination, he was carrying at least $200,000, probably more.

He signed the checks and I went to the cashier cage, where they called and verified that the checks were good as gold. Phony travelers checks were always a problem in Las Vegas, and some casinos wouldn't cash them on weekends for people they didn't know. Banks were closed on weekends.

When I returned to the table and gave him his cash ($10,000) he said he would like a room for the night and his (two) bags were at the bell desk. I knew this man deserved a suite but I didn't have the authority to comp rooms, so I called John Dixon. He came into the pit and I told him what had transpired. His reply was, "He looks like a fucking bus boy to me." I told him how much money he had with him, and John said, "He probably won it somewhere." to which I said, "What difference does it make where he got it? He's here and we have a chance to win it. John's answer was, "Well, I'm not comping any fucking rooms for him or anyone else." With that he walked away.

I stood there and couldn't fathom what I'd just heard. The only thing the room cost the hotel was the price of cleaning it, and they sure didn't need an expensive suite on a quiet night. After I got home, I tossed and turned and was generally agitated over the situation. At 6AM I called Lou Digreg, the assistant casino manager (hoping I wouldn't wake him) and informed him of the situation. He told me to call him at the hotel when I woke up and he would let me know what happened. Later that morning I called, and he told me that when he got to work and inquired, he found out that man had asked if his room was ready and was told he had to go the front desk and get a room. I guess he took his bags and left. He wound up losing $18,000.

Lou was a highly respected man in the business, and he told me that there's a different mind-set with corporate management, and just forget about it. Anywhere else John would have been fired as soon as it all came out into the open. The very next day, my brother who was a Baccarat dealer at Caesars Palace called me at home. He said, "Did you hear about Mr. Wahab?" When I asked if his first name was Bajumi there was a moment of silence, and he asked, "How did you know that?" I told him to tell me his story first, and then I would tell mine.

Bear in mind that Las Vegas was a huge rumor mill, and news traveled fast. If someone lost a lot of money in a particular casino, you would hear about it in a ho-hum way. If someone came in and tipped a huge amount of money to the dealers and employees, it was all over town in a flash. Of course, if you were one of the last to hear about it, the amount had probably doubled by the time you received the information.

Seems that after leaving the Frontier, Mr. Wahab walked into Caesars Palace, went directly to the cashier's cage, put a suitcase on the counter, and told the cashier he wanted to put the contents on deposit, and draw on it as he gambled. When they opened the case, they found one million dollars in cash, neatly strapped in $10,000 packets. Within a very short time they had a casino host take Mr. Wahab up to the best suite they had to offer. In the next few days, Mr. Wahab had lost the million, and they extended him $500,000 in credit. While he was there he purportedly gave the dealers in the Baccarat over $100,000. That came to about $4000 per man in just a few days. Not bad when $30 a day in tips was considered a desirable job. After I told my story, my brother commented, "Oh my God".

When you take into mind that in 1971 a $10,000 credit line got you the best the hotel had to offer, it makes you wonder.

131. Real Las Vegas Class

As an example of class and people skills, I recall a pit manager at the Frontier named Mario Romano. During an invitational when the place was full of invited high rollers, he was introduced to the wife of an insurance executive. She was a beautiful woman, had a head-turning body, and wore a dress so tight it looked like it was painted on. He looked her up and down, and the first words out of his mouth were, "I can see ya ain't carryin' a gun or nuttin."

132. A Medical Alibi

Dr. Harry Fightlin arrived in Las Vegas in 1946. He saw possibilities in the small town of less than 20,000 and opened his medical practice. At that time, he was the only doctor in Las Vegas who could correctly read an X-Ray, and actually mentored some of the other physicians. Harry was a physician *and* a surgeon, something you rarely see in today's specialty medicine. His practice grew and his reputation with his peers as a brilliant diagnostician spread. He was the house physician for the Flamingo, and on more than one occasion he made house calls at the hotel for Bugsy Siegel and his girlfriend, Virginia Hill.

Dr. Harry was also a personal family friend and spent quite a few holiday family dinners at our home. One night after a few martinis we asked him what the most interesting thing was he could remember in regard to his career in medicine. In spite of his medical accomplishments, the lives he saved (my wife's was one), the fact that he was the first chief of staff at Sunrise Hospital, and in the early years, he was not only the house doctor for the Flamingo, but the El Rancho and the Last Frontier as well, the only hotels on the Strip.

This is what he told us. On Friday night, June 20th, 1947 he received a call from the El Rancho hotel, that they had some ill guests in one of their bungalows (the El Rancho didn't have rooms, per se) and they needed a doctor. When he got to the hotel they directed him to the bungalow, and he entered to find four men sitting on a sofa, and several others spread out around the room. Harry described it as "a smoke-filled room full of men." They all claimed to be victims of stomach distress, (diarrhea, etc.) and they wondered if he could do something for them. According to him, these guys looked and talked like Murder, Inc., and none of them looked sick. He examined each one and could see that they weren't seriously ill. Each paid in cash and wanted a written receipt. Harry didn't carry receipts, and there was no stationery in the room, so they insisted he go to the front desk and get blank receipts. When he returned, he made out a separate receipt for each individual, each got a prescription for Donnatal (a stomach tranquilizer) or other stomach related meds. They thanked him and he left. The next morning it was in the Las Vegas paper that Bugsy Siegel had been killed in Los Angeles the previous night. Las Vegas had no television, and the LA times used to fly the paper to Las Vegas on a daily basis. The Los Angeles police claimed it was a Mob hit, and they had several suspects they planned on talking to, all reputed hit men for the Mob. Several of Harry's patients were on the list. They, of course had an airtight alibi, they were nowhere near Los Angeles on the night of the murder. Harry was their alibi.

The LA police flew to Las Vegas with mug shots that Harry identified. They were registered under their real names, and Harry could verify their whereabouts on the night of the murder. Curious that they all came to Las Vegas on that particular night and were all patients of Dr. Harry Fightlin. (must have been an epidemic of stomach flu).

It was obvious they knew something was going to happen, but of course they "din't know nuttin."

133. True Confessions

On May 10th, 1995, American Justice aired a documentary on women and the Mob, or “Mob Wives.” One of the women interviewed was Bea Sedway, the widow of Moe Sedway, one of the Mobsters who took over the Flamingo Hotel the day after Bugsy Siegel was killed. The interview ran the usual course, and then she was asked how she got “tight” with the Mob, and ultimately found a husband. She coyly intimated (on national TV) that it was her prowess at the art of oral sex that did the job.

In the Mob, if a man wanted to advance and maybe become a “made man” he had to “make his bones” or “do some work” for the outfit. This usually meant killing somebody or doing something equally as important. I guess you could say that she ate her way in.

After Moe passed, Bea remained in Las Vegas and her son went to Medical School and became a highly respected Optometrist. From there he entered politics and served several terms in the Nevada state legislature. There were several Mob children who grew into respectable citizens and served the state well.

Dr. Sedway has a middle school in Las Vegas named for him.

134. Rags to Riches, Las Vegas Style

Las Vegas is rife with rags to riches stories, some had circumstances, that played a major part in the success of the person involved.

Phil Cohen had what was thought of as a bad break that started him on his way to millions.

Lois Gottlieb was the wife of Jake (a.k.a. Jake the Fake) Gottlieb, one of the major owners of the Dunes. Jake was in the trucking business in Chicago and was able to get a huge loan from the Teamsters Pension Fund to purchase the troubled hotel. Everybody knew that Jake had a lot of hidden partners as a prerequisite to getting the loan. He was a large, heavyset man, always in a suit, who stayed out of the gaming area.

His wife, Lois, was a Roulette aficionada who played every day. She would come down each morning and order coffee, light a cigarette, and take a $500 marker. She looked like the wrath of God, dark bags under her eyes, hair not well kempt, and a persistent scowl. However, she was a nice lady, always left a generous tip when she left the game, and if you commented on a sweater, or a piece of jewelry when she sat down, the tip was larger than normal. She had unlimited credit and would sometimes get stuck as much as $3000 in a sitting. She usually played until she got even, which she was able to accomplish on numerous occasions. The reason she was able to do this so often was that her play did not count. Unknown to her, her husband made the arrangement that no matter how much she lost, they just acted like it never happened. If she were to win, they kept track of how much she cashed out, and Jake would pay the money back to the casino. We kept the buttons indicating how much she owed on the rim of the wheel, but back far enough so she couldn't see them. Consequently, if she owed, say $3000, and gave us $1000 in chips to reduce her balance, we would take $2000 in buttons off, as the sooner she got even the sooner she would leave. She could have owed $3000, and we would tell her she owed $1000. She never questioned it. She also played and had credit in a few other hotels, like the Sands and Riviera. If she lost in those places, Jake would go down and pay whatever she owed.

Phil Cohen was in charge of the Blackjack and Roulette pits at the Dunes. He was a WWII veteran and made the Normandy Landing on D-Day, something none of us knew at the time. He was an affable guy, who smoked a cigar. If you were losing, he would walk up and down the pit with the cigar in his mouth mumbling curse words under his breath. It was rumored that he drove a Good Humor ice cream truck when he got out of the army and then came west, getting into the gambling business. He learned to deal Blackjack and worked at the Flaming Hotel when it opened in 1948. He worked his way up from a dealer, became an exec, invested wisely, and supposedly had a small interest in the Riviera at one time, but the hotel went under and when it reopened he had to settle for far less than his investment. He was a fair-haired boy at the Dunes and was the only pit boss in town on a salary, instead of a daily wage. Supposedly $25,000 a year, a handsome sum in those days.

The Dunes at the time was preparing to build a huge tower with rooms restaurants and convention facilities, with another loan from the Teamsters. The added facilities would rival anything in town at the time, and everyone was talking about it. One day, Lois Gottlieb was playing the wheel by herself, no other players, and a woman sat down and bought in for $20, which would give her four stacks of 25 cent chips. She insisted on the brown wheel chips, which were the reserve chips, used only when all the other chips were in play. I tried to talk her into another color but she insisted, and Phil okayed it.

As it happened, the brown wheel chips were nearly the same color as the Dunes $5 chips at the time. Phil and I looked at each other, and we both knew what was coming. During the course of the play she accumulated about $50 in $5 chips which she had set aside from her wheel chips. She started small talk with Mrs. Gottlieb, and of course they became “Roulette buddies.” She was a local and said she was waiting for her husband to fill out a job application. Then here it came, I spun the ball and she grabbed her $5 chips and bet seven or eight different numbers, straight up, which meant that if one of the numbers were to hit, she would be paid 35 to 1, or $175. I called out to Phil, who was standing nearby, that there were $5 chips being wagered, which was standard procedure. She never batted an eye, and when she failed to win she said "Oh my god, I didn't mean to bet those $5 chips, I thought they were the 25-cent wheel chips." Of course, we knew what happened and we were expecting it, so Phil told her that if she had won she would have been paid $175 instead of $8.75, end of story.

Now she started to sob, the tears fell, and Mrs. Gottlieb tried to console her by saying that anyone could make a mistake. If they (the chips) had been any other color there would have been no "mistake." While the poor, distraught woman sat there and sniveled, Mrs. Gottlieb looked up at Phil and said, "You should give her, her money back, she made a mistake" Phil walked around the table, took the cigar out of his mouth, and whispered something into her ear. I was only a few feet away, but I couldn't hear what he said. Mrs. Gottlieb flinched, and her face went from the usual grey to a pale white, and she looked stunned. She sat there for a moment, and when I saw the tears start to form in her eyes, I knew there was going to be big trouble. She got up and went over to the dice pit and started complaining to Dave "Butch" Goldstein, who was one of the minor owners, and the shift manager. I don't know what transpired, but she walked away, and left her chips on the table. The next day, Phil was gone. It seems that they couldn't go ahead with the new tower without Mrs. Gottlieb's signature.

Across Maryland Parkway from the Boulevard Mall, (the biggest mall in town at the time), a new shopping center (anchored by a huge Wal-Mart type store called Wonder World), was taking shape in the center of what at the time, was the major shopping area in Las Vegas,

Phil got a gaming license and made a deal with the owners to open a slot machine arcade in the building. It was a huge success, upon which he got a liquor license and opened Wonder World Liquors, which became the biggest liquor retailer in town, perhaps in the State. Then he wisely started buying property, developing some major shopping centers on his own. When he died in 2011, he left over seven million dollars to the university, and also bequeathed substantial amounts to several other philanthropic organizations, beside taking good care of his family.

I never found out what he said to Mrs. Gottlieb.

Phil told us an anecdote about when he was dealing at the Flamingo. The pit boss in the Blackjack was a well-known bleeder who would throw tantrums (and other things) when a dealer was losing. His name was Gans and he wasn't a likeable fellow. One night, a dealer was losing hand after hand in a big game, and Gans was foaming at the mouth. He sent the porter back to the dealer's room to get another dealer (who was on his break) and he got Phil to come out. Gans put Phil on the game, and he kept right on losing, just like the other dealer. Gans started screaming and cursing the porter right there in front of everybody. When the porter asked what he did wrong, Gans replied, "I told you to go back there and get a dealer, and you bring me this ice cream sonofabitch!" referring to Phil's days as a Good Humor man. Changing dealers was a common practice in those days in a lot of places, and customers noticed it.

It never changed a thing.

135. The Father of His Country

Herbie Saul was the day shift boss in the Blackjack pit at the Dunes. Herbie was an "actor" and whenever the games were losing he would walk up and down, mumbling and cursing, but never abusively.

One day a player bet his case (last) $20 on my game, got a "push" (tie) and walked away thinking he had lost. I called him back to the game, and he took that last $20 and won $2000. Herbie was in rare form, he was livid. I was due for a break, and when the dealers came in to be assigned to games, he would say, "You take out so-and-so, etc." When it came to my name, he said to the oncoming dealer, "And you go down there and take out George Washington."

136. Storybook Beginning, Tragic Ending

Jerry Martin walked into the Flamingo hotel late one night in 1959. His pants were so long that he stepped on them with his heels and they were torn and soiled. He was wearing a short-sleeve shirt with some missing buttons, and he was carrying a wrinkled paper bag, which happened to contain everything he owned in the world.

He was a pleasant looking, rather chunky young man, and he had come to see his uncle, a fella by the name of Ray Miles, who was dealing at the Flamingo at the time. We came to find out that he had been working for a mining company in Tonopah, and that hard labor wasn't for him, so he managed to hitch a ride to Las Vegas. Ray took him in, fed him, bought him some clothes and petitioned the casino manager to give him a job as a shill and an opportunity to learn how to deal Blackjack. Jerry struggled with learning to deal, but he was always trying his best, and everyone liked him.

One night, a dealer got sick and had to leave, and we were busy, so they put him on an empty table, ready to replace him if the action got too heavy. He was standing there on the game and a woman walked up and started betting $1 a hand and having a drink. She was an attractive, well-dressed woman and they conversed back and forth as she played. Turns out she was a widow from Illinois, whose husband, a physician, had passed away about a year previous. She was in Las Vegas by herself, testing the waters, so to speak.

Long story short, they met for a drink when he got off, and a few weeks later they were married. Overnight, he was driving a Cadillac to work, and living in a lovely home in an upscale community. I guess that some property she owned in Illinois was leased to an oil company in hopes of finding an oil field in the area. Jerry opened a liquor store, called Jerry's Liquors, and followed it with two more. They built a swimming pool in their backyard and adopted a beautiful baby boy. A year later the baby somehow wandered into the yard and drowned in the pool.

They dropped out of sight after that, and I don't know what happened to them.

137. Here's to the Girls

As for the ladies, there was "Nightmare Alice," "Betty Boop," "Dirty Doris," "Big Fritzi" and "Little Fritzi."

Many of our local lovelies avoided being tagged with nicknames, but some of their exploits put the men to shame. More than once I had seen men, (not locals), who had never heard a woman use foul language, turn white when they happened to be around on one of those occasions. A sweet young thing, named Betty Petty (really pretty and demure), was losing a bundle at a Blackjack game at the Tropicana, and on one particular hand she drew a card that would have "busted" the dealer causing some players on the game to lose their money. A southern gentleman sitting across from her admonished her and told her how she misplayed the hand and what it cost him and others. She smiled sweetly at him and said, "I'm so sorry. Now why don't you go fuck yourself." Things like this were a common occurrence. The guy almost fell off the stool. Each one of these ladies were famous for one thing or another.

138. The Easy Southern Drawl

Jerri Stuckey was a cocktail waitress at the Dunes Hotel. She was in her mid 40s, had that "been around" look and, being from the south, had that easy drawl you hear in Texas. She was taller than most of the other waitresses and when she walked she had an easy gait that gave the impression that she didn't care whether school kept or not. Her claim to fame was that, as she was leaning over serving a drink at the Baccarat table, some drunk peeked down her top, and commented, not too quietly, that he would "sure like to get in your pants." She never blinked an eye, in her soft southern drawl she replied, "Honey, I already got one asshole in there, and I figure that's enough."

139. A-Team to the Rescue

The Baccarat table was just several feet from the cashier's cage. One night there was a commotion, and several of the big bosses surrounded a sweet young thing obviously in distress, with tears rolling down her face.

At that time some of the casinos, when replacing chips, would drill a hole in the old $100 chips, put in a chain and give them away as souvenir key chains. This young lady said that she had lost all her money, and some guy at the bar offered her $100 to go up to the room with him and trip the light fantastic. He seemed like a nice man, and she was desperate to have enough money to get home to LA. She had "never been to Las Vegas before," and had a boyfriend and would *never* think of doing what she did, except that she needed the money. So up to his room they went, she did whatever he wanted her to do, and when it was all over he gave her a black $100 chip and headed out down the Strip. When she went to cash the chip in, it had a hole in it and, of course, was no good. When she started wailing, they called in the A team and all these fat old farts were consoling her and drying her tears.

While this heart wrenching scene was going on, Jerri ambled along behind the table and said "Pore li'l ole thang, I'll bet she even wiggled." The end result was predictable Sid Wyman pulled a wad of C-notes out of his pocket, and gave her the $100, And took her up to the gourmet room for dinner.

I'm sure he wound up being dessert.

140. Nightmare Alice

Nightmare Alice's moment came one evening after drinking and gambling for several days and nights, she was broke and drunk. Her boyfriend gave her the pitch and she was afraid she was going to lose her job as a cocktail waitress. So, she went up to the Riviera roof (some say it was halfway up) and jumped. She landed on an awning near the front door, bounced, rolled off and landed near an astonished parking attendant. When an ambulance was called she got nasty with the EMTs and damn near went to jail. Anyway, she escaped with a broken wrist and some scuffs and scrapes.

Two days later she was back on the job with a cast on her forearm.

141. How to Clear a Table

Betty Boop waited on the nightshift dealers at the Tropicana. She was an attractive woman but would get into moods (always over men) that made her downright nasty. It was said that she had sex with practically the whole swing shift (married or single) at one time or another. This wasn't exactly like, say, the third Marine Division, but it was a respectable number. When she got going she would get repentant and would mention names, which scared everybody to death, especially if she had been drinking. The dealers table was in the rear of the coffee shop, a large round table that could seat at least 12.

It was customary for the oncoming dealers to have coffee and get the latest news before their shift started. Betty would serve the day shift dealers for several hours before our shift started, and if they saw she was in a snit, would bait her unmercifully, therefore by the time we got there she would be in rare form.

One evening a young dealer came in and asked for a cup of coffee. When she slammed it down in front of him you could see she was in one of her moods. He missed it. When he tasted the coffee, he made a face. She asked what was wrong, and he said that it tasted terrible. The conversation proceeded like this: She asked, "What's wrong with it?" He said, "tastes like you pissed in it." To which she replied, "Well, *you* ought to know." After a split second of stunned silence, one of the other dealers let out a guffaw. She looked at him and announced, "What are *you* laughing at?" In 10 seconds the table was empty, everyone scattered when they saw what was coming. She wound up breaking several plates purposely, then got sent home. It's a good thing, because we were afraid to go back to the coffee shop and would have gone most of the shift without food.

Then there was "Big Fritzi" and "Little Fritzi." Big Fritzi was a stocky, frizzed out blonde on whom the years hadn't worn well. Her face looked like a road map of Pennsylvania, and she was a charter member of the Red-Hot Stove Club. She should have been president. Her notoriety came when her daughter came into her teens. She showed her the ropes and they usually hustled as a team. In Las Vegas, anyone who would turn their daughter out to hustle was the lowest of the low. By the time Little Fritzi was in her 20s she looked like a woman twice her age.

They lived like vampires, came out at night, and were referred to as "bloodthirsty."

142. The Saga of Dirty Doris

"Dirty Doris" was a willowy redhead with some nasty habits. I don't know if she was really unclean or what she did for a living, if anything, just that the name stuck to her and she was forever known as Dirty Doris.

One night at the Stardust a young dealer was dealing to a full table when out of the crowd staggered Doris. She reached across the table and stuffed a piece of paper into his shirt pocket and wobbled off. The dealer was taken by surprise. He wasn't allowed to go into his pocket except for tips and he hesitated. A pit boss by the name of Harry "Cocky" Powers darted in and snatched the note from his pocket. He read the note and then made it public to anyone who was close by. The note said, "You fucked me up and now I'm going to fuck you up good."

Of course, the word got around the casino in a very short time. If a pit boss were to do that these days he would probably face a lawsuit. It seems that this young man got off early one night and went in search of female companionship. He went into a local bar and there was Doris, alone, having a drink. He bought her a drink. She moved over and a romance was set in motion. The more he drank the better she looked and in a matter of a few hours he was convinced that he'd found his one and only. I guess the feeling was mutual. Please bear in mind that these bars were quite dark and with the help of a large amount of alcohol it was easy to fall in love with a Miss America look-alike.

Anyway, they sat and smooched and planned for their future together until 8AM Now it was time to consummate this union. Out into the bright sunlight they walked and he got a good look at the love of his life.

When you go into a dark bar at night and drink until the sun is up you're in for a surprise when you walk out the door with the sweet young thing you fell in love with. It can be quite a shock, or in plain terms it can curdle your blood. This is a common occurrence in a 24-hr. town and it boils down to just how amorous, (horny), you feel as to whether you want to continue the relationship.

This young man, as he related to us, was horrified. All the desire fled in a matter of a few seconds and he decided to pass. According to him he couldn't get away from this apparition fast enough. This, of course, led Doris to become highly insulted and she let go with a stream of choice words and took a swing or two at him, which he ducked before running to his car. Which led to the note in the pocket the next night, after he'd told her where he worked.

Now it was time for the casino practical jokers to step in. When the young man came to work the next night, he was told that a security guard had caught a woman coming into the casino with a gun in her purse. She was drunk and very vocal about "killing a dealer." They also took the trouble to make out a phony security report which described Doris to a T. After reading the report (which looked authentic) the kid smelled a rat and asked the guard in question how he knew she had a gun in her purse. Without hesitation he said she was carrying a plastic "see through" purse (all the rage in those days) and he noticed because the gun was so large, probably a .40 caliber revolver.

That dispelled any doubt and he panicked. He called his brother and had him bring a .45 automatic pistol and leave it under the seat of his car. He wouldn't sit at the dealers table which was near a window looking out at the pool and, while dealing, he constantly looked around instead of paying attention to his game. The dealers were to keep their heads down and their asses up. Not doing so could lead to losing a job. To put it mildly he became a nervous wreck, even requesting a security guard to escort him to his car, and he made the statement that if he saw her first, not taking chances, he was going to shoot. There was no doubt that, in his frame of mind, he would do just that. Then he left for his day off after working six days.

When they (the pranksters) realized that this could lead to homicide, and some of them were complicit, they decided to call off the prank. He didn't answer his phone and nobody knew where he was. Now there was real panic. The town was pretty small in 1958 and the security guard and another prankster started out to find him.

They went in and out of every bar they knew of, and went to his apartment, but could not find him.

They considered calling the police. Nobody knew where Dirty Doris lived so they search every casino in town until 7AM with no luck.

That morning he came into the Stardust to pick up his paycheck and they took him aside and told him the whole story. He was not happy. Had it not been a payday and the timekeeper alerted to notify security if he showed up, it could have been a real disaster.

Not all practical jokes in the casinos had happy endings.

143. A Practical Joke Gone Awry

John Acuff was a floor man in the dice pit at the Stardust. Like many others he was working at the casinos in Havana, Cuba when the revolution took hold and Fulgencio Battista was ousted. As Castro and his forces neared the city, everybody got out fast as they could, many leaving clothes, boats and other possessions behind. Some of the major bosses flew out in private aircraft or escaped by yacht or speedboat, carrying millions in cash that was used to bankroll the gaming operations.

Almost all of the Americans and quite a few of the Cubans wound up in Las Vegas and were assimilated into the Las Vegas work force. John wound up at the Stardust. A highly capable and well-thought-of man in the industry, he had no trouble finding a job. However, he had a habit of complaining long and loud about everything: working conditions, not enough breaks, and the rate of pay, to name a few.

Just before Christmas of 1959 it was obvious that there was no bonus forthcoming, not even a fruitcake. One thing about the Mob, they never liked to pay anybody for anything. Of course, John moaned and muttered over this slight, and at one time accused the owners of "violating the child labor laws" by not giving enough breaks to the pit personnel. Seizing upon this opportunity several of the other pit bosses got together and got five $100 bills, put them in an envelope and left it with a casino cage cashier who was in on the prank. The cashier would call into the pit and the person who answered the phone would call out that he has to go to the cage and had someone cover for him. When he returned he had the envelope in his hand and made sure to open it where John could catch a glimpse of the bills. After counting it he would remark to a nearby floor man, "Not bad, this is a surprise." The man would reply, "yeah, I got mine earlier." Then they would find a way to get the money back to the cage, where the cashier would put it in another envelope, write a name on it and call the pit. This they repeated several times until everyone got called to the cage except John. They all let it be known that they were not to talk about it amongst themselves because everyone wasn't included.

Finally, John couldn't stand it anymore so, calling for someone to cover for him, he headed to the cashier's cage. When he asked if there was an envelope in there for him, they made a production of looking all over and told him there wasn't. He made them look twice with the same result. He was livid. While all the other floor men were getting a good chuckle over it, Johnny Drew and his wife Jeannie were walking through the casino on their way to dinner. Johnny Drew was about five-three, his wife considerably taller, and he wore suits with shoulder pads like a pro football player. He represented the Chicago outfit's (Mob's) interest in the hotel and reputedly had five "points" (or 5%) in the operation.

Johnny and Jeannie (his wife) were usually drunk, and although Johnny generally had a big smile on his face it was said that he had a terrible temper. As John turned to leave the cashier's cage he spotted Johnny Drew approaching and made a beeline for him. Before the horrified conspirators could stop John, he started to berate Johnny and the rest of the big bosses.

The conversation, (according to those who heard part of it), started with "You fuckers" and went from there. The smile left Johnny Drew's face in a hurry. His wife stood by, wide eyed. Grabbing her, Johnny stormed off and, within a very short time, John was gone. Fired.

When the guys who instigated the joke tried to appeal for him they were told that if John had talked to Johnny Drew like that in Chicago, he would be dead before morning.

John went on to open a bait shop, store and bar on the Boulder Highway at Tropicana Avenue, called the Sportsman. Soon he and his wife, Gladys, split the sheets, and she wound up with the shop and bar. She got licensed to install a Blackjack table and had some woman come in on occasion and deal the game. Gladys, an ex-cocktail waitress, knew some of the hustling girls around town, and they would find these lonely guys, get them drunk, take them down to the Sportsman's and relieve them of their hard-earned money. The ladies who steered the guy down there got a percentage. Gaming Control got wind of it (through a complaint) staked it out and shut her down. The place is still there today, although considerably larger.

I don't know what became of Gladys or John, for that matter.

144. The Man Who Died Laughing

The boat kept on coming. It raced past the "No Wake" signs at the entrance to the small harbor and never slowed down. It was only a few hundred feet to the rocky beach and gravel launching ramp. We stood there watching, as the boat ran aground with a sickening crunch. The outboard motor flew up into the air and the force of the impact broke the propeller off.

It was mid-June and a friend and I were securing my boat on the trailer after a morning's fishing on Lake Mead. We looked up to see two people in the boat, the driver and someone on the bench seat in the back holding the head of a third, inert figure lying on the floor between the seats. The driver leaped out of the boat and ran over to us practically incoherent. You could smell the whiskey ten feet away, and even though it was barely mid-morning, it was brutally hot and he could barely catch his breath. He said he had to get to the ranger shack which was just a few hundred yards up the road, and he was in no condition to run or walk. I got him into the car and we went racing up to the station while he told me that their companion was having a heart attack and may be dead.

Luckily, the ranger was there and immediately radioed the Boulder City hospital for an ambulance. The hospital was just a few miles up the road in Boulder City and by the time we got back to the scene you could hear the sirens. When they arrived they immediately started CPR and oxygen and got him into the ambulance. Before they took off they asked some questions and told the ranger they would need his report, they didn't think the man would make it.

They were right. He was dead on arrival at the hospital. The ranger took his companions up to the station and asked that we come along as witnesses to the statement. The story that unfolded got many a laugh in the years to come, but at the moment it didn't seem funny. The unfortunate person was a dealer at the Sahara Hotel, a practical joker, and a heavy drinker. The day before their fishing trip he took a red broom handle and sawed it into several pieces. He then went out and bought several short dynamite fuses, the kind they used in construction when they were loosening up caliche (rock hard clay) that was everywhere throughout the valley. After drilling holes in the red cylinders, he inserted the fuses and put the sticks in his tackle box. After several hours fishing they had no luck and were sitting dead in the water several miles from the dock, finishing the last of whatever they were drinking.

It was calm, not a breeze or a ripple on the water. At that time, our joker announced that he was tired of not catching any fish, and he'd be damned if he was going home empty. As his companions watched, he reached into his tackle box and brought out two of the fake sticks of dynamite and lit the fuse on the one in his hand. He made as if to throw it into the water and let it purposely slip out of his hand and roll under the floorboards of the boat. His friends saw the burning fuse, and while he made like he was frantically clawing at the floorboards to retrieve it, they did what anybody would have done, they abandoned ship and started swimming for all they were worth. When no explosion was forthcoming, they stopped swimming and looked back. The joker was sitting in the boat howling with laughter, doubled over with glee, stomping his feet and pounding on the side of the boat. Luckily the guys in the water didn't drown. When they swam back to the boat, their friend was having trouble catching his breath, and they thought it was from the laughter. It wasn't.

He was going into cardiac arrest.

145. Big Game Hunter

Everett Strong was Wilbur Clark's bodyguard before the Desert Inn opened. Wilbur started building the Desert Inn in 1948 and ran out of money. He was originally from San Diego, and, try as he may, he couldn't raise enough to continue the project. He finally took in some "partners" from Cleveland and they made him an "offer he couldn't refuse."

Wilbur wound up with 25% and no say in management or operations. And a beautiful home on the golf course. The large sign on the Strip read "Wilbur Clark's Desert Inn."

Everett, as payment for his years of service, was taught how to deal Blackjack and given a job at the DI. He wasn't your average looking dealer, his countenance was frightening. His head was lopsided, he had a huge brow which was mostly scar tissue and lumps, giving him a Neanderthal appearance. To top it off he had two "cauliflower" ears and a nose flattened and off to one side. Throw in the scars and it was hard not to stare when you saw him for the first time. His hands and knuckles were so misshapen from years of bare-knuckle club fighting that it was a wonder he could hold the cards.

But Everett was a gentle soul, albeit a little punchy. His favorite prank was, on his way to the table or going on break, he would sneak up behind a dealer on a game and tap him on the toe of his shoe with his comb. This feels just like a chip falling off the table and hitting you on the foot. Consequently, the dealer would step back and start looking under the table. If large denomination chips were in use, the dealer would sometimes call the pit boss and start to crawl under the table. He was told it was just Everett and to get on with the game. Everett was told not to do it anymore, but he couldn't remember from one day to the next, so they tolerated it. Then on his way to a break or back to the game he would stop and ask the dealer if he found the chip. He thought it was the funniest thing he'd ever seen.

One day three of the dealers went Quail hunting in Overton, a farm town about 90 miles north of Las Vegas. Near a large rock outcropping they came upon a huge bobcat, obviously dying, most likely from old age. The poor beast was pretty mangy and could barely muster a feeble growl as it lay there and stared at them. They put it out of its misery (with a shotgun) and threw it in the back of their pickup truck. They stopped at a bar on the way back and being winter it was dark when they emerged and they were pretty tipsy.

Everett had a home in Huntridge, the oldest subdivision in Las Vegas. It had a huge tree in his front yard with a branch that jutted towards his front porch. Arriving in Las Vegas, the three dealers crept up to his house, propped the poor dead bobcat on the branch and made their getaway.

It was Everett's night off and he was not sober (he never was when he wasn't working). He let the dog out later in the evening and of course the dog went bonkers. When Everett went out to see what the commotion was, he spotted the bobcat and ran into the house for his shotgun. It took about three blasts before what was left of the cat finally tumbled out of the tree.

Neighbors, hearing the shots, called the police, reporting gunfire in the area. As it happened, a lady reporter for the Las Vegas Sun was at the police station looking for a story and followed the cruiser that answered the call. When she found out what had happened she called a photographer to the scene and they took a picture of Everett holding the cat up with two hands. During the interview Everett was quoted as saying that the cat "was snarling and spitting and was ready to spring when he pulled the trigger.

When the truth was known around the hotel, they made poor Everett's life miserable. When he was on the table they would growl in his ear on the way by, or if he was on a break they would snarl and pretend to claw at him.

Finally, he took a week off and went to Bullhead City (which at that time was a couple of double wide trailers and a bait shop) and stayed drunk for a week until things quieted down.

146. Gotcha

One busy summer night in 1960 I walked into the Flamingo Hotel Blackjack pit, signed the payroll sheet and started to go for a cup of coffee before my shift started.

Waiting at the entrance to the pit were the shift manager and the pit boss, who motioned for me to come over. They told me there was a big player in the hotel and his wife played Blackjack. They wanted to introduce me to her so I would know who she was if she came to my game, and to be extra nice to her. They took me to a table where a woman in her late 50s was sitting in the end seat, wearing an expensive beaded dress and decked out in what looked like expensive jewelry. She had reddish hair and her makeup was perfect. They introduced me by name, and she said (in a haughty voice), "It's so nice to meet you, young man."

She offered her hand and, when I did the same, hers darted between my legs and locked onto my scrotum. Hard. She pulled me close so it wouldn't be too obvious, and I was shocked and speechless. She held on, I tried to wriggle loose, and the two pranksters ran down to the other end of the pit screaming and howling with laughter.

I was glad they did because everyone was looking at them instead of noticing my predicament. The dealer on the game was shaking with mirth, and I was begging her to let me go. While she was holding me, she was still playing her cards with her free hand. Any attempt by me to grab her arm or get free resulted in more pressure applied to my family jewels. I stood there and tried to look nonchalant so nobody would notice. Finally, after what seemed like an eternity, and seeing that I was liable to do something drastic, she let go. The shift manager and pit boss were practically on their knees with laughter. I was so mad I was shaking like a leaf when I started my shift.

Later, when I calmed down, I laughed too, despite the fact that I was pretty sore.

147. Classifications

The ladies who were regulars around the casinos were generally broken down into three categories. There were the “hustling broads,” the “hookers,” and the “semi pros” (who were somewhere in between depending on the circumstances)

The hustling girl would walk into a casino and look for a table with a man with chips in front of him (the mark). If she could get a seat next to him she would make casual conversation, usually making him feel like a big shot. In short order, she would lose all her money, and instead of letting her leave, the guy would give her a few chips to play with. Then the romance began, it was like boyfriend, girlfriend, and the more the men had to drink, the more they loved it. During the course of the play, these women would slip chips into their purse, their pockets or wherever their MO dropped them. It was amazing how some of them did it. Then they would have no chips left (they were all in her purse) and the mark would give her some more to play with. They would make arrangements to spend the evening with each other, or anything the girl would have to promise to keep the chips coming. A little under the table squeeze of the guys package went a long way.

Usually, when they had their load, they would excuse themselves to go to the ladies’ room, and that would be the end of the romance. They just never came back. The men usually acted nonchalant about it when they realized their sweeties weren’t coming back, not to be looked at like suckers.

The casinos weren’t happy with these women, but once they were on the game, if you removed them, they risked the customer getting up and leaving with them. I have seen on many occasions where a guy would buy in a few hundred, get lucky, and have several thousand in front of him when the hustler and he got friendly. Over the next few hours the girl would slip lord knows how much into her purse, and when the smoke cleared, she’d be gone. The guy had lost his several hundred, and the house would lose a large amount because the girl had the money.

This was not good business.

148. Disappearing Chips

A cocktail waitress from another hotel came into the Flamingo with a "live one" she had scooped up (probably from the Stardust where she worked). They sat on my table, where she was well known to everybody, and she took the end seat, next to the inside of the pit. When the waitress would bring the drinks she always stopped for a few minutes and made small talk. It was several hours later that they realized that several thousand dollars in chips were missing from the game, and nobody knew what happened to them. We were watching her like a hawk, but she never slipped anything into her purse or pocket, and he was not taking anything off of the game.

After about three hours, everyone was nuts trying to figure out what was going on, and then they nailed it. When "Little Elsie" the cocktail waitress would drop off the drinks and make small talk, she would rest her tray on the edge of the table and using that for cover the girl would slip her a handful of chips, under the tray. If someone was watching, Elsie kept both hands on the tray, and there was no exchange. Elsie was barely over five feet tall so the fit was perfect. When the girl realized they were catching on, she got up and left. She made several thousand dollars, and I'm sure Elsie got her share.

The guy never knew what hit him, and there was nothing illegal about it. It was money they had won, and the only person that got fooled was the mark. The only thing was that the casino had no chance to win the money back. Elsie, of course denied it, she would hand the chips to the hustler in the rest room, or somewhere. She never really had them in her possession for any length of time.

When you think of some guy from Kissmyass, Oklahoma, who's in Las Vegas alone or on a convention without his wife, this is what he dreams about, and he's vulnerable to the advances of a pretty girl. There is no end to the number of "marks" who come to Las Vegas. Some of these girls actually got "friendly" with these guys and the guys would let them know when they were coming to town. They would go to dinner and gamble the night away. It was a lucrative situation for these ladies.

In rare instances a marriage would result if the guy were wealthy enough.

A hooker is a prostitute, plain and simple. They go from casino to casino and try to stay under the radar. For a town like Las Vegas, there are few incidents of robbery, or someone getting "rolled." If a girl is arrested for soliciting, she goes downtown (in a paddy wagon) pays a fine and goes back to the job. Sometimes women come in from Los Angeles for the weekend and try to make extra money. They could be wives, mothers, or any number of legitimate employees. These were known as "Librarians from Peoria".

The best place to find a hooker was at the casino bars in any hotel. Some worked days, maybe turned a trick or two, and were home by nightfall when the vice squad was at its busiest. Others preferred nights when there were more drunks, and more money flying around. If a john had enough to drink the lady didn't have to be beautiful. She could have been downright ugly and it wouldn't make a lot of difference.

When I worked the day shift Baccarat at the Sands, the Vice squad would make a sweep at least four times a week. "Sergeant Dave" (Dave Hanson), as we called him, would walk into the place, and in a very short time (on a good day) he would have four or five girls in tow. They knew better than to run because the police had a couple of guys outside, one driving a paddy wagon.

Dave would come into the Baccarat with the girls in tow, have them sit down, and he would pass the time of day with the bosses, and have a drink. When he was through, he'd say, "Okay ladies, let's go." He would walk out the door with the girls following behind like ducklings following mama duck. Then it was into the paddy wagon, and off to the station, where they were booked, photographed, posted a very small bail, then back on the street. They would lay low for the day, it was not good to be caught twice in a short period. Sergeant Dave would also take care of traffic tickets for some of the personnel in the hotel.

He would take the citation, put in his jacket pocket and it would disappear.

149. Dave Forgot

Juan Del Prado was a boss in the Baccarat at the Sands. Hailing from Cuba, he was an Al Capone look alike, damn near a twin. Juan, however had a very shrill voice, almost like a woman's. He was a nice person and would give you the shirt off his back. One day the chief of security came into the pit and told Juan that his new Lincoln was on fire in the parking lot. Juan jumped out of the chair and headed out to investigate. He didn't come back. The fire department put out the fire and they towed the car, but no Juan. They looked everywhere, called his house, but he was gone.

The next day we found out that when he got to the parking lot, the police were there along with the fire department. They asked him if it was his car, and he said yes. They then spun him around, cuffed him, and took him to jail. Seems like there was a warrant out for his arrest for failure to appear in court for a speeding ticket. He had given the ticket to Sergeant Dave, and Dave forgot about it.

On occasion there would be three or four hookers in "Hookers' Nook" when we would come to work. You could see that part of the bar from the Baccarat. Just for laughs someone would get on the phone and have the operator page Sergeant Dave over the page system.

In 20 seconds all the stools in Hookers' Nook would be empty. The drinks were still on the bar but the ladies vanished.

Several years later I was up for a gaming license and had to be fingerprinted and processed. When I arrived at Metro, they took me into the back room so I wouldn't have to wait in line. While I was waiting for the fingerprint lady I happened to glance at a computer screen and noticed my name and pertinent info about me. It had me classified as a narcotics informant. I almost had a heart attack. When I mentioned it to my next-door neighbor, who was a Metro police officer, he told me that's what Sergeant Dave would tell the judge, or his secretary, when he would fix a citation for someone. Seems that's one of the perks of being an informant. When I mentioned it to my lawyer, he said he'd take care of it. He did.

A "semi pro" was a girl who adapted to the situation. She didn't specialize. The high-priced hookers (some went for $500 a night) were run through the bell captain or, in some cases the casino. Five hundred dollars was a lot of money at that point in history. These girls would hardly ever be seen. They led private lives and quite a few of them wound up wealthy, with investment portfolios, and some invested in real estate. Others just piled up the cash. There were those who gambled away everything they made and wound up old and broke. They would end up as streetwalkers, turning $10 tricks.

One night, unemployed, I picked up my wife at work and went to the Dunes Hotel to see about a job. The man I wanted to talk to wasn't there yet, so we sat at the bar and had a drink. The bar was full, and the only empty seats were at Hookers' Nook. We sat down, ordered a drink and then I saw the man I wanted to see come into the casino.

I told my wife to go ahead and have her drink and wait until I got back. She said, "What happens if someone comes up and propositions me?" I told her, "Tell them that you get a thousand dollars and that will scare them away." She replied "what if it doesn't?"

I told her I'd wait down here until she got back.

Then there was the Sands cocktail waitress who, at the request of some Saudi Princes, had sex with a German Shepherd while they watched. They had promised to set her up in a Beauty Salon and were true to their word.

Her salon became quite well known in Las Vegas. How she acquired it was *not* common knowledge.

150. A Lesson Learned

Among the most frequent questions I have been asked is, “What are your most embarrassing moments?” Do any incidents stand out? I recall dealing on a Blackjack table at the Tropicana. The man in the end seat was tipping generously, so I made a special effort to establish a rapport with him. Out of the crowd staggered a woman who was sloppy drunk. Her speech was slurred, her hair, a mess, her makeup, smeared something awful. She plunked down some chips and remained standing while I dealt. She weaved back and forth trying to focus her eyes on the cards, took a card and went “bust.” She threw the cards in, called me an asshole, and staggered off. I leaned over to the man I’d been talking to and said, “How would you like to be married to that?” He replied “I am. That’s my wife, she didn’t see me sitting here.”

I never made that mistake again.

151. Refusing to Admit Defeat

I've seen countless incidents where a player will go off the deep end. They can sit and play a few bucks, have a good time, then suddenly go nuts. We called it "Taking the steam, or the heat."

The games have a way of making a person lose control of their senses and do things they wouldn't normally do. I've seen people buy in with a $20-dollar bill and start betting a few bucks, lose the $20 and start to chase it, losing everything in their pockets and whatever else they could get their hands on. I've seen huge sums lost after which a player would sit and stare at the table, a look of severe distress on his face. One, a furniture store owner, looked at me and said, "What do I do now? I just lost everything I own." He walked away as if in a trance.

Sid Wyman, a Dunes owner, came into the Baccarat pit at the Sands when I was working there. On his arm he had a big showgirl. They had just had dinner in the Gourmet room, and he stopped by to thank one of the bosses for the "Comp" He took a $20 bill off a wad of bills and bet it on the bank. He told his sweetie, "You keep the winner, I'm going to the rest room." They lost the bet and when he returned, he bet $100, trying to win the twenty back, plus a few extra bucks for her. When the smoke cleared he signed a marker for $20,000. He went across the street, brought back the cash, paid the marker and lost another $10,000. That was $30,000 chasing a $20 bill.

He wasn't real happy, but to him it wasn't critical.

152. Not So Silent Movie

This incident I will never forget. I was dealing double deck Blackjack at the Stardust. The year was 1958 and I was 22 years old. Double Deck is dealt face up, and the game is four times faster than regular Blackjack because the player never touches the cards.

A young couple sat down, broke a twenty and began to play a few dollars at a time. They looked to be no older than 30, she, a pretty girl in a cotton dress, while he looked like a farmer, stocky with a plaid shirt and work jeans with cowboy boots. She got up to play the slots, and he started playing two hands. He lost the money he had in front of him, and bought in another $20, lost it quickly, and came out with $80 in twenty-dollar bills, bet $40 on each hand, and lost it. When he didn't make another bet right away, I started to deal the cards. Without saying a word, he held his hand up to stop me, and took off one of his boots, came out with a handful of hundreds, and bet $100 on each of the hands. When he lost that, his whole body flinched, and he started to shake. I'll never forget the look in his eye. It was like he was hypnotized. The next bet was $200 on each hand, which he lost. He couldn't win a hand and you could see it coming. He started betting the limit, $500 on each hand. Every time he lost a bet he would moan and sob and a crowd started to gather. When the money was gone, he took off the other boot, took out a large wad of $100 bills and kept on going.

About that time his wife returned. It took her a minute to realize what was happening, and when she saw the boots on the floor, she went crazy. She screamed, "What are you doing? It's all we have!" She tried to reach for the money and he pushed her away. She started to cry, went down on the floor and wrapped her arms around his legs and screamed to the crowd, "Please, stop him! We sold our home and are going to California to start a business and buy a house!" It was like a scene from a three-penny opera, or the old silent movies where the daughter tries to keep the father from drinking up the rent and food money and he pushes her away and keeps on drinking.

Meanwhile, he continued losing, she kept crying and the noises he was making were unearthly. Finally, he put up what looked like their last thousand dollars on two hands. The crowd was mesmerized, she made a dive for the money and he pushed her down again. He was shaking to the point of convulsions. I hesitated for a second, and the pit boss said, “Deal the cards.” I dealt the cards and he lost both hands, it was over, and it happened fast. I don’t think he won a hand. Then he just sat there with a look in his eyes of someone in a nightmare trying to wake up. She stood up and just stared into space. He sat for quite a while, then she helped him out of the chair and they started to walk away, leaving his boots under the table.

A woman who had been watching, retrieved the boots and gave them back to the couple, who had sat down at a table on the edge of the lounge. She asked the girl “Do you have any other money? She replied, “That was everything we had in the world, I don’t think we can buy gas.” People were crying out to the pit bosses to give them money to get out of town, some wanted them to give it all back. The total was over $12,000, a whole lot of money in 1958. I don’t recall whether they offered them dinner or a room for the night. It was a horrible sight, the worst in all the years I was in the business.

I knew what it felt like to wake up broke after a night of drinking and gambling and hoping it was a bad dream. I would get up and look on my dresser, where I put my money, and realize it wasn’t a dream.

I can’t even imagine what they must have felt like.

153. Humiliation

Humiliation is another story altogether. There are times when you see someone being humiliated and, as a result, you, yourself are humiliated.

In the 1950s African Americans were not allowed in the hotel casinos. The workers and the top name entertainers had to leave by the back door when they were through for the night and go to the "Westside" of town where the whole black population of Las Vegas resided. Blacks did not hold any of the better paying jobs in the resorts. They were limited to being porters, kitchen help, maids . . . general clean up positions.

The "plum" jobs were the attendants in the men's and ladies' rooms. This was a festering situation that simmered for years. Finally, Frank Sinatra and his "Rat Pack" refused to perform at the Sands unless the hotel gave Sammy Davis, Jr. a room at the hotel for the entire engagement. It created quite a stir at the Sands, but finally the hotel relented, insisting that Sammy stay out of the public area between and after the shows. The Rat Pack said, "No, he goes where we go or you turn out the lights in the showroom until you can get someone else."

That was the beginning of the end. No longer would famous black personalities like Lena Horne, Pearl Bailey, Nat "King" Cole and others have to leave the hotel after their show. The Mob, mostly the Italian factions, were furious and contemplated some type of retaliation.

Meanwhile, the NAACP and other civil rights groups were starting to get involved in the Jim Crow policies, and Las Vegas Sun publisher Hank Greenspun, and Mayor Oran Gragson were meeting with Bob Bailey, a former star singer with the Count Basie Orchestra, a college graduate, radio personality and part owner of the Moulin Rouge Casino on the West Side of town. Bob was also related to the great Pearl Bailey. Many of the white entertainers and show people from the Strip would go there after hours and have a good time. The hotel was owned by a group of black businessmen, and counted on black business to sustain the venture, but it was patronized by whites as well, mostly after hours.

The Strip hotels posted notices in the dressing rooms, mostly directed at chorus girls and dancers, that anyone seen at the Moulin Rouge would be fired. That set things off. The NAACP and other groups planned a big march down Fremont Street and on to the Strip in protest of the policies. Every African American in Las Vegas planned to participate. Some whites not employed in the casinos were going to join them. Young blacks started barging into Strip hotels, forming long conga lines and dancing through the casinos and into the showrooms while the show was on. They would march right across the stage during the show, stopping everything, and hurling epithets at everyone in sight. Security had orders not to interfere, to prevent violence. They would even march right through the middle of the pit, pinning the pit bosses up against the tables. It got nasty, and they ignored pleas by Bob Bailey and his groups to stand down. Then the rumor started that carloads of blacks were on their way to Las Vegas from Los Angeles to participate in the March, and to generally create chaos. Some said there were thousands on the highway.

Finally, the rumor started that our fearless sheriff was at the state line with a posse, armed to the teeth and with orders to "Shoot to kill" any black who crosses the line. That rumor, of course, was false, but it gives you some idea of what was going on. The only posse that interested our sheriff was spelled with a U and a Y.

Governor Grant Sawyer got involved, and a meeting was held with Bob Bailey, McMillan of the NAACP, Hank Greenspun, Mayor Oran Gragson and a handful of white politicians, and that was the end of segregation in Las Vegas.

All segregation.

The march was called off and everyone stepped back to see what would happen. It was that easy. Years of Jim Crow policies ended in a matter of minutes. The Mob-owned casinos were livid. They contended that it would be the end of the industry, people would just quit coming. They said that all the wealthy Southerners and Texas oilmen would not mingle with blacks. They overlooked the fact that to gamble and find the amenities Las Vegas had to offer, they had nowhere else to go. Some of the hotels gave their employees orders to offer no courtesies to black patrons and ignore them when possible.

On the other hand, people like Al Benedict, a Stardust boss, set up a school and solicited a staff to teach blacks how to deal and help them find jobs. They hadn't gotten around to women yet, but that's another story.

Black customers began to filter into the casinos and restaurants, in most cases it was not a problem at all, but in some places (mostly Strip hotels) it got ugly at times. The dealers of Italian descent (mainly Sicilian) or those with family connected to the Mob, at times refused to deal to a black person, and instead of being fired were just sent to another game. Everything began to return to normal, except for a few diehard resorts who refused to extend any courtesies to blacks unless forced to.

That brings us to humiliation. One evening I was dealing Blackjack at the Flamingo Hotel. There were three players on the game, and the biggest wager was $3. A black couple sat down on the game. They were in their 40s. She wore an evening dress and he, an expensive suit. They said, "Good evening." and bought $300 in $25 chips. I had orders not to respond. They each bet $50 and the cocktail waitress came around. She took drink orders from the three white customers and ignored the black man and his wife. As she started to walk away the black man said, "Excuse me, but we would like a drink, too." She took the drink order, and when she returned she placed the drinks down in front of the players, and said to the black couple, "That will be $5 please. The black man didn't bat an eye, he said "I thought the drinks were on the house." The waitress replied, "Sir, we have the right to choose who we supply with complimentary drinks." Which is what she had been told to say. The man took a $25 chip and asked me for change. I gave him $5 chips, and he asked me for five silver dollars. Without comment, he paid her $5 for the drinks, and gave her a $2 tip. He was the only player on the game who tipped the waitress. Her face turned red and she glanced at me.

I just lowered my eyes and kept dealing.

I won't go into a lot of detail, but two years previous I had been involved in a boating accident on Lake Mead. My best friend, Danny Kolod, and I had spent the night on the lake and were on our way back to the Marina when we spotted a small boat with four black people in it, and they were towing another small boat which was obviously disabled. The water was getting rough (Lake Mead is a treacherous lake) and we offered to take some of their people with us to the harbor and send assistance out to them. They declined, and we took off at full speed. We were sitting on top of the seat, holding on to the windshield, when we hit a large wave, and both wound up in the water. The boat was an 18-ft. Chris Craft speed boat, and it took off at full throttle, and started running in circles, coming right back at us. We were not wearing life jackets. We were separated in the rough water, and I had to concentrate on ducking the runaway boat. The steering wheel was jammed to the side and the boat was going around 45 miles an hour.

In 1958 you could go weeks without seeing a boat on the lake, but this was Saturday and there were a few boats around. Whenever the boat hit a wave the rudder would shift so it wasn't doing perfect circles and being in the water I couldn't see it until it was almost on top of me. Then I would pull myself underwater until the boat passed overhead. It made a high-pitched whine and after it went by, I would surface.

It took 50 minutes for the boat to run out of gas, and during that time nobody could get close enough to help for fear of getting hit by the boat. Soon the only boat around was the one with the four black people in it. They attempted to get close enough to throw me a rope, but I missed it and they had to beat a hasty retreat. They had untied the boat they were towing and stayed out there in spite of the high waves which could have swamped or capsized them. They were the only ones who stayed. They could just as easily have continued on and left me to my fate, and I couldn't blame them. I had survival training in the Marine Corps, and it probably kept me from panicking and saved my life.

When the boat finally did run out of gas they came in and threw me a floating cushion. It felt like an island. They flagged down a passing cabin cruiser, which took me aboard and back to the marina.

My friend didn't make it. His body was never recovered.

The point I'm trying to make is the people who risked their safety to stick by me were black, the hand that threw me the cushion that saved my life was black, and now I had to stand behind that table and be part of this injustice. I was the one who was humiliated. At the risk of my job, I leaned over to the couple and said, "I'm sorry, not all of us feel that way". The man looked up at me and nodded.

When I went to the coffee shop on my break the cocktail waitress was there. She saw me and started to cry. Her name was Donna.

154. Systems

Down through the years, I saw countless systems on every game. Contrary to TV, none of them worked. And they never will.

With the advent of personal computers, systems have become more elaborate, and they still don't work. That's not to say that people playing a system didn't win. Of course, they did, but it wasn't the system, it was the way the game was going at the time. The worst thing that could happen to players with a system is that they would win the first time they tried it. When the cards or the dice or the wheel, or whatever a man's poison, finally begins to bite him (very few women are system players) he can't believe it and keeps at it until they he's broke.

In the pre-computer and "counting" days, progression was the integral part of most systems. Some used the term "double up" in describing the technique. It was pretty simple, bet $1 and lose, it was time to double your wager 2, 4, 8, 16, 32, 64, 128 and 256. The only rub was that if you lost the $256 bet, the limit was $500. To double $256, you had to bet $512. If you do the math, here's how it played out. When you bet the $256 you could either lose $511 or win $1. Those aren't very good odds. People refused to believe they could lose that many bets in succession.

Should they lose, a lot of progression players would then bet the $500, meaning that at that point they stood to either lose $1011 or $11, and they figured that the $11 could be made up. On rare occasion some would "take the steam" and just bet whatever they had left. All discipline would go and human nature would prevail.

There were two progression players who came to Las Vegas frequently. They were known as "System Smitty" and "System Shorty." Their target was to win $50 a day, whereas arriving at that figure, they would either quit or go to another casino. Back in the '50s and the '60s, $50 a day was a decent living. The thing they didn't seem to realize was that if you lost over $1000, it would take almost a month, at $50 a day to make it back. And losing nine bets in a row in any of these games really wasn't a rare occurrence.

Anyhow, "System Smitty" carried a large, well-worn leather billfold, and when he ran out of money he would turn it inside out and upside down, and then would stand in front of the table and stare at you for 30 minutes before he would leave, as if to accuse you of cheating him. “System Shorty” was barely five feet tall, and he would do the same, except that if another player took his seat, all you could see was his head and those eyes burning into you.

System Smitty lost all his money one day at the Flamingo then came back the next day and lost his first 11 bets, he never won one hand and ran out of money. That was the last time I ever saw him. He stood and stared at me until I went on my break. They weren’t the only ones who used that system, but at the time they were the most well-known. Though they faded out of the picture after a few years, plenty of others stepped up in their place.

My first exposure to a system was at the Thunderbird in 1957, where I was breaking in. Everything was new to me, and my mentor was the father of a girl I knew in high school. He took a liking to me and it saved me having to go downtown and shill for $8 a day, then try to learn to deal on my own time, *if* they’d let me. My education was first rate, from seasoned professionals, and I was considered extremely fortunate.

One day a man came running through the door and up to the Roulette wheel and bet $32 on black. He won, grabbed the money and left. The next day he came in again made a bet on the black, lost it and headed out the door. George Rosen, the shift manager and my benefactor, asked him what he was doing. His system was he’d bet red or black, or odd or even, but never the same thing two days in a row. His first bet would be $2. If he lost, he would bet $4 on another wheel, if one was open. If none was, he’d go to another casino and make his bet. If he lost, he’d get in his car and drive to yet another hotel to make his next wager. In those days there were very few cars on the Strip, gas was 15 cents a gallon, and he could run back and forth in a very short time. His rationale was that by doing so it would prevent any one wheel from “getting a streak on him.” One day he ran in and made a $64 bet on red, lost it and flew out the door.

Never saw him again.

155. The Unsolved Casino Mystery

A year after the Stardust opened, two couples came in, stayed at the hotel and played Roulette on two wheels, betting a "section" of numbers, which was not uncommon. For example, one couple would sit at one wheel and bet the numbers 1, 13, 36, 24 and 3, which are next to each other on the wheel. The other couple would sit at another wheel and bet a different section, and both played the same group of numbers every time they played. Their section was 2, 14, 35, 23 and 4. They began to win a lot of money. They played for hours, if they lost at first, they would wind up winning every time. The bosses went crazy. They checked the wheels for every possible discrepancy, and then wound up putting on brand new wheel heads, with the same results. It made no difference. They checked the balls, they checked the frets (the metal spacers between the numbers) a loose fret can make a big difference in a section of numbers as the ball wouldn't bounce when it hit a loose fret, it would just slide off. They did everything possible to figure out what they were doing, to no avail. There was a lot of discussion in gaming circles around town about the situation, and when they played they began to draw spectators around the game, quite a few who worked in the casinos themselves would sit and play the same numbers, but if they caught a losing streak they didn't have enough money to stick around.

Finally, after about three weeks, the Stardust had enough. They told the people that they weren't welcome anymore and suggested that they take their business somewhere else. I don't know if they ever played anywhere else, I *do* know that the Stardust lost a substantial amount of money to them. If they were cheating, nobody ever figured how, and that included the biggest experts in the gambling world.

It was said that they had "the hooly" on the game for the lack of any other explanation.

156. Real Estate Financing

Two couples walked into the Desert Inn and bought in for several thousand dollars on the Craps tables. They played a type of progression but alternated from the Pass line to the Don't Pass line. The Pass line was considered with the house, and the Don't Pass, against the house. The only thing that kept the Don't Pass from being the same as the house odds was that if the dice rolled 12, (two sixes, or "boxcars") you lose.

These couples played a $25 progression. Starting at $25 if you lost 6 times in a row you were past the limit and out of luck, unless you started all over again, and then it would take you all night to win your money back *if* you were lucky. They would bet $25 on Pass. If they lost, they would bet $50 on Don't Pass. If they lost that, they would bet $100 back on Pass, etc. They played for about three weeks, and won a lot of money, and told everyone that they had bought property in Las Vegas with the money they had won. They were the only smart system players I ever saw. To the best of my knowledge they didn't play again.

Several dealers thought it was the best system they had ever seen and tried it themselves. One dealer at the Desert Inn wanted me to chip in with him and play the system and I refused the offer. The next night I saw him and asked him how he did.

He replied, "It was just too slow, and I couldn't stand it anymore, so I started to play the way I usually do, and I lost a thousand dollars."

157. Scientific Pipe Smokers

The first computers were mostly for commercial and scientific purposes. Few individuals had one. One day a group of "scientists" came into the Dunes and asked if they could stand and record every spin of the Roulette wheel 24 hours a day. They were given permission, but they had to stand to the outside. They had notebooks and pens and worked in two-hour shifts. They wrote down the number that came up on every spin, day after day, and night after night. They said they were going to feed the results into a computer and come up with a system to beat the house.

Several were pipe smokers, and pipes in a gambling house were said to be bad luck, so some of the bosses wouldn't let them smoke in the gaming area. When they finally got all the info they needed, they disappeared.

About a month later, back they came, armed with the results of their efforts. One man would play, and there were about ten behind him feeding him the info on what to bet next. They didn't last very long and went home to refine their system. I imagine that they went the way of all systems. Of all the casino games, there were more systems on Roulette than any other.

It was the worst game to play a system on.

158. Crack Goes the Meerschaum

The most notable of all the progression players was the singer, Bobby Darin. Bobby was the headliner at the Flamingo in 1959, and he was filling the showroom every night, both shows. He was an intense young man, likeable, and his wife, Sandra Dee rounded out what everyone referred to as a storybook couple. He would play Blackjack between and after the last show, and he always attracted a crowd. Sandra Dee would sit next to him while he played, and if the table filled up she would stand up, so a customer could sit down.

Everyone wanted to sit at the same table with Bobby Darin. He played the standard progression, starting with a $2 bet. He won a few dollars every time he played for close to a week and began to think he had found the goose that laid the golden egg. He was good for business, people would crowd around the table when he was playing, he kept a lot of people in the casino, which was the object for an entertainer. He also smoked a small ceramic pipe, shaped like a Meerschaum, and would clench it between his teeth while he played.

One night, after the last show, he started to play, and immediately a crowd formed. I was dealing on a table several feet away, and I heard murmurs from the crowd. That told me the cards were starting to bite him. Then I heard a collective groan from the crowd, and heard the pit boss call Chester Simms, the casino manager, and tell him that Bobby wanted to bet $512, and the limit was $500. Chester talked to him and told him it was okay this one time, after that he was subject to the house limit. The holy grail for a casino in those days was to get an expensive entertainer to gamble and lose his salary. Then they got his services for nothing. It happened more times than you think. Joe E Lewis worked the El Rancho for years and they never paid him a cent.

There was silence as the dealer dealt the cards, then I heard a loud CRACK! Bobby bit his pipe stem in half when he lost the bet. The bowl fell into his lap with the tobacco still lit, he jumped up, Sandra Dee brushed him off, and they left. He didn't take the bait, he accepted the loss. Most people with his available credit would have chased it with more money.

159. The Las Vegas Manhattan Project

That brings us to the "Count," tracking the cards and tailoring your wagers when you think the odds are in your favor. Not too long ago I saw my one and only episode of "Breaking Vegas" on TV. They featured a bunch of engineers from MIT who fashioned a system of counting and by the time they were discovered won a huge sum of money. They were supposedly tripped up by a stern looking pit boss who followed one of them into the rest room, or something of that nature.

About halfway through I couldn't take it anymore and turned it off. To begin with, maybe they *did* win a large amount of money, but it wasn't the system that won it for them. No matter what your style of play, there will come a time when you will win playing in that manner. But you won't continue to win. Period. Then came a deluge of books on how to use the count to win, each using different ways to count the cards. It was good press and really helped the casino business, everybody read the books, practiced religiously, and headed for Las Vegas.

For years and years, there were players who would sit and play, sometimes for hours, and their bets usually would be in a particular range. Then, suddenly, they would get a "message" from above, (or wherever these messages come from) and bet almost everything they had in front of them.

Sometimes they won, sometimes they lost. They were what we called "impulse bettors." There were a lot of people like that. Sometimes the free drinks would bring forth the "revelation," but nobody could figure out what motivated them to take the risk. Once the counting craze started, these people became notorious counters. A lot of them were told that the casino didn't want their business anymore, in spite of the fact that they had been playing there for years and had lost quite a bit of money in the establishment. Suddenly, counters were spotted everywhere. If you fit a certain criterion, you immediately came under suspicion, and if you won, they probably would say you couldn't play anymore.

The criteria some of these dopes in the pit used were as follows. If you had kinky or long wild hair or wore thick glasses, looked the least bit "scientific," or bookish or generally nerdy, you were probably a notorious counter. Some people played a money management system, changing their bets to make money last longer, they were also discouraged from playing. There is no telling how many legitimate customers were run out of the major casinos. Another fact is that anyone who plays Blackjack likes to watch the cards. If they win, it makes them feel smart. That's one of the draws to the game.

A guy by the name of Joe Bernstein started it all. In the late '50s and through the '60s, Joe gambled all over town. He was a sharp Poker player and managed to win enough to keep on gambling. He was almost a lifetime resident of Las Vegas. He had a great mind for cards, and actually was the one who started the whole counting craze, although he was doing it for years before it caught on. He worked with a woman named Betty, who everyone thought was his wife. He made no bones about what he was doing, and nobody told him he couldn't play. He began to attract attention, and the Stardust Hotel invited him to play exclusively in their casino, and they would advertise the fact that he was gambling there. Sometimes people would come and watch, and the Stardust would take care of his meals, etc. After a while he started gambling in different casinos. When he won, nobody told him not to come back. Betty sometimes would play alongside him helping him count, which made it easier for him to win. They were dealing single deck Blackjack to him, and if he jumped out and made an exceptionally large bet after several small bets, they would shuffle the cards.

Remember, just because you have the odds in your favor, it doesn't mean you're going to win.

160. Seniority

In the mid '60s, Las Vegas saw an influx of new residents, mostly from California, the East and Midwest. By the 1970s they were pouring in at an unprecedented rate. The town became the fastest growing city in the United States due to the weather, the clean air, the cheap property taxes, the low crime rate, the availability of employment (nobody went without a job), affordable housing and the casinos.

The result of the explosive population was a higher crime rate, increasing air pollution, gridlock traffic, higher taxes and the usual urban headaches. A large proportion of the new residents had been to Las Vegas over the years, and they all liked to gamble. That resulted in the construction of giant off-Strip casinos that catered mainly to locals, such as Sam's town, the Coast casinos and the one that started it all, the Palace Station, the first of the many Station Casinos located throughout the valley. They all featured first rate buffets and restaurants that offered Mexican, Italian, Chinese, steaks and seafood; excellent food at reasonable prices. The lines waiting to get into all of them, night or day, proved it.

They featured bingo, and slots that were loose, compared to the Strip hotels. They could afford to be, as they had a captive audience. The slot business in the Strip hotels was transient by comparison. Money won on the slots at a Strip hotel may never come back to that hotel. Money won at a local establishment *by* a local would most likely come back the next day or sooner. Most featured movie theaters and fast food courts. The competition for the local buck was fierce, but there was plenty of business to go around.

No matter where you lived in Las Vegas, there was a first-class hotel and casino a short drive away. These were not neighborhood dives, the casinos were huge, and most featured a minimum of 2500 friendly slot machines. On some days you couldn't find an empty machine. The rooms were cheaper than the Strip hotels and were a bargain for the money. The residents, new and old, were known as "locals." When it came to playing the "system" they knew every trick and angle in the book. For newcomers, there was always someone they knew to teach them the art of the finagle. Especially the ones from the East, New York, Connecticut, Boston, and the big cities in the Midwest.

They wore the years they lived in Las Vegas like the "hashmarks" on the sleeve of an old soldier or sailor. They would constantly lord it over the newcomers, who would soon have seniority on the new people constantly moving in. They were the most jaded, argumentative, and conniving people I have ever met. If you were a casino executive in one of these places, you had the toughest job in town. The day was one beef after another, working on the Strip was a piece of cake by comparison, and 99.9% of all the beefs were over "comps," complimentary food.

Because local business was in high demand, the local-oriented casinos bent over backwards to accommodate the whims of their patrons. To a point. For example, one elderly woman would come into the Boulder Station, usually early in the day when it wasn't real busy and play the quarter slots. On the bank of slots, she liked to play on, there were about 12 machines. She would go from machine to machine, and if another customer tried to play one of the machines, she would announce that she was playing all the machines and tilt the stools so nobody else would try to sit down. She was told she couldn't do this, but she would do it anyway. She always got a complimentary lunch, and when she got hungry she wanted "reserved" signs put on five machines. The policy was that no more than two machines could be reserved for a lunch break.

Every day she would complain to the slot floor supervisors, who would then contact me. When I reiterated the policy, she would threaten to take her business somewhere else or call my boss and have me fired. I don't know how many times I told her that we hate to lose her business, but policy is policy. There were always a few other dowagers within earshot, and as soon as she left for lunch, they would move onto the disputed machines, strictly out of spite, and then smile at her when she returned. This spurred her on to greater efforts.

One day she came in, sat at her usual machines, and when she went to eat, she glanced around, reached into her purse, and came out with no less than eight "Out of Order" signs and placed them on "her" machines. This was all caught on surveillance tape. The slot supervisor noticed the signs, collected them and took them into the coffee shop and returned them to her. She denied that they belonged to her and went back to the grins of her fellow slot degenerates.

Multiply that by 30 and you've had a busy day.

161. Everybody Likes to Eat, Nobody Likes to Pay

Then there were the complimentaries. With several different restaurants in the establishment, including a gourmet steak and seafood house, fine Italian and Mexican rooms plus Chinese, a high-end coffee shop and the best buffets in town, everyone of course would demand the best. Before we would comp them in the gourmet rooms, we would ascertain whether or not their casino play warranted it. This was done in several ways, by computer, verification, with floor or slot personnel, or personal observation.

Most places knew their better customers by name, and whenever someone took credit or sat down at a game to gamble they would be rated by the floor personnel in that section. A rating card was kept on the desk with name, how much cash they bought in or credit taken, the amount of the first bet, the amount of the average wagers, and the won or lost results, along with the amount of time spent on the game. A common ploy was to walk up to a table and bet a $100 bill. This got the floorman's attention and if they won, they could continue to play and possibly win some money. Either way, they would ask for a comp in the steak house. If they got lucky on the $100 and have, say, $1000 in chips in front of them, it would be difficult to turn them down. If they lost, or only made the one wager and you turned them down for the steak house (where two people could easily run up a tab of $200 or more) and offered a buffet or coffee shop, the doo-doo would fly. At the end of the day the ratings were entered into the computer, which could go back several years on any given individual. It really gave you something to base a decision on.

If it were a new customer, you had to base your decision on their performance on that particular play. The typical encounter (a nightly event) would begin like this: The customer would approach and you would ask, "May I help you?" They were usually women and would stand there and look at you as if you were some subspecies of amoeba, as if the very sight of you nauseates them. This immediately tells me that they're locals, surely from the Eastern part of the country. Then begins a choreographed dialogue that starts with the comp request. If you tell them that their play doesn't warrant a high- end restaurant comp, and offer the buffet, invariably the next comment would be; “You know, this town was a much better place when it was run by the Mob.”

My standard reply was, did your husband work for the Mob?” “No, but we knew somebody . . .” “Oh,” I would reply, “that sounds great.” The next comment would be, “These corporations ruined this town, they don’t care if you come into their casino or not.” I wouldn’t bother to comment, and I knew what was next, which was my favorite part of the whole dialogue. After addressing me with the amoeba stare for several seconds, they would pop the inevitable, “I’ve been in this town since 1969.” My standard reply was, “Gee, you’re practically a native.” And then I wouldn’t say another word.

Finally, here came the high point of my day. The next question, of course, was, “How long have *you* been here?” accompanied by the look. “1950,” I would reply, “and I worked for the Mob.” That usually ended the conversation.

Sometimes I would add, “I got paid minimum wage, no insurance, no vacation-pay, no time-and-a-half for overtime, no days off for weeks sometimes. And if you wanted a meal, you paid menu price for it, including a cup of coffee for 25 cents.” And to top it off, they could fire you on a whim, and you had no recourse. These conversations all followed the same pattern, as if someone was handing out a new resident handbook.

They always settled for the buffet or coffee shop.

162. Working the System

The Palace Station installed a computer system that tracked complimentaries on an individual basis. You could bring up a name, and see each comp with the date and the amount. Since management was always complaining that comps were too high, they figured a running record would rein in a lot of the abuse.

As it happened, I noticed that every morning at precisely five minutes before the day shift took over, a little elderly man and his wife would walk up to a Craps table, break a $5 bill, and he would bet $1 on the pass line. He would then ask the graveyard dice pit manager for a comp for breakfast. It was the cheapest meal in the place and with the specials it really didn't amount to much. But I noticed that he came in every day.

One day, questioning the pit manager about the daily free meal, he replied, "They're a nice old couple and they play the slots (which wasn't the case) and they have the 99-cent special, which doesn't cost us anything." For all I knew they might have been his mom and dad.

A few hours later I saw the old man go to another pit boss, who then directed him to me. He asked for an upgrade from breakfast to lunch, which was just a matter of crossing out "breakfast," circling "lunch" and initialing the change. The comp was credited to the original signature. Any pit boss would do it, as it didn't reflect on his comp report. I refused him, and I saw the name on the slip, Richard James. I went to the computer and brought up Richard James, and there was a whole string of comps, mostly for lunch, which was considerably more expensive. But I noticed that the dates weren't consecutive, there were no amounts for days that I knew he had gotten a complimentary. Upon further research, I found that slips were made out to Richard James, Rich James, R. James, Rick James, Dick James, and to the wife, Dora James, D. James, etc. All in separate places in the computer.

On further investigation, practically every name in the computer (and there were hundreds) had the same situation. The cost to the casino in unwarranted comps was enormous. Some people would get two or three comps on the same day. If they had an extra, they would probably give it to a friend or relative.

I don't know how they finally fixed it.

163. The Big 360

The biggest changes in Las Vegas occurred in the late '50s through the late '60s. In the '50s, the busiest time for the casinos was summer. They advertised "Fun in the Sun in Fabulous Las Vegas." If you worked in the casinos and asked for some time off, the reply was, "Wait until after Labor Day, and you can get all the time off you want."

Several years later it was just the opposite. June was the slowest month, and business was slow in the summer. After Labor Day, the town would fill up and stay full. People didn't care to put up with the heat. December, close to Christmas, was pretty dead, and Thanksgiving was the same. By the late '60s both these holidays were major events in the town, and New Year's, which was the busiest time of the year, was becoming more peaceful.

Before the change, we would stand by our games just before midnight on New Year's Eve and tremble, waiting for the showroom curtains to open and the drunken horde would roar out with their hats and noisemakers and head for the nearest tables. In most cases we would stay busy until eight or nine in the morning, with drunks blowing those things that unravel in your face. In the early '50s, there weren't enough rooms in town to house all the visitors, and the local radio stations would plead with people to rent rooms in their homes (no TV). Tents would pop up on the courthouse lawn, and on the grass in front of the train depot. People slept in their cars up and down Fremont Street.

164. Las Vegas Mother's Day

If you worked as a casino exec in the places that catered to locals, Mother's Day was a day more frightening than New Year's Eve used to be in days gone by. Everyone had a mother, everyone took their mother out to lunch or dinner for Mother's Day, and everyone's mother was too infirm to stand in line. So, the lines in the restaurants would wind around the casino, and everybody requested, and received, a line pass. When a valued customer requested that you walk them to the front of the line, the objections, and other invectives would assault you from every direction.

The lines would look like the old refugee newsreels from WWII. These same ladies, just the day before, with cigarettes hanging out of their mouths and purple bags under their eyes would bolt out of the bingo room when the session was over and race down the long hall into the casino headed for their favorite machines. It looked like a senior 10K. Now, on Mother's Day, it was the lame, the halt and the blind.

When the day was over, the walkers, crutches, oxygen caddies, wheelchairs, casts, canes and orthopedic shoes would go back into the closet until the next Mother's Day.

165. Power of the Pen

The pen is mightier than the sword. These words were penned by Edward Bulwer-Lytton for his play “Richelieu” in 1839. Never was the expression more evident than in early Las Vegas where it had morphed to “power of the pen”, or in short, “the pencil.” This simply meant the power to grant or sign for complimentaries in the casinos. Older people, when denied a free dinner or show, wail that Las Vegas was so much better when it was run by the Mob.

This is basically true. The Desert Inn cost five million dollars to build in 1949 and 1950, and they “won it out,” or paid for it in the first year of operation. This didn’t count the money that found its way east or the contents of shoeboxes taken out of the counting room. Everybody in the Mob was happy and anybody who asked for a comp usually got it with a smile. Bear in mind however, there were no gourmet restaurants in the hotels at the time. The showroom had no cover and no minimum for the late show and during the dinner show the most expensive thing on the menu was a filet mignon or New York Steak for $5.50. The Chuck Wagon buffet was a steal for a buck and comps weren’t an issue for the bottom line. There was excellent food in the restaurant and it was inexpensive, more like a coffee shop. Then the gourmet rooms started to appear with the junkets, the first being the Candlelight room at the Flamingo in 1960. Food and beverage costs were rising and the corporations were moving in.

Enter the bean counters. Now the complimentaries were entered as casino expenses and had an effect on the bottom line. The mantra was “Cut down on the comps.” and it was heard over and over. Then they narrowed down the number of people who could sign. A pit boss couldn’t sign for drinks at the bar and shift managers and assistants were the only ones who could sign in the showroom and the restaurant, though most took a certain amount of latitude. Those who could sign constantly received gifts from good customers and one shift manager at the Frontier was caught selling comps to the gourmet room. Give him $50 and you could have a complimentary $250 dinner.

For example, my father opened the Desert Inn in 1950 and had power of the pen until he retired in 1986. I wore suits for at least 25 years during my career and never bought a tie. If I needed a tie, I would go over to my dad's house where in one closet there were boxes and racks of ties never worn, all gifts. There were literally hundreds. In another room were two closets full of any kind of booze or wines you could imagine, by the case and shelves of appliances, golf clubs, free invitations to pro-am golf tournaments all expenses paid, shirts, sweaters, jewelry and apparel for my mother. The list was endless. As a teenager I could go to the Desert Inn pool and have a beverage and the waitress would take the check into the casino. Our high school prom dates were at one of the major shows, and always complimentary. There was reciprocity among the Strip hotels, and one hand washed the other. The Stardust Hotel had the best Polynesian food in town at their Aku Aku restaurant and, as a family, we would go there almost weekly. With the drinks and food for five, six or seven people, the bill would be pretty high but, for 20 years, we never got a check. One night my dad and I tried to estimate how much in comps we got at Aku Aku over the years, and a conservative estimate was $120,000. That didn't count the gourmet rooms in different hotels, anniversary parties, etc. I came to realize that food tasted much better when you didn't have to pay for it.

166. Intramural Competition

Someone at the Flamingo organized an oral sex contest which was to be between the dice dealers and the Blackjack dealers. Everyone chipped in $25 for expenses (the contestant from each pit got $100). Between $100 and $200 was for the lady who was to be the judge. Separately there was a $500 wager between the pits. The winning side got about $25 per man, and of course bragging (?) rights. They put up a betting sheet in the dealers' room complete with changing odds. For example, if the dice pit rep burned his tongue on hot soup, the odds would change.

Finally, came the big night. They rented a cabin at the old Alpine Village which was quite a way out of town, and set the contest for 2AM Of course, everyone was inebriated and there was some side-betting going on. One of the Blackjack dealers was given $200 to go find an attractive judge (which, given the sum, wouldn't be difficult). It seems that too much alcohol made him feel lucky, and he stopped at the Horseshoe Club and lost the whole $200. In a panic he borrowed $40 from a friend at the club and went to find a hooker. He showed up late with a streetwalker that made Dirty Doris look like Miss Universe. Everyone wanted to kill him, and the Blackjack pit representative withdrew from the contest. The dice dealers claimed they were entitled to the money by way of forfeit, but the other side said they wouldn't pay until the dice pit did the deed. (No one from the Blackjack pit was willing to substitute). The poor guy wanted to back out but it was agreed that all he had to do was make contact. Well, after much shouting and cajoling, he did and, at the same time, the police pulled up outside.

In the ensuing stampede, one of the Blackjack dealers broke his shoulder, and there were plenty of cuts and bruises as everyone scrambled to get away. The only arrest was the poor hooker who had nowhere to run.

When Chester Simms (the Flamingo casino manager) heard about it he was furious. (To him oral sex was a felony.). He moved heaven and earth to find out who was involved, and since he couldn't fire everybody he fired the champ, who went to work at the Tropicana. In a discussion some time later he was heard saying,

“Now the Tropicana has the champ.” The guy who lost the $200 was on everybody’s’ “shit list” for months.

167. Carpet vs. Sawdust

Back in the day, the "Million Dollar Golden Nugget" in downtown Las Vegas had wooden floors. In the card room (Poker, Pan, Faro, etc.) they had some sawdust on the floor and it was covered with peanut shells, cigarette butts, and the like. The constant traffic back and forth moved the peanut shells and other debris out into the main casino area. It qualified as a "sawdust joint"

A sawdust joint is the opposite of a "carpet" joint" (a casino with a carpeted floor). All the major hotels were carpet joints. Dealers in carpet joints looked down on dealers in sawdust joints. After a while it became an expression, even if a casino had a carpet floor, if it wasn't on the Strip, it was a sawdust joint.

All the casinos in Reno were sawdust joints compared to Las Vegas. If a dealer from Reno went to work in Las Vegas, everyone kidded him, and asked if this was the first carpet joint he ever worked in.

There were no women dealers on the Strip. The only place that had a few was the Monte Carlo club downtown. Blackjack only. In the late '60s some women activists were making a lot of noise about the fact that they were being denied employment opportunities, etc. etc. Carl Thomas, casino manager At Circus Circus came into the Baccarat one night and told us he had been at a meeting at the Riviera with owners and Casino Managers and although they knew they would eventually have to hire women, they could slow the process down for years. They would take employment applications from women and just not act on them. A few days later one of the lady labor agitators went into the Tropicana, one of the better jobs in town, and approached Don Speer, the casino manager. He was on his way to a meeting, and when she stopped him and asked for a job he replied, "We don't hire women". And the walls came tumbling down.

Meanwhile women were every bit as able and reliable as men, maybe more so. In truth, some of my best employees were women. When the Mob still had influence, the no-women policy was a macho thing, nothing more.

168. Everyone Wore a Belt

There were no $1 chips anywhere in town. Everything was dealt with real silver dollars. The businesses in town all used the silver dollars, and if you wanted paper dollars, you had to request them. Ten silver dollars had enough weight to pull your pants down, but in a lot of places there were *no* paper dollars available. The silver dollars were also hard to deal with on the gaming tables, as some were warped and some were worn thin, which made dealing very difficult. The largest gaming chips were $100 and, since there were no color regulations, they could be any color the casino chose to make them. This caused no end of problems (and scams). For example, the Dunes Hotel decided it would be a good idea to make their $5 chips black, the same color as most of the other casinos' $100-dollar chips. The rationale they used was that it would make the customers "feel like big shots."

The result was it drove everyone in town crazy. Even though the inserts (the markings on the side of the chips) were a different color, when they were mixed with other black chips, it was impossible to differentiate. So, some people would take stacks of chips (20 to a stack) to the cashier's cage, with the Dunes $5 chips mixed in with the house $100 chips and if the cashier didn't check closely they would walk away with $2000 for, say, $480. Even worse, the chips were practically legal tender in Las Vegas, they were spent in stores, the Casinos would accept chips from other casinos and they were accepted by cab drivers, restaurants, bowling alleys, etc.

Another example: A player could walk up to a gaming table and bet, say, two black chips, one worth $5 and the other $100, the $100 chip on top. If he loses, he loses $105. If he wins, he has a good chance of getting paid $200. These are pretty good odds, and you would be surprised how often it was successful. If the player was questioned the reply was, "I just got them mixed up, they were all in my pocket" or, "I knew what they were worth but it's not my problem."

And they were right.

169. A Classic Mix-up

The Flamingo Hotel had White $100 chips, the only place in town that did so, and the chips were old, warped and worn, some so smooth you could hardly read the denomination. They were what was called a "hot stamp" chip; no logo or round center insert, just "Flamingo Hotel" and $100 stamped into the chip itself. They were inexpensive to make and were only used occasionally. When there were several big Blackjack games going, they would bring out a rack of $100 chips ($10,000) and place it on the Roulette wheel apron to use at a moment's notice if needed. There was very loose documentation in those days. The practice ended a few years later but, one busy night, they had the white $100 chips on the apron and, during the course of the hot, hectic evening, with mountains of ten-cent chips being played, the $100 white chips got mixed in with the practically identical ten-cent white chips.

All the Roulette chips were ten cents unless otherwise indicated by a marker button on the rim of the wheel. There was no denomination designated on the chip. This resulted in a 20-cent wager possibly being paid with $7000 instead of $7. Even with two or three $100 chips mixed in a stack of ten-cent chips, a huge overpay was certain. You could take a small amount of $100 chips to the cashier's cage and cash them out without any verification. Finally, a dealer realized the error and pandemonium ensued. They stopped the game and went through the players' chips and all the unused white wheel chips. When the smoke cleared there were four $100 chips missing.

I suppose the player noticed the discrepancy in the chips and stuck them in his pocket.

170. The Industry Changes

The gaming industry began to see major changes in the late '60s and early '70s, and it wasn't long after that it had literally evolved 360 degrees. Craps was the main game in the '50s. (the casinos had more crap tables than Blackjack) Then the dice games began playing second fiddle to Blackjack, and with the proliferation of Baccarat, interest in Roulette waned.

Before Baccarat, Roulette was the main game for South American and Mexican customers. With the concept of a global economy, and huge dollars coming from the Pacific Rim, Baccarat became the game of choice for high rollers. The fact that the game was dealt with cash, by dealers in tuxedos in an opulent setting, and had a higher limit than the other games, helped bring this about. In Mexico, among the affluent, the game was the national pastime. If someone were to win a lot of money at Baccarat, the news was all over Mexico within two hours after he cashed out.

The biggest change of all was that the slots had become the biggest source of profit for the casinos. New technology, more customers, and the advent of multiple coin machines made the casinos more money than the table games. You don't have to pay a machine, provide benefits or worry about it stealing from you, it never calls in sick and, in most cases, it's reliable.

Slots in the '50s were mostly one-coin mechanical machines, with the jackpot in a transparent chute on the front of the machine, which would open and drop the money when the jackpot was hit. The common jackpots were about $5 for nickels, $10 for dimes, $25 to $35 for quarters and $150 silver dollars for the $1 machines. With the advent of progressive jackpots and multiple coin machines, the payouts got larger along with the amount of people who spent every waking hour trying to figure a way to cheat them. And there were a lot of ways. This began the cat-and-mouse game between the slot manufacturers and the cheaters, of discovery and prevention. The cheaters would figure a new wrinkle, and the companies would find a way to prevent it, etc. etc.

It was a constant game of leapfrog. The old mechanical slots were really vulnerable.

171. High School Education

When I was in high school, the main hangout was the Roundup Drive-in at Main and 5th (now known as the Strip). The Stratosphere tower now sits across the street. The Roundup had three slot machines, about a foot from entry, a really stupid place to put a gaming device.

One night, five of us were crowded around the quarter machine, blocking the view from the counter and the kitchen. We had a "spoon" made of semi soft plastic, that, when inserted into the coin slot and twisted slightly, caused the reels to float freely, almost like they were anti-gravity. We would pull the handle of the machine down, and when a payoff would line up in the correct position, we would pop the handle back up, and the reels would "index"-or lock into place and the payout would fall into the tray. Then the procedure would be repeated. You could empty the machine in 20 minutes or less, and we would take our load of quarters downtown to the Boulder Club and the change booth would cash them out for us. Then we would most likely head for the brothel in Searchlight. At the very worst it was beer money.

Another night we were doing our thing on the machine and I looked back and saw the cook running from behind the counter with a huge cast iron soup ladle. I sounded the alarm and we ran, except that we all hit the door at the same and got briefly stuck. We finally broke free, but the last one out was unfortunate. I heard a loud *boink!* and a curse and I kept moving. The guy behind me was moving too, but on wobbly legs. It's a good thing that teenage heads are hard or he might have been seriously injured. We headed for the Boulder Club with our meager "winnings" and hadn't gone three blocks when the police pulled us over. They were called by the manager of the drive-in, and of course they found the quarters. Some of us had prominent parents, both in local business and casinos, so they took our names, and the quarters (maybe $80) and told us that if we were caught again were going to jail, and worse, our parents would be notified.

The kid who got bopped with the ladle wound up running his family's casino (the world-famous Horseshoe Club) and owned several other casinos over the course of the years. I don't know what the cops did with the quarters, but a short time later, on a busy night, the quarter machine disappeared. Instead of trying to cheat it, someone just picked it up and walked out the door.

He must have been one strong dude.

172. Cheating the Slots

As the slot business started to progress, the technology leaped ahead. The old mechanical singe-coin machines were passé and, more and more, casinos featured multiple coin machines. Most of the machines early on were five-coin machines, however, to receive the maximum payout, you had to have five coins in the machine. People always had stories about hitting the jackpot with their last few coins and not getting the larger payout. A bonus was always offered with the fifth coin; a powerful incentive to buy more change if you only had only four coins left. Then again, feeding these machines five coins every time you pulled the handle came to be expensive.

Some local entrepreneurs came up with a good idea. They would take a coin (generally a quarter), drill a tiny hole in it and tie it to a piece of monofilament fishing line. On the opposite end was a loop which fit loosely on the end of a finger or thumb. They would drop the coin into the coin slot until it registered on the machine, and proceed to move their string up and down, which tripped the "coin in" lever and enabled you to get five coins on the display and the max payout for nothing. This was called "stringing." It required very little movement of the offending finger and was very hard to detect in a busy casino. If the culprit thought he may have been detected, all he had to do was let the loop slip off his finger and the coin and the string would drop down into the machine. Most of the fruits of their labor were not large amounts but multiply that by hundreds of "stringers" around town and total revenues (and taxes to the State) were taking a big hit. It didn't take long before slot personnel were finding coins with strings attached in the coin buckets under the machines and the alarm went out. Dropping the coin and string into the machine eliminated any evidence if you were detained and searched.

All the slot manufacturers operated under the auspices of the State. If the State decided to suspend their license they were out of business. Remember, Nevada was the only legal gambling venue in the United States. So, the State told them to fix the problem, and quickly. The slot companies fitted all their new and old machines with a device that cut the string the minute it was introduced into the machine. They went from casino to casino and installed thousands of them in just a few weeks. So much for stringing.

Some of the more enterprising cheats had different MO's. They had small, high-powered drills which could drill through the side of the machines and misalign the reels. The only evidence was a small amount of sawdust which could be swept to the floor or blown away with a "sneeze." The slot companies countered this by installing metal plates inside the machines which eliminated that threat. The holes these drills made were so small they were, for all practical purposes, invisible. Not to be discouraged, those who made their living outside the law started drilling the machine's door lock. They were adept enough, after hours of practice, to quickly reach in and do any number of things to the mechanism, close the door and win the money. By the time the slot personnel realized what happened, they were long gone, on to the next casino. The antidote to this was the "idiot bar," a steel bar installed on a loaded spring which leaped out when the door to the machine was opened and needed a special tool to reset. Now, they could get the door open, but they could not get it closed. This simple apparatus resulted in some convictions, which in Nevada could mean considerable prison time. The idiot bar caused panic to the cheater and caused many to turn and run out the door.

Some didn't make it.

The coin receptors on the old electro-mechanical machines weren't foolproof. Sometimes a dime machine would take pennies. A flattened-out nickel would pass for a quarter, but usually they would get stuck and you either called the slot mechanic or walked out the door. Since you couldn't string a machine anymore, those so inclined had to figure out a way to get a maximum payout for free.

The answer was slugs. By this time casino operators were realizing the huge potential in the machines and were doing everything they could to make them exciting to play. Almost all the casinos did away with the payout tray attached to the machine and inserted large metal bowls into the slot stands. The coins would fall farther and make a lot of noise when they landed in the bowls.

Especially the dollars. The noise from dollar tokens falling into the bowls was deafening and attracted attention. Some places removed the screws that held the bowls in place to increase the noise. About this time the slugs started to appear. Lead was cheap, and for a while there was an epidemic of lead slugs showing up in the dollar machines. Cheaters wouldn't bother with smaller denominations, as it wasn't worth the possible jail times if they were caught.

The major drawback to the lead slugs was if a payout were hit, the machine would mix some slugs with the payout. When the dollar tokens hit the bottom of the bowls they made a loud ringing sound. The lead slugs would fall with a dull thud. The difference was noticeable anywhere in the dollar slot area. This, of course, led to many an arrest, and a quick stop to the lead slugs. Then they tried mixing different alloys with the lead, but it wasn't good enough, so the lead was eliminated altogether.

Next came the pure alloy slugs, more expensive to make, but still cheap enough to be practical, and they were pretty successful. To counteract this threat, the slot manufacturers came out with the "coin comparator," a unit with two distinct purposes. The casino would install one of their tokens in the comparator. When a coin was fed into the machine, it compared the coin with the token, electronically. If it didn't match, the machine would reject it, or, in some cases, eat it.

Then came the comparator that sensed not only the casino token, but different alloy compositions. This was space age technology in those days. Finally, the only thing that would work in the machines, beside the legitimate token, was stainless steel washers, available in any hardware store. They really worked. The only drawback was that they were so expensive (especially in Las Vegas) that they were too costly. Some new comparators could be tuned to reject stainless about 50 percent of the time. Counterfeit tokens were next, but the mints were able to vary the composition of the tokens, and the comparators improved to the point that losses to slugging were negligible. How was a slot cheat supposed to make a dishonest living?

With the progressive machines paying bigger and bigger jackpots, the temptation was too great to just walk away.

173. Believe It or Not

In 1980 I attended a seminar conducted jointly by the Metropolitan Police and the Gaming Control Board. Both had departments that dealt with slot cheating, however the State Gaming Control had the final authority. The loss in tax revenue to the state was enormous due to cheating, and the slots made up the biggest share of the revenue.

Admission to this seminar was by invitation; only licensees and owners were invited. We were allowed to bring either our slot managers or an assistant casino manager, not both. The invitations had to be presented at the door along with proper identification. There were about 50 attendees.

Some of the things presented were like a movie, only real. There were teams of slot cheats driving around in vans, equipped with the latest in slot repair and test equipment. Along with the toys, they had shirts and work uniforms from every major casino in both Reno and Las Vegas. On a really busy night in a large casino they could blend into the mass of humanity. One team had an individual who had total recall, and then some. They would put a bent coin into the machine and call the attendant when it got stuck. He would reach out with the key to open the door and clear the jam, something he did a hundred times a night. This individual would look at the key (they were a complex design) and go out to the van and fashion a duplicate from memory.

The same key was used on almost all the machines. You can imagine what they were capable of doing with that key. I imagine that some of the underpaid slot floor persons would be approached and, if they decided to go along, would press the key into a block of wax held by the cheater, who would then make a key from the impression.

In another caper, a crew of cheaters went into the Riviera Hotel to "take off" a progressive quarter machine that held a jackpot risen to nearly $12,000, only to find the machine turned around with an "out of order" sign hung on it. It was a Saturday night, the place was jammed, and they needed the money. They went out to the van, put on the maintenance uniform that resembled the Riviera's, came back, and with the help of three "blockers" who crowded around the machine to impede the view, removed the machine from the stand and carried it out to the van in the rear of the parking lot. Using their test equipment, they diagnosed and repaired the machine, and being familiar with the time of the shift change, waited until the change was in progress, took the machine back into the casino, set it up and hit the jackpot. They yelled and screamed like any customer would with a jackpot that size, waited for the verification, then waited for the attendant to get the money from the cashier's cage. Once they were paid, they tipped the slot personnel, and headed for the coffee shop, then immediately beat it out the door. The theft wasn't discovered until later when the incoming slot mechanic read the previous mechanics log, and saw the machine was listed as out of order. Upon checking the machine, it was in perfect working order, no sign of tampering. They called the mechanic from the previous shift who had shut the machine down, and he told them that it needed parts that wouldn't be available until Monday, so he shut it down. These guys had the parts, the hotel didn't.

It was a lengthy seminar, with a lot of incidents recounted, and with help as to how to protect yourself, but the main line of defense was the manufacturer's technology. Most of the machines were what they called "electro-mechanical" with supposedly all the goodies to protect them from cheaters, which we could see wasn't working as well as they wished.

Abe "Botts" Goodman, a former casino exec at Caesars Palace was hired by Bally, the biggest slot manufacturer in the world at the time, to liaison with the casinos and help their sales. We called him "Botts from Bally." He had been spreading the word to the casinos that Bally was putting the finishing touches on a machine that was foolproof; couldn't be compromised. At the seminar, he showed us schematics of the machine. This was before computers were common and, when spread open, the hundred or so pages of the schematic stretched out over 16 feet. If you'd never seen a schematic with all the diagrams and lines you might as well be looking at the secret designs of a rocket to mars. All of us felt "so what?"

Then they told us that, a month prior to this meeting, Gaming Control and Metro cooperated in bringing down a ring of slot cheaters flying their own plane back and forth between Reno, Tahoe, and Las Vegas. They were looking at some serious jail time. They fingered the brains of the operation, the guy who figured out how to beat the safeguards, a genius gone wrong. While in jail awaiting indictment, he was approached by the state, which offered him a deal: work for them (on probation) or do a lot of years. He would be paid like any other employee, but the rules of probation would apply. I don't know how long the deal was to last, but he took it. The other three got reduced sentences for fingering him, but still did several years in the state penitentiary.

The Gaming Board had been testing Bally's new unbeatable machine prior to clearing it for sale, and they agreed it was safe. They then decided to test their new employee. They showed him the schematics, he studied them and said, "Let me take some time with these." Still under arrest, they put him in a hotel room and had a guard on the door. If he got hungry they would bring food to the room, and there he sat for three days, poring over these schematics. Finally, he knocked on the door, they opened it and he said, "I can beat it." They got all the Bally techs together from various locations and he proceeded to show them how he could do it.

This guy could have had a legitimate career, but he chose the excitement of cheating a casino instead. He did stay with the Control Board for quite a few years, and rumor had it that the New Jersey Gaming authorities had approached him. I don't know whether he accepted or not. The slots had entered the Video stage and that was a whole new world.

174. The Living Dead

In the early 1980s, Las Vegas was in a rut. Interest rates were at an all- time high, and several resorts, the Riviera included, filed for Chapter 11 bankruptcy. It seemed like the whole country was at a standstill. At that time IGT (International Game Technology) was putting a new machine into casinos for trial, the first new wrinkle in the industry in years. It was called Video Poker, and it created a whole new legion of zombies.

They offered to put the machines in a casino, and for six months they would take 40 percent of the win towards the cost of the machine. If the machine didn't pay for itself in six months, the balance would be paid at 12 percent interest. Not a bad deal, except for the fact that the percentage for the house on the machine was around 2.5 percent and IGT claimed it would "hold" 5 percent. Everybody predicated their purchases on the 5 percent, and they came up short in a lot of cases. The 12 percent interest negated almost all the win. The screaming was long and loud.

The machines in the local oriented casinos stayed full almost all the time, and they had so many machines that they were quite profitable. One local casino decided to add a program, which would increase the percentage for the house by around 2 percent. They had their slot manager come in at 4AM and change half of their Poker machines to the higher percentage program. The change consisted of *one* coin on the payout for a full house. It was called a "visible" change as it sat right on the face of the machine where it showed the payouts for each hand, as one pair, two pair, three of a kind, etc. That one coin was the only change. The machines required five coins to get the top payoff on a royal flush.

The next morning, they had one complaint after another, protesting the change, and while the unchanged machines were full, the ones they had changed stayed empty. For one coin, and it was spotted immediately. They changed everything back in a hurry. Video Poker became an epidemic, and when IGT originally approached me to try the machines in a small off-Strip casino I was managing, they referred to it as a "disease," and they were right. In a town full of compulsive gamblers, and a lot of sad stories, this took it to a new level. Video Poker caused more divorces, bankruptcies, job losses, and financial hardship than all the other games put together. Most of the local casinos allowed their employees to play the machines during their off hours. It was a way to win back the paychecks and to inadvertently reduce labor costs. They assumed that they were going to play someplace, so why not there?

I recall getting off work at the Palace Station at 6PM, and on my way out I noticed a dealer, just off work, sit down at a Poker machine and buy a roll of quarters. When I returned to work the next morning, she was still at the same machine. She looked at her watch, got up, signed the payroll sheet and went to work another shift.

This was not an isolated incident. There were people who played all night and didn't realize they hadn't shown up for their next shift. The local operators recognized what these machines represented and came up with variations on the machines. For example, a royal flush with five quarters played paid $1000. The cards didn't have to be in sequence. Station Casinos came up with "reversible royals." If you got a royal flush in sequence, 10JQKA, or AKQJ10, they paid $50,000. Before long, you could go into any local bar (and there were a lot of them) and in the counter in front of each barstool was a Video Poker machine. You would pay for a drink and drop the change into the machine in front of you. It was irresistible. If you played enough, they would buy your drinks. Along with the bars there were banks of Video Pokers in every grocery store (they were allowed 10 machines). It was not an unusual occurrence for a woman to lose her grocery money in the grocery before starting to shop. The stools were always full, even during the wee hours of the morning. The amazing thing about it was that the machines in the stores didn't pay as well as the machines in the local casinos. Strangely enough, this phenomenon only occurred in Las Vegas. The Strip hotels did moderate business on the machines, and the local-oriented casinos in Reno did well with them, but not anywhere near what was going on in Las Vegas.

For some reason Video Poker's hypnotic effect made degenerate players out of people who'd never gambled in their lives.

175. Just What Is Random?

A random generator is the program in all Video Poker, Blackjack, and Keno machines that guarantees that the cards are shuffled electronically in a random manner. The state authorities guaranteed that if you sat down to play one of those machines, you were getting a "square gamble." They were wrong.

Take the case of the American Coin Company in Las Vegas. They were the fourth biggest slot route operators in Nevada with over 1000 machines in bars, restaurants, markets, etc. One of their programmers had a twinge of conscience and informed the authorities that he had been told to eliminate the Royal Flush, or jackpot from the programs. The Gaming Control Board and law enforcement officials checked their machines and found out his allegations were true. A person who played these machines had no chance of ever winning a jackpot. They revoked the license of the company and brought charges against the owners.

Before the trial, the whistleblower, Larry Volk, was working on his car outside his home when someone walked up and shot him point blank in the head. One David Lemons was tried for his murder in 1993 and acquitted. The coin company's owners were fined one million dollars and barred from ever operating in Nevada. In 1998, David Lemons, in prison on another offense, confessed to the killing of Larry Volk. Since he was acquitted of the charge in 1993, he couldn't be tried again.

He named the people who paid him $5000 for the hit and they were jailed on conspiracy charges.

176. Nerves of Steel

This next example could have taken all the prizes. In Atlantic City in 1995 a man walked into the casino at Bally's Park Place and marked eight numbers on a Keno machine. Incredibly, he caught all eight numbers for a jackpot of $100,000. When he went to collect the payout, he asked to be paid in cash, showed no emotion, and had no identification. New Jersey law states that any jackpot over $35,000 has to be verified by the casino Control Board.

The officials were notified, and since it didn't seem right, they asked him what room he was in. They went up to the room and encountered a man who gave his name as Ron Harris, a friend of the winner. They went back downstairs to question the winner whose name was Reid MacNeal and found out that Ron Harris was an employee of the Nevada Gaming Control Board. Returning to the room to question Harris, they found him gone. Searching the room, they found computer chips, and documents pertaining to hacking into computer programs. Harris had been an employee of the Nevada Control Board for 12 years and was one of the individuals who would travel the state from casino to casino and checking slot computer programs for compliance with state regulations. He had access to the random generators and other programs. He had found that certain combinations of numbers would precede jackpot payouts on some Keno machines. He transferred the info to his own computer and worked out the plan. They went to Atlantic city, created the right situation, and hit the $100,000 jackpot. MacNeal was arrested on the spot, and Harris when he deplaned in Las Vegas. Upon further investigation it was found that Harris set up jackpots in several machines in Northern Nevada, by a unique system. For example, if you played five coins, then three coins, then five coins again, then one coin, the jackpot would hit on the next play. He had "beards" (people who play and take down the jackpots), he wouldn't do it himself. It was almost foolproof. Had MacNeal had identification with him, and acted like he was excited, it may never had been detected. Imagine how much money they could have made. MacNeal testified against Harri and wasn't charged.

In 1998 Harris was found guilty of racketeering and sentenced to seven years.

177. Surveillance

I'm sure most of us have seen the "inside" scenes from the surveillance rooms of the Strip casinos on television. The surveillance director would show a few grainy videos of a culprit trying to cheat the house, grabbing chips from the rack on the table and attempting to run, with the security guards to the rescue, and various other devious and ingenious ways to cheat the house. He would then give you a lesson in sleight of hand which would make the average individual ooh and aah. The implication was that these were common occurrences, and every night was a "circle the wagons" situation.

Truth be known, 99 percent of that stuff was passé 40 years ago. It looks good on TV, though. If you saw it being done on an actual game, chances are it was a training video used to indoctrinate most of the surveillance personnel. Actually, unless a person has dealt the games for years and developed an instinctive reaction to unnatural moves, *there is no way to know what's going on. Period.* You don't learn that stuff from books or videos.

After years of dealing and observing from the floor level some people develop a sixth sense, their gut telling them when something is amiss. Surveillance room panels have hundreds of screens, every inch of the tables and the surrounding casino are covered by cameras. Almost all are "pan and tilt" which means they can be moved around to cover every angle on the game and zoom in so close you can see the lint on the table. I have observed videos of card switchers, past-posters on Roulette, dice "scooters" and various other underhanded tactics and, even knowing the cheating occurred, there were occasions where I had to watch the tape numerous times to finally see what happened; and I spent a lot of years on those games and did a little cheating myself. A lot of these things have moved to a different level, but the basics remain the same.

The most expensive equipment money can buy is no better than the person using it.

178. Eye in the Sky

Before the days of high tech surveillance, casinos mainly relied on the "eye in the sky" or the one-way mirrors in the ceiling, above which were cat walks that ran the length of the casino. On different occasions there would be a gaming genius up on the catwalk, observing the tables below. They weren't always staffed. Actually, they were seldom used in the casinos I worked in. The identities of the persons in the "eye" were highly classified, or so everyone thought. But it didn't take long to find out who they were, as very few people in the business could keep their mouths shut.

These clandestine endeavors were filled with people who couldn't get a job on the casino floor, much more lucrative than walking around in the dark. In certain situations, they would bring floor men in on their night off to work in the sky, and they would be more effective. There was one element that rendered the eye in the sky practically useless, it was the nemesis of desert living: dust. When the wind blows in the desert, which is most of the time, the dust that comes with it permeates everything. Even when the wind *doesn't* blow, it permeates everything. Most of the casinos at that time were older structures they kept adding on to as the town moved forward, but they always added on to the casino areas, older buildings not up to the newer building codes. In short, the area above the casino ceiling was extremely dusty. When there was someone in the eye, you could mark his position by the dust falling through the light fixtures and the seam around the one-way mirror. You could literally stand and watch the dust filter down as he would make his way down the walk. The dealers and the customers would look up, and brush the dust from their clothes and hair, and blow it off of their glasses. The players would get a laugh out of it, the dealers didn't think it was funny. The only thing accomplished was that if a dealer was about to do something he shouldn't be doing, he'd be forewarned that he was being watched.

With the coming of the corporations, and top-level management that had no gaming background, a lot of emphasis was on surveillance. When the eye would call down and make a report that he saw a dealer make a mistake, or a wrong payoff, for example, his word was taken without question. Many dealers lost jobs when accused of wrongdoing in the written reports from surveillance. There were no tapes, no defense, no recourse. Dealers terminated in this manner usually had a "jacket" hung on them, and had difficulty finding work.

I remember a specific incident at the Frontier Hotel in 1971. I was the wheel boss, responsible for two Roulette wheels and two Blackjack games on the night shift. I had two Roulette dealers working on the games who had around 100 years' experience between them, and their reputations were impeccable. On a busy Saturday night, the casino manager came up to me, handed me a slip of paper and said, "Here, sign this." It was a discrepancy slip from the man in the sky, saying that one of the dealers overpaid a customer by 150 chips, and I stood there observing the transaction without correcting it.

The chances of one of these men overpaying someone by that amount, and me not seeing it are about the same as hitting the lottery. I asked the casino manager what the qualifications of the observer were, and maybe *he* made the error. He said, "I can't tell you that," and I refused to sign.

There was a big to-do over it, and it wound up in the corporate general manager's office. This was a Summa Corporation (Howard Hughes) hotel and the general manager's name was Schwind, from Germany, and had never seen the inside of a casino prior to this position. I was in his office and looked him in the eye and told him that if my accuser had the credentials to question my ability, I would sign, under protest. I made it clear that I wanted to know who it was and gave my word that I would never confront him. To my amazement, he told me. It was a security guard who couldn't find his ass with both hands and had never worked behind a gaming table in his life. He and I had a previous altercation when I saw him shove a woman out of his way when he was on his way to the pit with some chips from the cage. He lost. After that, no documentation was given to any personnel to be signed. That gives you some idea of how tenuous job security was in those days.

When the Mob was in charge, the people in the eye were mostly qualified individuals, and I never saw any written reports, ever.

179. Dangerous Paranoia

The Dunes hotel had more catwalks and one-way mirrors than any place on the Strip. Major Riddle, the owner, was paranoid, and the whole place could be observed from above. This included the restaurant and cage cashiers, the bartenders, and probably the rest rooms. After Little George the Greek was fired for rubbing his shoulder on the Big Six wheel to prevent a winner, while Gaming Control agents watched, he and his wife would come into the casino every night and sit at the bar. They would always take the two end seats, right in front of the cash register. The bartender would put their checks in a glass, denoting that their drinks were complimentary. They were there every night, all night.

One night the eye-in-the-sky came crashing through the ceiling and landed on top of George. Poor George was taken to the hospital in an ambulance, along with the guy who fell through the ceiling. The next night he was back in the same seat, with a cervical collar around his neck, and he'd filed a suit against the Dunes. They had repaired the ceiling in one day. I don't know the outcome of the suit. It's amazing that more drunks didn't fall off the catwalk onto someone's head.

To some of them, it must have been like walking a tightrope.

Some of the casinos, especially Summa Corporation, used "outside men" to observe the games from the floor. They were known as the "eyes in the rug" or the carpet baggers. They were usually retired dealers or floor men, and I promise you that none carried a Phi Beta Kappa key. They would plant themselves outside the tables and stare so hard they could burn a hole in the felt. If you stopped dealing for a second and looked at them, they would stop and look right into your face, then get pissed off because their cover was blown. They were really easy to spot. The Frontier had two on the night shift, and they rotated nights. One was a little Jewish guy who'd been around town a hundred years, and he would stand there with his arms folded and stare at the dealer instead of watching the game. The look dared the dealer to make a wrong move. Some of the older dealers would look at him and just shake their heads. The other was an Italian gentleman with wavy gray hair cut close to his head, and a huge pinkie ring. He wore his pants around his tits and leaned back so far you would think he would fall backward. It was a comedy, and the whole issue was like a scene from the cuckoo's nest.

The truth of the matter was that most of the scams between dealers and agents or customers were spotted by a person playing on the game and reporting it to a pit boss.

180. In Union There Is Strength

Al Bramlet was the head of the culinary union in Las Vegas, which he ran with an iron fist. If you were to open a restaurant and not sign with the union, you were subjected to fires, bombs and whatever labor delights Al could contrive.

The Alpine Village restaurant was a good example. Just minutes before they were set to open, Bramlet paid a visit to owner Herschel Leverton, and told him that if he didn't sign with the union, he was going to picket the place. Leverton told him to get lost, and the pickets appeared 20 minutes after they opened, remaining for 20 years, along with bombings and fires which caused the restaurant to move several times.

The Culinary Union under Bramlet was as corrupt a union as you could find anywhere, but that's all been documented many times over. Besides having a harem that would put 1001 nights to shame. He could give you the best job in town with a wave of a finger or you could serve drinks in a coffee shop and wind up with sore feet and a few bucks a night. Nobody ever complained twice. Al married more than once, and one of his exes was a young cocktail waitress I'll call Sharon. Sharon was a little on the wild side, and the marriage wasn't destined for longevity. Several years later, a friend and I got off work at 5AM at the Flamingo and stopped for a drink. We were told that Sharon was having a party at her apartment so we decided to go see what was going on. When we got there, the door was open, there were three or four guys drinking in the living room, and Sharon was nude on the kitchen table, taking on anyone who was interested. We decided to get out of there fast. My friend had a gray Corvette, and we had the top down. As we rounded the corner the apartment sat on, here came Sharon, buck naked, waving her arms and hollering for us to stop. It was broad daylight, kids outside, people watering their lawns, not a good place for us to be. We stepped on it and went on our way.

The police were called, and when they got there Sharon climbed a tree and had to be dragged down. While this was going on she was professing, at the top of her lungs, her love for a married shift manager at the Stardust. It was said that she tried to kill herself by lying down in front of a semi on the Strip in front of the Stardust. When the trucker stopped in time she got up and made it to the front door of the hotel before security grabbed her, all the time screaming for her "Georgie" who was inside working.

Al made good choices.

In 1977 Al disappeared for three weeks and everyone assumed he moved in with Russian Louis, however his body was found in the desert, naked, with three bullet holes in his head.

One in the front and one in each ear.

181. Overheard

Two young busboys, standing at the end of the coffee shop counter at the Dunes, were discussing a young pantry girl who worked in the kitchen. I arrived in time to hear, "Yeah, really, you could go out in the car with her during your lunch break, or after work, and she'd do almost everything. She would let you see everything, and you could even touch it if you wanted. It was great She would go out there with anybody." "Can you still do it?" "No, she doesn't work here anymore. Besides, Louis ruined it for everybody. "What did he do?" "He bought her a pizza."

182. The Best Retort

Dunes Hotel, 1963. I went to work at 10AM and, as I was heading to the game I was assigned to, I noticed a player at the end of the table wearing a Texas ten-gallon hat, and his head was hanging down so you couldn't see his face. The outgoing dealer told me, "He's been here all night, over eight hours, and he's drunk. I asked, "Is he awake? The dealer replied, "Yes, he's been awake all night, you just can't see his face." When he finishes his drink he just raises his finger and the waitress brings him another. He tips her a $5 chip for every drink, so she's paying good attention to him."

The man sat in that seat all day long, nobody saw his face because of his hat and the fact he never raised his chin off his chest, kept on drinking, didn't get up to pee and he played liked he was sober, no trouble at all. He never said a word.

I happened to be back on that game around 6PM, when the place started to fill up with people coming in for the show. Two women sat down at the game, ordered some fancy exotic drinks and played $1 a hand. When the drinks arrived, one of the ladies stirred her drink, and her straw had an ice cube sliding up and down on it. She said, "Look Gladys, must be something new, an ice cube with a hole in it." For the first time, the guy with the big hat looked up and said, "That ain't nothing new, lady, I've been married to one for 30 years."

I have to rate that as the best retort I've ever heard.

183. The Sex Kit

Frontier Hotel, 1972, 3AM: My friend and co-worker, Ken Coburn, and I got off work, and decided to have a drink in the casino lounge before we went home. As we were sitting there, here came two ladies of the evening, attractive, well dressed, one carrying a small suitcase, like an attaché case. We invited them to sit with us, and they saw the signed check on the table and knew we could sign for the drinks. It would save them some of their hard-earned money. So down they sat. We drank and chatted longer than we anticipated, and we were getting pretty well fried, when Kenny jokingly asked the girl if the case was for her money. She replied "that's my sex kit, I never leave home without it". We got her to put it on the table and open it. There were the usual sex toys, a few S&M gadgets, which we got a kick out of and, pressed around the perimeter, were two large feathers with quills on the end. They looked like small ostrich feathers.

This was not your usual show-and-tell. The lady told us they had a customer (?) who had some strange requests. One was that as a prerequisite to sex, he had her insert the feathers into his rear end, quills first, of course, and he would run around the room making noises like a chicken while she followed him, hitting him on the ass with a leather strap. Well, we started laughing so hard we were screaming, and I was holding onto the chair for fear of falling out. I guess we were too noisy, as the graveyard shift manager sent security over to tell us to vacate the premises *right now!* When we walked out the door, it was daylight, so we decided to call it a night. I laughed all the way home.

About five hours later, I awoke with a hangover, showered, dressed and went to work. The casino was busy. As I walked into the pit, the cocktail waitress handed me a glass of coffee and said, "You look like you need this."

The first thing an oncoming floor man does is check the tables he's responsible for to make sure there're enough chips on the games. I went to one of the Roulette wheels first, tried to clear my head and took a big sip of coffee. As I brought the glass away from my mouth I glanced down the middle of the pit, and there stood

Kenny Coburn, my partner in crime from the night before. He's about 5-8, with curly blond hair, cut short, and the girls love him. He had his fists against his chest with his elbows sticking out and, with a huge grin was pumping his elbows up and down emulating a chicken. He looked like a little banty rooster. Here came the coffee, out of my nose and mouth and right into the Roulette wheel. It took over 15 minutes to bring a spare wheel to replace the one with the coffee. The customers weren't happy, and the casino manager was plenty pissed. You only had a certain amount of time before people head for the showroom, and I wasted it. I wanted to kill Kenny.

We tried not to look at each other all night.

184. The Pineapple Caper

When the Hawaiian junkets came to the Frontier Hotel, they brought cases of fresh pineapple for the bosses, including the floor men and box-men. It was a custom. As it happened, the previous junket brought a load of pineapples, and by the time some of the big bosses went to get theirs, they were all gone. They complained long and loud. When the next group came in a few months later, the casino manager had a clipboard put up on the door of the bell closet, which was right near the front desk, and it was used to store luggage, uniforms, etc. If you wanted a pineapple, you had to sign for it to make sure you didn't take more than one. All the pit bosses and floor men were highly insulted, and the word was out to boycott the pineapples. The guys were saying, "Shit, you can buy a pineapple for a couple of bucks, and they want us to sign?"

The bell closet was in front of the lobby, and its back wall was the outside of the building. It got godawful hot in there, especially in the summer. Well, the pineapples sat in there and stewed in the heat, and if you haven't smelled rotten pineapples, you're lucky. The smell permeated the whole lobby, and the adjacent casino, and began to trickle into the restaurants. The casino manager kept asking everyone if they got their pineapple, trying to get them out of there, and the stock answer was, "Not if I have to sign for one." They finally threw them out but it literally took weeks before the smell went away.

185. Local Svengali Exposed

It was in the early ‘70s that Las Vegas had its first case of PTSD. A dealer by the name of Carter Danis (Da-Nay) lived in one of the luxury apartments on Sahara Avenue just down from the Strip. He and his girlfriend had been together for a while, and they supposedly were making plans for the future. Carter was a Robert Redford look alike, and he had a way with women; he never lacked for female companionship.

One night his elevator got stuck between floors. It took several hours before they could get someone to fix it. I guess Carter was traumatized, as a few months later he filed a lawsuit against the building’s owners. The premise was that he was so traumatized, that he could no longer get an erection, and he wanted compensation. When the case went to court, his lady love testified that Carter had lost his prime asset, and they could no longer enjoy sex. The defense brought in a string of witnesses, ladies that were seduced by Carter since (after?) the elevator incident, and they were pissed because he loved ‘em and left ‘em. Reading about the suit in the papers they called and volunteered to testify. After about the fourth female witness for the defense (with several more in the wings), the judge threw the case out. It had been in the papers, and everyone was watching for the outcome. Carter’s landlord advised him that his lease wouldn’t be renewed, he lost the suit, and his sweetie left him.

Who was it who said, “Hell hath no fury, etc., etc.?”

One morning at 2AM I was sitting on a stool at an empty Blackjack table at the Desert Inn. When there were no players we were allowed to sit. A fight broke out in the lounge and security had to subdue the instigator and eject him from the casino. He was a large, menacing man. I was sitting just about 20 feet from the front door. A short while later, Sonny Barnett, a pit boss, got off work and headed for the front door with his newspaper under his arm. He said goodnight to me, and out of nowhere the man they ejected appeared and put a gun to Sonny’s head. Sonny was one of the few survivors of the infamous Bataan Death March, and his face turned the color of his teeth. The guy turned him around and marched him out the front door. Bob Bergin, another pit boss was walking through the pit when he saw the gun, and said, "Uh oh," and turned around and went back to the other end of the pit. Bergin was billed as "the world's oldest living pit boss." he was actually a veteran of WWI.

Then Sonny came back into the casino and told Security that this guy had grabbed a hostage and had him in his car with the gun to his head. He told Sonny that if they didn't send the guy that he had been fighting with outside in ten minutes, he was going to kill the hostage. Meanwhile security had called the sheriff's department, and then we heard the squeal of brakes outside the door and several gunshots. I came out of the stool and hit the floor, those walls weren't very thick. It was over in minutes. The deputy, our future sheriff, and his partner went to both sides of the car, the little guy who was the hostage dove out the door and they shot this guy five times in the torso, and three times in the head and neck. He survived. He was an accountant by the name of James Vincent Carter.

The Las Vegas sheriff's department didn't fool around.

186. Credentials

Read an interesting article in the Seattle newspaper not too long ago. It seems that a local gaming genius was applying for a license to open one of the small neighborhood casinos popping up all over the area. Asked what he intended to do about problem gambling (a really stupid question), he replied, "If the friends or family of the individual with the problem contacted me, I wouldn't let him into my establishment."

If you believe that, then you are personally acquainted with the tooth fairy, and Santa Claus. If he operated a neighborhood casino, he would make his living off these so-called problem gamblers, who would only go to another neighborhood casino and lose their money. Gambling is a disease or, if you will, an addiction, no less lethal than any type of drug, I don't care what it is. Meth addicts lose their teeth, gambling addicts wouldn't spend money on a dentist, so the end result is the same. Heroin addicts sometimes die of an overdose. Nevada for a long time had the highest suicide rate in the nation though, since gambling went nationwide, its lead in that category has been substantially narrowed.

Before legislation was passed to permit this "limited" neighborhood gambling, I wrote to the state senator sponsoring the bill, stated my credentials, and told her that, if passed, it would open a Pandora's Box that could never be closed. She called me, and we discussed the issue. They passed it, and the casinos are sucking the lifeblood out of the communities they're located in. Unlike Las Vegas, which is a reasonably affluent tourist area, these casinos, for the most part were in blue collar, or working-class neighborhoods, where the population was heavily immigrants from Asia, the Pacific islands, and other venues. These people are highly susceptible to the lure of gambling and make up a large segment of the clientele of these establishments. These are definitely not destination resorts. Hence the failure of small businesses, the increase in crime, divorces, domestic violence and everything that goes with poverty.

When Las Vegas was the only game in the country, people could go home, lick their wounds, save some money and come back for another fix. Now, there's nowhere to hide. According to statistics recently published, when a casino opened in a new area, over the ensuing two years suicides increased by 213 percent.

187. Local Loan Sharks

There were several shylocks, or “shys,” who hung out on the Strip and downtown on Fremont Street. In plain speak, a “shy” is a loan shark bankrolled by Mob money from the East. They were always available for a loan, and you had to pay five percent interest on the loan *weekly* until you paid it off. And believe me, you paid.

A favorite shy was Jasper Speciale, who owned a restaurant out on the Strip called the Tower of Pizza. Jasper was a well-mannered, classy guy who had a lot of money on the street. But like anyone else, if you owed, you paid, and he didn’t like to have to go looking for someone. The Tower of Pizza and the Loan Sharking business changed hands when Jasper went to jail on a racketeering charge. Tony “the Ant” Spilotro took it over. If you want to see how “the Ant” wound up, you can see it online. It’s not pretty. After Tony took over, some of the collecting fell to some pretty mean guys. A Craps dealer by the name of Joe Caprio owed quite a bit of money and was having trouble paying the weekly interest, he was a player and was always broke. When things got bad, he left town, supposedly home to New Jersey. We heard later that he “committed suicide.”

That kind of news made payers out of owers.

188. My Credentials

Before we go further, let me offer my credentials so I can speak with authority on the subject. First, I'm not an anti-gambling crusader. I earned my living and raised and educated my family in the gambling business. Second, my father provided us with a good living, which he earned in the business. He opened the Desert Inn in 1950 as a casino exec and was considered a "pioneer" in the Las Vegas gaming industry. We as a family owe a lot to the industry. I owe a lot to what I learned from my father.

From the day I turned 21 I worked in gaming, spending 40 years of my working life in Las Vegas Casinos. I learned to deal all the games and did so for 12 years. Then I worked as a floor man, pit boss, casino shift manager, Baccarat shift manager, and casino manager. I had an interest in and ran the gaming in a small off-Strip hotel, casino and truck stop for over ten years. During two of those years I managed two different off Strip casinos. One is now owned by Station Casinos. I believe it's called "The Wild, Wild West."

I finished my career as a casino shift manager with Station Casinos. More than 25 years of my career were in positions approved to issue credit and tend to credit matters. Therefore, I dealt with "problem gamers" and "gaming addicts" on a daily basis. There is nothing I haven't heard or encountered. And foremost, I myself had a gambling problem for over 12 years.

After 12 years earning an excellent living, being single with minimal expenses, I wound up broke. I drove a nice car, had a boat (which I hocked several times to get money to gamble with) but couldn't put $200 together if I had to. So, the icing on this cake is the fact that I know how a player thinks. That puts me ahead of all the psychologists and experts who pontificate on the subject. I was there myself, I am an expert. Anyone who thinks they're more qualified than me to discuss these matters better offer some very strong evidence. That being said, let's continue into some case histories that will give you an idea of what the results of this illness can bring.

They come from all walks of life, professional and working class.

189. Art Schlichter

Scott MacGregor, in a July 2000 article in the Cincinnati Enquirer, said, “This is where gambling addiction will take a man. He will steal from anyone, even his family. He will trash a promising professional football career and waste a powerful charisma.”

He was referring to Art Schlichter who, coming out of high school, was sought by every major college in the country. He opted for Ohio State where he immediately became their starting quarterback and was first team All-America two years in a row. He took an unbeaten team to the Rose Bowl, where they lost to Southern Cal by one point. Supposedly, he was a shoo-in for the Heisman trophy, but some rumors and some of his associations were made public, and he wound up in the top five, not number one. In a college biography he was referred to as “Straight Arrow.”

He was selected No. 1 in the 1982 NFL draft by the Baltimore Colts, who later moved to Indianapolis. He received a $350,000 signing bonus and a lucrative contract. This is where his gambling addiction caught up with him. An old, wise gamer once told me there was “a paddle for everybody’s ass.” Some people need the table games, some the slots, some are addicted to the ponies, Schlichter’s paddle was sports betting, not a good selection from his perspective.

He lost the $350,000 signing bonus halfway through his rookie season. Rumors flew, he wasn’t performing to expectations, and some bookies threatened to expose him if he didn’t pay up. The NFL suspended him for 18 months. He had gone to the FBI for protection from the threats, and everything came out. He was reinstated to the team, but when it was learned that he gambled while on suspension he was barred forever. As a result, he lost his family, stole cash and credit cards from his father, said to be over $40,000, and his career was history. His father later committed suicide. He spent a large segment of his adult life in prison, all related to gambling and was just recently sentenced to ten years in prison for a ticket scam. Previous convictions included bank fraud, tax evasion, and a plethora of other felonies

At one time he lived in Las Vegas, which was like an open cookie jar to him. Any form of gambling was available on a 24-hour basis; all he had to do was cash bad checks, steal from friends and relatives and con people out of their money so he could stay in action. Every casino in town knew Schlichter and he couldn't cash any checks or get credit.

On opening night at the Boulder Station, I was the shift manager on the night shift. At around 3AM here comes Schlichter, saying, "I'm Art Schlichter, I played quarterback for Baltimore, and I really like this place. I think I'll start doing my gambling here." He forgot that he tried the same thing with me at the Palace Station and got nowhere. He figured that I would do anything to get a famous athlete for a customer. He said, "I have some checks here that you can cash for me, and I'll do some gambling." "These checks are good, no problem."

Of course, it was a Saturday night, and all the banks were closed. No way to verify the checks, and I don't think he ever cashed a legitimate check in his life. I turned him down, and then went to the cashier's cage and told them to pull his card from Central Credit, and, put on it in bold letters "DO NOT CASH UNDER ANY CIRCUMSTANCES, per me. He came in several hours later and approached the graveyard shift manager, (it was his first time in that position) and gave him the same spiel he gave me. The shift manager, guy by the name of Joe Stenger, walked Schlichter over to the cashier's cage and when he read my directive on the card he said "It's my shift now, and I'm going to override this. Go ahead and cash these checks." As expected, the checks were phony, and they bounced.

He's lucky it was only $5000.

Pete Rose was banned for life from major league baseball for gambling. He bet on some games his team was playing. The ban will keep him out of the Baseball Hall of Fame, where he really should be, if not for his indiscretions. He thinks he was treated unfairly, yet he disgraced the game that made him famous.

Sports betting was his paddle.

190. The Medical Professionals

Medical professionals who gamble may not only jeopardize their career and reputation, but also their patients.

An anesthesiologist from a hospital near the Palace Station had it bad. I had seen him many times, pounding the table and talking to himself when he was losing. He was almost a daily player, I didn't know what he did for a living until someone told me. Then, on more than on occasion, he would come flying in the front door in his green scrubs, replete with the shoe coverings and hat, rush over to a Blackjack table and start betting hundreds. He never sat down, and when he lost he would bang on the table and yell profanities. Then he would look at his watch, turn around and run out the door, most likely to assist in a surgery, where a miscalculation in anesthesia could result in disaster. We used to comment on what it would be like to be awaiting surgery and have him come in and introduce himself.

I would get up and run out the door.

There is (or was) a husband and wife team of psychologists who played Blackjack frequently in the Palace Station and other casinos. They had a credit line and if one were to come in alone and use some of that credit, the arguments nearly came to violence. They played all the time, and how they stayed solvent was beyond me. One late night at the Palace Station she got up and literally ran to the ladies' room. She came back in a hurry, lest she miss something, but this time there was a trail of toilet paper starting under her dress and going back all the way to the ladies' room. I had one of the female floor persons go and whisper in her ear. She reached behind her and tore it off under her skirt and jumped back onto the stool. The trail sat there until we had a porter remove it. Incredibly their specialty was counseling people with gambling problems. Several of their clients were dealers at the Palace Station and on occasion, would deal to them. They were of Asian descent, Filipino, I believe, and they had hundreds of Asian clients. This was not an isolated event in Las Vegas.

Years back, a young promising ophthalmologist and eye surgeon, Dr. Gingrich, started a practice with a Dr. Shepherd, who eventually opened several eye clinics in Las Vegas. The clinics are still in operation today. My wife was one of his patients, Dr. Gingrich was married with young children, and had a brilliant future in front of him. However, he had a gambling "problem." Without anyone realizing it he went deeply into debt, and finally the distress and pressure were too much. He committed suicide.

An OB-GYN played in the Sands Baccarat on a constant basis. His license plate read STORK. He would sit and play $25 and $50 a hand until his beeper sounded. Then he'd jump up and rush out to bring another customer into the world. He was subsequently disciplined by the medical board and lost his license on a temporary basis and couldn't perform any medical procedure without another doctor standing by. He was eventually forced into retirement.

191. School Days

I received a call from the cashier's cage at the Palace Station. A woman wanted to talk to me. I walked over to the cage and met with a woman I would take to be in her 40's, well dressed and obviously in distress. She was a principal at a local elementary school and had just cashed a check for $200 then lost the money playing the slots. She begged me to have them hold the check for 30 days before depositing it. I went to the cashier's cage to look at her card and saw there were three cards, filled out front and back then stapled together. This is indication of a lot of transactions. In several places on the cards were notations in red stating, "Cash no more checks, per customer request." This is the sign of a person with a gambling problem. Underneath each of the "Do not cash" entries, were the words, "I wish to reopen my check cashing privileges as of (date), and her signature. Then there would a series of cashed checks until the next "Please do not cash anymore checks" notation. This is a cry for help, but as long as a person rescinds the request, and the checks clear. They'll keep cashing.

She said to me, "If you deposit that check, I'll lose my family and maybe my job." Then she burst into tears. I told her that we would hold the check for 30 days, if she didn't come in and redeem it, we would put it in for deposit. When she heard the word "deposit" she started crying again. I had the cashier's look up her record with credit central and found that she had checks on hold in several local casinos. I had toyed with the idea of shutting her check cashing privileges off permanently until I saw that she owed in several other places.

As long as we weren't the only place she gambled, to try to help her was an exercise in futility.

192. Those It Hurt the Most

Senior citizens often fell victim to the gambling bug. The El Cortez Hotel, located downtown away from the main clubs, had a special promotion. Every week they had "Social Security Night" where you could cash your social security or welfare check, get a coupon for a free drink, and have a stub put in a large bowl. Then, a few hours later they would have a drawing where check cashers could win cash prizes up to double the amount of their check. The wait before the drawing got a lot of the old folks to the games and the slots. They even had penny slot machines, which at the time were single-coin machines and they were always occupied. The jackpot was, I believe, three dollars. Any transient in the area who happened to find a "lucky penny" in the street would put it into those machines.

This promo, more than anything, got a lot of seniors in trouble.

193. The Businessmen

Directly across Fremont from the El Cortez was the Outdoorsman, the only sporting goods store in town. There were two partners, George Knipp and Ralph Wilson. George was in his late '70s at the time and had a problem. It was called Roulette. One afternoon I needed some fishing line, and when I went to the store there was a sign on the door that said, "Be back shortly." The door was ajar and I walked in. There was an area in the back of the shop with some old chairs and a couch around a wood stove. I called out, but there was nobody home. They not only sold fishing equipment, but they had guns and ammunition on the racks. I couldn't believe they would leave the place unattended.

I walked out and closed the door. In small print on the bottom of the "Back shortly" sign it said, "If you need service now, I'm across the street." I crossed the street and walked into the El Cortez, here was George sitting at the Roulette Wheel smoking a cigar. When I told him that I needed some line he acted annoyed. When I told him the door to the store wasn't locked, he *really* got annoyed. His partner finally got out of the business and started his own store. He told me "that old fart" didn't want to do anything but play the wheel, and some days he found out that if he (Ralph) wasn't there, the place wasn't even open.

I wonder what would happen if you left a place like that unattended in these times.

194. Not Our Problem

There was a young dealer at the Frontier in the early ‘70s who quit to go into the construction business. He shook my hand, and I wished him luck. Eight years later he came into the casino I was managing and asked me not to cash any more company checks for his partner. When I looked into it, his partner proved to be one of our best customers who would come in almost weekly with large company checks made out to himself, usually between three and six thousand dollars. We always made sure the checks would clear before we would cash. He would come in, cash the checks, and get so drunk he would be almost incoherent, and invariably lose the money. I told this young man that we made our living from people like his partner, and I had no intention of turning the checks down. He would only go somewhere else and do the same thing. It was something they would have to work out themselves. He told me that if it continued to go that way, they would be out of business. All I could say was, “I’m sorry.” His partner continued to come in.

I don’t know how it ended.

195. Keep the Faith, Baby

Men of the cloth were not exempt. In 2006, a widow whose husband had left her $350,000 in cash approached priest William Kenny, whom she loved and trusted implicitly, to manage her financial affairs, pay her bills and take care of all financial matters. She gave him access to her bank account, and authority to write checks to see to her finances. She volunteered regularly at his church and, to her, Father Bill could do no wrong.

She didn't know that Father Bill had a gambling problem. He was addicted to Blackjack. It wasn't long before he came to her and confessed to losing all her money, leaving her practically penniless. It all came to light when relatives came to Las Vegas and told Father Bill they would take over her finances in order to take care of her. She was in her late eighties at the time and suffering from acute dementia. It was against the law for a priest to handle a parishioner's money without the bishop's permission. Kenny didn't bother to ask. The family sued after promises by Kenny to repay the funds didn't materialize. Had she not declined to press charges if the money was repaid, Kenny would have been off to the slammer. As it happened, a wealthy parishioner bailed him out, paid off the debt plus, I'm sure, attorney fees and some hush money on the premise that the records would be sealed. Shortly after, Father Bill was reinstated by the bishop, who undoubtedly was offered an "incentive" in the way of a large donation to do so. Today, Father Bill holds a prominent position in the church.

This is not an isolated incident. In 2012, Father Robert Petekiewicz resigned from Our Lady of Las Vegas Church over allegations of financial misdealings after a lawsuit filed by three employees of the church, including the bookkeeper who claimed they were fired when they tried to bring the misdealings to light. Any time they can't explain where the money went you can assume it was gambled away.

There were numerous occasions where men of the cloth would come to Las Vegas and whoop it up. We had a player in the Baccarat at the Sands who got chummy with one of the dealers dealing a little cocaine on the side to pay for his own addiction. I saw them conversing in the lobby on more than one occasion, and once saw him heading for the rooms with a lady of the evening.

When I asked the dealer what this guy did for a living, as he was a good player, the dealer told me he was a priest.

196. No Discrimination

The Las Vegas influence could affect those in high religious standing without relating to gambling. For instance, Rabbi Aaron Gold, head of Temple Beth Sholom, got into some shady real estate deals with several local businessmen, one being the head of the Temple Hebrew School, Abe Schwartz.

They were invested in several properties, one of which was a run-down motel in North Las Vegas where street-walking prostitutes would take their "johns" for a quickie, and addicts would rent rooms, to use as "shooting galleries" (places to cook and inject heroin). Several articles were written in the paper, and Abe Schwartz was found in the desert with a bullet in his head.

Not the least bit embarrassed, Rabbi Gold entered into an affair with a Baccarat shill at the Sands. Her notoriety came when she severed her relationship with a Sands shift manager, took a scissors and cut all his expensive ties in half. Anyway, the Rabbi's wife took the kids, left town and divorced him. Still, he continued to lead his flock, supposedly mouthing, "I love you" to his sweetie, sitting in the front row at services (She wasn't even Jewish). One Friday night during services, Abe Schwartz's wife walked down the aisle and said to the Rabbi, so everyone could hear, "You are a murderer, you killed my husband."

These are people who counsel others on human weakness.

197. Imagine Yourself in His Place

Fred Hardy started out in the business as a dealer. Unlike most of his peers, he was a frugal guy, scrimped and saved every nickel he could. After years of saving and sacrificing he managed to accumulate quite a bit of money, in cash, in a safety deposit box.

At that time dealers were not in full compliance with the tax codes and didn't want any excess cash to be visible. It was a joke within the business that some guys had it buried in coffee cans in their backyard, though it wouldn't surprise me.

When Fred was dealing at the Frontier, he called in sick one night. The next night he told us his wife went to the Showboat Hotel for the early bingo session and bought $20 worth of bingo cards. She didn't win a thing, and on her way out the door she made a $20 bet on the Blackjack table to try to get her $20 back. She lost. She then proceeded to chase her $40 with everything she had in her purse. When she ran out of money she went to the bank and raided the box. When the smoke cleared, she came home about the time he got off work and informed him that she had lost everything he had worked for, all those years.

He was in shock and couldn't work for a few nights, then back he came to stand behind a table in a noisy, smoke filled casino, for $22 dollars a day and tips. But now he was broke, and, had no other options. He said that it was close to $100,000. It's impossible to imagine how he felt.

In some cases, it was grounds for suicide.

198. Airsick Bag

Mel "Red" Greb was a Craps dealer and a boxing promoter. He promoted several second-rate fight cards in Las Vegas, in places like the Silver Slipper and the Showboat. Mel was also a degenerate Craps player. He came into the Dunes one day as I was standing on an empty Roulette wheel. He stopped by to say hello and I asked if he was going to shoot a little Craps. He told me he doesn't gamble anymore, that he had been seeing a hypnotist who, after several sessions, had convinced him that whenever he thinks about shooting dice he would get deathly sick to his stomach. He said that it felt great to always have money in his pocket. A few weeks later I came off of a break and, as I walked into the pit, I heard retching sounds coming from the dice pit. There was Mel, standing at the Craps table, throwing the dice with his face in an airsick bag. They told him he could do it if he was the only player on the table, if another player came over, he'd have to quit, because the noise and the smell was disgusting.

I guess he got himself de-hypnotized as I saw him many times later doing what he did best, with no obvious physical effects

199. An Honest Politician

Right here in Washington State, the head of the Democratic Party financial apparatus was caught embezzling a substantial amount of money and was forced to resign. He acknowledged that he had a gambling problem.

Las Vegas was rife with similar stories. Where a guy stands in a casino with smoke coming out of his shoes while his wife is out gambling, if not that instance, he goes out and loses his paycheck. I know of one incident where a friend of my wife's parents died and left her a paid-for house. Her husband was a Craps dealer with a Video Poker problem. The end result was that the house wound up fully mortgaged and was consequently repossessed by the bank. They divorced and went their separate ways.

It was a nice house, too.

Then, there were the countless wives and mothers who would go into a market to buy the family groceries. All had slots and Video Poker at their entrance. Many of these women never got past the machines. Credit cards were not in fashion at the time, and someone who decided to risk a few dollars wound up without groceries. At this point they would frantically search for a place to borrow money. Some lost track of time and would sit for hours and not make it home for dinner.

If I were to recount all the stories and heartbreak I'd seen through the years, this book would never end. People I knew would win huge amounts of money, and wouldn't pay off a car or the mortgage, and lose back every cent. Legal gambling provides revenue and taxes, and in the case of tribal casinos it's been a saving grace.

You never hear of the downside and the human cost. But you're hearing about it in these pages.

200. The Upper Class

Celebrities and the wealthy are not immune to the disease. A recent article in the AARP Bulletin dealt with problem gambling. They offered a few examples. Actor Ben Affleck checked himself into a $34,000 a month rehab center in Malibu for gambling and alcohol addiction. Charles Barkley, the former NBA star, lost $2.5 million in six hours at the Blackjack tables and figured his total losses to be in excess of $10 million. A man the New York Times described as a "relentless moral crusader" in 2003, acknowledged losses of at least $8 million. His name is William Bennett. Golfer John Daly claims to have lost $50 million in a 12-year period. Gladys Knight, the "Empress of Soul" would lose $40,000 a night playing Baccarat. She sought help from Gamblers Anonymous and kicked the habit. Movie Star Omar Sharif spent most of his career in heavy debt because of his addiction. One Terry Watanabe, a wealthy businessman from Omaha confessed to losing $205 million over time in Las Vegas. It was rumored that Milton Berle had an expensive weakness for the horses.

201. Her Honor, The Mayor

Maureen O'Connor was the mayor of San Diego. She was heiress to a huge fortune (over $50 million) left to her by her husband who founded the Jack in The Box fast food chain. She lived in a waterfront mansion in La Jolla, California, a high rent district even in Southern California.

She caught the Video Poker disease and wound up living with her sister. Casinos in Las Vegas would send private jets to pick her up and fly her to the resort. When she ran out of cash she took several million from a charitable foundation her husband had set up, and it had to be shut down. She was prosecuted but did no jail time. The accounts are endless. My father once told me that there was "no bottom" to the drop boxes on the tables, and "no limit" to what a machine can absorb. I've seen it to be true many times over. A lot of Las Vegas residents who made a good living for years and years, wound up old and broke.

Not a good place to be.

202. Rank Has Its Privileges

A newspaper article brought to light the story of a U.S. Navy Vice (three-star) Admiral caught counterfeiting $500 Poker chips at the Horseshoe Casino in Council Bluffs, Iowa. Three stars, in both the Navy and the Army means there are only two ranks above you.

This particular Vice Admiral, Timothy Giardina, happened to be the No. 2 commander in the Strategic Nuclear Command. At this lofty position he was privy to highly classified and top-secret information dealing with U.S. nuclear strategy.

At first, he denied altering $1 chips with counterfeit insert stickers to make them look like $500 chips. He claimed to have bought them in the men's room, then claimed he found them in the same men's room. The men's bathroom is the number one alibi in many a casino scam.

When investigators found his DNA on the *bottom* (sticky side) of one of the phony inserts, they started looking into his gambling habit. Further investigation showed he'd spent 1,096 hours at the Poker tables, or an average of 15 hours a week for the 18 months prior to his being caught. That was just at the Poker table. I'm sure he had other gaming related diseases such as Blackjack and other table games. He was known as 'Navy Tim" in the casinos in the area and was also seen on surveillance Video from the casino taking cigarette butts out of public ashtrays and smoking them.

A Vice Admiral's salary would enable him to purchase all the cigarettes he could smoke. Could this be an indicator of financial problems? The implications are serious. Would a person with a gaming habit sell U.S. nuclear secrets for the right price? Could he be blackmailed or compromised? The answer is, he's human; consider the possibilities.

Even after he was caught, he continued to gamble at the local casinos, and finally was banned from gambling at Harrah's and the Horseshoe for 90 days. True to form he returned several times to play before the ban was up. As a result, he was banned from any Caesar's Corporation casino for life. Less than a week later he was kicked out of the Hollywood Casino in Kansas City, Kansas. No reason was given for the expulsion. Remember, a player will do anything for money to gamble with, just like a junkie without dope. His gambling days are not over. The Navy covered up as much as they could, and the press used the freedom of information act to get the little information they were privy to. The Navy decided not to hold a Court Martial as they say they weren't sure of a conviction. A court martial would be public and the Navy didn't need that. In the end, they charged him with conduct unbecoming an officer, demoted him to a two-star Admiral (poor guy), and a loss of $4000 in pay. They also moved him to a desk job. He was never charged with counterfeiting (he could have been prosecuted at the state level) and clamped down hard on anything else about the case. I would like to wager that the Navy and the FBI now have to subject him to constant surveillance.

Some governments or clandestine groups would pay a ton of money for the information he possesses.

203. Enter the Suits

Nothing good lasts forever. The gambling business started to change into a corporate atmosphere. It was inevitable. Had Howard Hughes not bought those hotels and opened the door for other big corporations, eventually the government would have taxed them out of existence.

The Mob, of course, was happy to sell as the heat was becoming unbearable, and they already had more than they ever thought they would; it was time to move on. Everything had become so big that the Mob wasn't prepared to manage under those circumstances. It was too much for them. Fresh young faces began to appear, and for some reason, college degrees became a requirement to obtain an upper level management position. The University of Nevada had a course on casino management taught by a guy who never ran a casino. The young Turks attempted again and again to reinvent the wheel. They did some ridiculous things.

For people like me who started out in the Mob-run casinos (and they did know how to run a casino) moving into the corporate era, was a difficult transition. When you get older your body and mind start sending you different messages.

A good example of this happened one night at the Boulder Station. A gentleman asked the assistant shift manager for a comp in the steak house, the most expensive restaurant in the place. She explained that his play didn't warrant it, but he'd be welcome to the buffet or the coffee shop. He asked her who was in charge, and she gladly pointed me out. He was a big man and made an effort to be intimidating. He put his hands on his hips, leaned over and said to me, "You're nothing but a fucking flunkey, do you know that?" Those were his first words. He also gave me the amoeba look, and I knew I was dealing with a local. I replied, "You're absolutely right about that, sir." I'd arrived at the point where I didn't care what they called me. His next statement was, "I know your boss and I can have your ass." I said, "That wouldn't surprise me in the least."

After I reiterated the invitation to the buffet or coffee shop, he really let loose. I became "a monkey on a string" and a few other choice epithets, and a crowd began to gather. Security inched in and stood at the ready. I let him rave on until I noticed that the dealers were starting to turn, and players on the tables were starting to watch. Now he was disruptive. I pointed my finger in his face and told him that if he said one more word, just one, or even made a sound, I was going to have Security take him downstairs, photograph him and read him the trespass act, and he would never be able to go into a Station Casino again. The penalty for doing so was jail. His face puffed up like a red balloon, and I reiterated, "Not one sound." and told him to leave quietly. His wife came over, put her arm in his, and said, "Let's go." He hesitated for a second, then walked out the front door.

As I walked away, my beeper started to vibrate, and I knew I had a repeat performance coming up somewhere in the hotel. Then I heard a small voice behind me saying, "That was wonderful." I kept walking, and here it came again. I turned around and here was a young woman in her early '20s standing there. She said, "You look tough" and all I could say was, "I look tough?" She introduced herself and told me she was looking forward to having me in her seminar next week. Those corporate seminars, especially the motivational ones, could turn your stomach. When I asked her what seminar she was referring to, she said, "It's on how to deal with difficult customers." I thought at first, she was joking. I said, "You're going to tell *me* how to deal with difficult customers?"

Her reply was that it was a mandatory seminar and all senior casino execs were required to attend. I just kept walking and didn't make the seminar. I never heard anything about it but I knew that the end of my career was imminent. The younger up-and-comers, who didn't realize they were alive, really ate that stuff up. Rah, rah yay team. All this taught by people who never spent one day in a casino. So it goes.

I might add that a short while after the above incident, a woman came over to me and said, "I thought you would like to know that I play at Sam's Town and the Showboat (both major local casinos) and that guy has been thrown out of both of them and told not to come back.

He was running out of places to gamble.

204. The Original MGM Grand

The original MGM Grand Hotel was hiring for its opening, employing a hiring process that was the most demeaning practice I had ever seen in all my years in business. The original hotel opened in 1973. It was about that time that things in the corporate world began to change. Not only in Las Vegas, but the whole country. There were no more employees, they'd become "associates" and supervisors and bosses were "team leaders." Motivational speakers were coming into vogue, and the younger set, were becoming believers. I recall calling my bank's account manager of my IRA in regard to a transaction. He had been with the bank for 20 years and held a decent position. When I asked a question that he wasn't sure of, he told me he would talk to his team leader and get back to me. It was the first time I had heard the expression. When I said, "Team leader?" he replied, in a sad tone, "That's what it's coming to." It hadn't come that far in the gaming industry yet, but it wasn't far off.

Case in point, the MGM Grand. The personnel department, aka "Human Resources," was hired by corporate headquarters in California. These young people didn't realize that, when hiring in Las Vegas, you're dealing with a different breed of cat. They decided that instead of employees, they were going to hire "cast members" and one of the requirements at an interview was that you had to sing a song, act out a movie scene or do a little dance. They called themselves "talent scouts."

It was hard to imagine a grizzled old box-man, pit boss, or dealer doing a sophisticated soft shoe or tap dance in front of people who looked like teenagers to them. More than one of them said it was so humiliating they just walked out. Not only did it keep people who needed the work away, but it cost the organization good experienced help, which was hard to find, especially for a place that would have the biggest casino in town. But it was good for the other hotels; they wouldn't be losing some of their employees to the new hotel. When upper level casino management got wind of it, they appealed to the main headquarters, but to no avail. Finally, they agreed that the practice could continue, though it exempted casino personnel.

Entertainers and Celebrities

205. Frank Sinatra and Ava Gardner

It was summertime in Las Vegas. I was stretched out on a towel on the grass at the Desert Inn swimming pool. The scent of sun tan lotion was in the air; the piped in music sounded tinny and distant. The hot sun bore down without mercy, and the thump of bare feet on the diving board was followed by a loud rattle as the diver became airborne. Seconds later there was a splash and by the reaction of the poolside spectators I knew that the diver was the lifeguard, Jerry Tenney, a onetime Olympic hopeful. He put on several exhibitions every day, and it was part of the Desert Inn experience. Jerry wasn't real tall, but had a great body, a head of blond tousled hair, a Coppertone tan and a gleaming smile. This made him a target for 99 percent of the women who visited the hotel. It was said that he did a lot of diving in and out of the rooms in the hotel.

But I digress.

Breaking through my teenage stupor was the sound of angry voices, seemingly trying to keep it quiet, but they were only 15 feet from me and they got louder and angrier. I opened my eyes and glanced up in time to see Ava Gardner jump up from her lounge and empty a drink into the hair and face of Frank Sinatra. She then half ran towards the hotel, while he sat there with a perplexed look on his face. He got up, jumped in the pool to wash off the pineapple juice and whatever else was in the drink, then followed her. The year was 1951, and he was the headliner in the showroom. I was 15 years old. The only thing I knew about Frank Sinatra was that I had two cousins in Cleveland who would run to the radio when he was singing and sit there and swoon.

I could tell by the chatter around the pool that I wasn't the only person who'd witnessed the event. Since there was no television, there was a blurb about it in the paper the next day. Besides the actual throwing of the drink, the only thing I remember was her ass wiggling in a one-piece black bathing suit heading for the hotel. Another match made in heaven.

Through the years, I had occasion to interact with some of the celebrities on a professional level and, since this was one of the most frequently asked questions during my years in the business, I will relate some of the things that stand out in my memory Since the queries usually fell in the category of what they were like, how they acted, etc., I will try to categorize, beginning with the ones I disliked the most. Please bear in mind that in casino work you are viewing and interacting with people at their worst, either drunk, losing their money, or both.

This combo does not produce happy campers.

206. John Berardino; The Worst of the Worst

John Berardino was an ex-major league baseball player before he made a name for himself in films and television. As a kid, I remember him playing for the Cleveland Indians in 1948, the year they won the World Series. He was an infielder, and was described as good field, no hit. (today he probably would have been a superstar). The last team he played for was the Pittsburgh Pirates, who released him in 1952. On to Hollywood and bit roles in movies until he became a TV star as Dr. Steve Hardy in "General Hospital" A soap that lasted 33 years, and only ended when he became ill. He obviously was a man of many talents.

He was also the most miserable, obnoxious sonofabitch I ever dealt with in Las Vegas. He would have been a strong candidate for the biggest prick in town award except that he wasn't a local, so that disqualified him. There were occasions when, at a blackjack table, the pit boss would offer to take the dealer off the game after a short time, as the abuse was nearly unbearable. The level of abuse tolerated from a player was commensurate with the amount of money he was playing.

John was a decent customer with a $5000 credit line, which entitled him to a higher level of tolerance. But he was brutal. One night at the Frontier He was in rare form, having lost his credit line, and demanding more money. I was a floor man at the time, and quietly explained to him that I didn't have the authority to approve credit. He accused me of lying to him, and then added, "If I don't get more money, I won't pay what I owe." Being fed up with his antics over the past hours, I replied, "You'll pay." That was a mistake, as he jumped up and let out a yell, "Are you threatening me?" Which made every head in the place turn and look I felt like a fool. I then told him that the only person who could approve credit was the credit manager, one Milton Frank. Milton Frank was a little guy, who's main endeavor was to keep a low profile and do as little as possible. He was famous for wearing brightly colored suits, and on this night was decked out in bright yellow. He looked like a little Tweety Bird.

Berardino headed off to find tweety, and finally got him to emerge from his office. He cornered little Milton and bullied him into raising his credit line. You could hear the shouting all the way from the cashier's cage. He then returned to the table, took a marker, and started his shenanigans all over again. Milton came up to me, white as a sheet and sweaty, and said, "Young man, you undoubtedly have a great future in this business, but you have to learn not to give out confidential information." When I asked him what confidential information I had disclosed, he replied, "My name"

John Berardino might have been a great guy sober but, in Las Vegas, he was despised.

207. William Talman; The Prosecutor

William Talman was an actor who had a varied and highly successful career. He was best known as the prosecutor on the "Perry Mason" TV show, and for his roles as a deranged killer and bad guy in some Hollywood productions. He started on the show in 1957, and in 1960 was arrested in a raid at a private home where marijuana was present and everyone in attendance forgot to put their clothes on. As a result, he was fired from the show. A deluge of viewer mail in his support led to his reinstatement months later and he stayed with the show until it went off the air in 1966. Nothing ever came of the arrest.

Mr. Talman was a highly talented individual, but his demeanor in a casino was atrocious. On New Year's Eve of 1960 I was dealing roulette at the Flamingo and he was one of the players on the table. I had come to work at 10AM and it was now 2AM; I'd been there 16 hours with at least another three to go.

The commotion and the noise from Harry James and his big band had me groggy, Mr. Talman was drunk and out of line. He purposely hesitated to put his bets down and then accused me of not giving him enough time to do so. Finally, I told him that I would wait until he said okay before I would spin the ball, drawing protests from the other players who wanted faster action. And all this time he was calling me a "fucking monkey" and other choice epithets. I ignored him. Chester Simms, the casino manager, happened to be in the pit and I was unaware that he was standing directly behind me. I spun the ball and Talman purposely waited until the ball was ready to fall, and then tried to put another bet down, but it was too late, I handed his chips back to him. He leaped up, causing the stool to fall over, leaned toward me and screamed, "You do that again and I'll slap your goddamn face."

That did it for me, I leaned over to say, "Here it is, go ahead." Had he done it, I was going to go around and knock him on his ass. As soon as I started to react I felt a hand grip my arm and heard Chester's booming voice telling me, "Say nothing."

Chester was an intimidating presence, and he told Talman that if he didn't behave, they would ask him to leave the table. He said he could gamble anywhere, and Chester walked out of the pit. They moved me to a different wheel and I was able to stay reasonably calm the rest of the night. I didn't see Talman the following night. There's no doubt in my mind that I would have lost my job, but after 16 hours I didn't care.

To his credit, when he was diagnosed with terminal lung cancer, he did a video on the dangers of smoking cigarettes and used himself as an example. The videos aired until he died in 1968. One of them is still viewable on the Internet.

208. Jerry Vale; Tighter Than Two Coats of Paint

Jerry Vale was a famous singer loved by the Italians. But he was a mooch. At the Frontier Hotel he would appear at the roulette wheel before, during and sometimes after the show. He would stand there and watch until somebody recognized him and they would invariably ask him if he was going to play. He would reply that he was broke or didn't have any chips and somebody would throw him a couple of 25-cent chips, just to be able to say they gambled with Jerry Vale. Then he would bet the chips and if he won he would make another bet or two and leave.

He never offered to pay the chips back. Should he lose, he would stand there with a smile on his face, hoping someone would throw him another chip or two. Anyone else doing that would be escorted out of the casino for hustling. He took advantage of his celebrity status for a couple of bucks, if he was lucky.

One extremely busy night he showed up and nobody offered to sponsor him. After waiting a while he took a dollar out of his pocket and asked the dealer for four 25-cent chips, figuring that if he lost the buck someone would throw him a chip or two. As it happened the game was full and there was just one set of colored chips left. I told him it was the house policy that if the game was full he would have to buy a whole stack of chips ($5). He mumbled something and walked away, nobody paid any attention to him. A few minutes later Howard (Hickey) Kamm, the shift manager, or a semblance thereof, came over to me and said, "Let this guy buy in for anything he wants, understand?" Mr. Vale was standing behind him with a grin on his face. I nodded and he immediately threw down a buck and asked for four chips. He promptly blew them and waited around for a sponsor. Nobody offered him any money, and he walked away. I had been down a lot of roads in the business, and if this wasn't a classic example of a mooch, what is?

209. Milton Berle; Hidden Talents and Then Some

Milton Berle was known as "Uncle Miltie or "Mr. Television" the man who started television on its way to becoming what it is today. I remember when my Uncle Joe (who lived upstairs) bought the first television in our family in 1948 and, as a result, began to see relatives he hadn't seen or heard from in years. The TV was as big as a dresser and had a 10-inch screen. He then bought a TV magnifier which, placed over the screen had the effect of a magnifying glass. In actuality it made the picture worse than it already was, but nobody knew the difference back then.

I can still recall, on the night of the Milton Berle show, the living room being packed with people sitting on the floor, and Uncle Joe stretched out on the couch. On Milton Berle night the living room was always standing room only.

In 1960, Berle was the headliner in the showroom of the Flamingo hotel, and I was a dealer in the casino. The casino was less than 3500 sq. ft. and it didn't take much to make a crowd. Milton filled the showroom and, consequently, the casino, every night. Most evenings between shows, He'd would come out to the casino, always to the front table, which usually was mine. It was a $5 minimum table, which was hot stuff in those days and as a rule, there were empty seats. He would move me aside (okayed by the shift manager) and start to deal. Then there would be a rush to get a seat at the game, as no matter what the cards said, Milton would just pay everybody with $5 chips, every hand. It was great PR, and the people loved it. And, Milton could deal.

His brother, Frank, also his manager (?), would appear just before the show broke, and stand and watch to see which game Milton was headed to, and rush over to get a seat. The way he (Milton) was throwing chips around, everyone wound up with $20 or $30 dollars. Frank wasn't bashful, and I never saw him playing at any other time.

Milton's wife, Ruth, was a lovely woman. She was pleasant and there was a sense of class about her. She would play for hours on my table and always showed an interest in the way Las Vegans lived. She would even ask about the fishing, as she knew we would sometimes head for the lake after work to fish for a few hours.

On one unusually slow night, the Berle family and friends were having a late snack in the restaurant after the last show. Milton came out to the casino directly to my empty table, picked up the cards and began to show me some card tricks, and he had some dandies. Then manipulated the deck, and I was taken aback at his dexterity and skill. He could deal seconds, deal from the bottom of the deck, false shuffle, and he was quite good at it. When I asked where he acquired this skill, he told me that it was one of his hobbies, and when he first got into show business he considered a magic act as a backup if everything else failed. I know how many hours of practice it takes to perfect some of the things he was doing, and I really had to respect what it takes to be successful in the entertainment business.

In the showbiz circles there was a strong rumor that Milton had the biggest penis in the entertainment world. I don't know whether that included some of the porn stars, but Milt's shlong was the subject of jokes at the Friars Club roasts in Hollywood, and amongst other such gatherings. One anecdote stated that Milton and a friend went into the steam room at his health club with towels wrapped around them. A guy on the second tier of benches (also wrapped in a towel) wanted to bet $100 that his shlong was bigger than Milton's. Milton declined, but his friend said, "Go ahead, Milt, I'll put up the money and you only have to take out enough to win."

In a memorial service after his death, which was held at the Friars Club, one Freddie Roman solemnly announced that Miltie's penis will be buried on May 1st and 2nd.

210. Andy Williams

Flamingo Hotel, 4AM, summer of 1960. I'd just gotten off work, and there wasn't a soul in the place, which in those days wasn't unusual at that hour. I walked into the lounge. It was dark, and I had a quick drink before heading for home.

As I kibitzed with the bartender, I noticed a figure sitting in a chair in the corner of the lounge. He was wearing chukka boots (in vogue at the time) and he was sitting with his head practically between his knees and his arms dangling to the floor, obviously passed out or sound asleep. I told the bartender he had a customer who may have to be sent to bed, and he replied, "That's Andy Williams." When I asked who Andy Williams was, he told me he'd just opened as the headliner in the main showroom. I had never heard of Andy Williams and when I asked what he did, the bartender told me he was an up-and-coming singer. The graveyard cocktail waitress told me he was like that the night before and didn't wake up until security woke him and helped him to his room.

Curious, I walked over to see what he looked like, and he looked up and saw me staring. At a loss for words I said, "Mr. Williams, a bunch of us sometimes go to the lake and swim and water ski after work, the chorus girls ski topless, we get some morning sun and then go home and get some sleep before coming to work. I wondered if you would like to join us one morning." He said he would like that, but in a way, he didn't seem sincere.

That night at work I mentioned it to Dick Mead, the pit manager and a regular on our morning trips to the lake. We flagged down one of the chorus girls and told her to ask him (Andy) if he would like to go this morning. If so, come out to the casino and let us know. Between shows, he appeared and told Dick that he would like to go and asked when and where. We had three cars with boats hitched to the back and all three cars were full of showgirls, night shift waitresses and Dick and I, along with a couple of dice dealers. We stopped for some cold beer and were at the lake an hour after sunrise. Lake Mead was at its best at that time of the morning. Cool and colorful, and absolutely deserted. We skied and laid around a couple of floating rafts, courtesy of the park service, and then headed for home. Andy was returned to the hotel, and everyone went home to bed. He went with us one more time, and I never saw him in the lounge after the late show again.

He had discovered showgirls, and started dating Claudine Longet, who was a dancer with the Folies Bergere at the Tropicana. She was slender and naïve, supposedly just 19 or 20 years old, and looked like a boy, until she got her clothes off onstage, and then the whole perception changed in a hurry. She was a sweet person and was seen around town with Andy on a regular basis. It was said that they were in a serious relationship. But I guess when it came to marriage, Andy wasn't about to budge. Then Claudine went out with Vic Damone a few times, and Vic was a formidable opponent when it came to vying for a lady's attention.

Andy had a rapid change of heart; he and Claudine tied the knot. On occasion through the years when I would stop at the Desert Inn after work and have a bite with my father, they would come in, and she always made it a point to come over and say hello. I really liked her. Several years later Andy Williams was headlining the show at the Desert Inn. Claudine would come into the showroom and wait for Andy to finish, then go backstage.

One evening, my wife was in the showroom celebrating the birthday of a friend. When the show ended they got up to leave. As she ran up the aisle she collided with Claudine who was headed towards the stage. They were both wearing the identical dress. They looked at each other and Claudine remarked, "Nice dress," and hurried on.

211. Traian "Ted" Boyer; This Takes the Cake

In the late '50's and early '60's, hypnotists were popular in the Las Vegas lounge scene. Pat Collins (a woman) was appearing at the Sahara and other resorts, and the Dunes had Traian "Ted" Boyer (Boy-a) booked into the lounge as "The Great Boyer." And being the egotist that he was, he really believed the "great" part.

Boyer was in his late 40s, about six feet tall with a perfectly coiffed snow-white head of hair. He was always dressed in a dark blue or black suit and, of course, had the deep Las Vegas tan. The shows were in the lounge and made a lot out of audience participation. We always felt that the people who did the funny things purportedly under hypnosis, were shills, but it was never proven.

During one of Boyer's gigs at the Dunes, he was winning at blackjack, and it seemed that every time he played, he won. He, of course let it be known that luck had nothing to do with, that it was his superior intellect that enabled him to overcome the odds. He never tipped anyone, and when he left the table he would smile at the dealer as if feeling sorry for him. To sum it up, Traian (try-on) Boyer was a schmuck.

During his shows he never failed to make mention of the fact that he was a winner at blackjack, and he felt that it was due to his "sixth sense." Add that to the fact that he was a "stiff" (someone who never tipped), some of the employees found it annoying. The game was designed to make a winner feel smart, and when the cards finally started to bite them, they refused to believe it, and that was a recipe for financial disaster. Then, as if sent from heaven, poetic justice paid a visit to the Dunes Hotel. In the small casinos in those days, it was not hard to notice customers who spent three or four days at the hotel. As it happened there was a young couple from some burg in Oklahoma, spending their honeymoon at the Dunes. She was a plain girl who loved to play the nickel slots, and he was a stocky young man who looked and talked like a farmer. He spent his gambling time at the blackjack table, was a one and two-dollar bettor, had two free drinks and was intoxicated, but always polite.

One night they went into the lounge to watch The Great Boyer do his thing. They were seated ringside, right against the stage. Boyer entered, got a few volunteers (men and women) from the audience (could they be shills?) and proceeded to put them under hypnosis. When he was finished, they would sit there with their heads hanging down, and wait for him to give them post hypnotic suggestions, then he would awaken them and the fun would begin. Some sang, some danced, some imitated strippers (of course he would stop them before it got too racy). It was comical to see a 60-plus woman start to strip and act like Gypsy Rose Lee. Just as he proceeded, the girl from Oklahoma stood up and waved to him and pointed to her husband, who was sitting there with his head down, obviously hypnotized. Boyer stepped off the stage, examined the kid and realized that he was really under. He whispered something in his ear and the young man snapped awake. Boyer, seeing that the lounge was full and the curtains to the casino were opened, with people standing outside and watching, decided to do something spectacular.

I was standing on an empty blackjack table looking directly into the lounge. The distance to the stage couldn't have been more than 50 feet. Bringing the young man onto the stage, Boyer put him under, and standing behind him with his hands on his upper arms proceeded to tell him that his body was becoming stiff, every inch of him was rigid and unbendable, and kept up the dialogue, becoming louder and louder, and the kid was so stiff he was shaking. The stiffening process didn't discriminate, and this young man had an erection. He was wearing a pair of orange slacks, and as it happened, he was extremely well endowed, and here was this huge bulge sticking out not far above his knee.

In spite of a few titters from the audience, Boyer soldiered on. He took two armchairs and with the help of two stagehands laid this young man, face up across the space between the chairs. Realizing what was causing the titters from the audience, Boyer took a white linen napkin and placed it over the bulge. The effect of the white napkin on the orange slacks really enhanced the spectacle. It looked like a picture of Mount Fuji from a tourist magazine.

But the show must go on, and Boyer continued. He got on a stool, and then stepped onto the young man's stomach. The young man didn't even begin to sag. It was quite a trick and would make one a believer in hypnosis. When he stepped down to acknowledge the applause, he woke the subject up, and then decided to take further advantage or the crowd that had gathered outside the lounge. The young man stood there with a dazed look on his face. Boyer then reached into his pocket and brought out a money clip stuffed with $100 bills. He made a production of showing it to the audience and announcing" this is $2500 I won playing blackjack, I win $500 a day *every* day. Then, turning to the young man, he said, "This money clip is red hot" and I'm going to put it in your hand, and it will burn you terribly." If you can hold it without juggling it for 45 seconds, you can keep it" Even in his hypnotized state, $2500 was a huge sum to this kid. Boyer put the clip in his hand and the kid flinched noticeably. He was in obvious pain and Boyer started looking at his watch and counting. At 20 seconds the kid was on his knees one hand holding the hand with the clip from underneath. His face was beet red and he was trembling like someone enduring the tortures of the damned. His wife screamed for him to drop it. As Boyer continued counting he was getting louder and louder, then went to his knees at 35 seconds and gesturing with his forefinger commanded the kid to drop it. He didn't. The audience was cheering the kid on and the tension was unbearable. The young man held on and, when the time was up, the audience cheered and his wife again begged him to drop it. He finally did and, soaked with sweat, stood up and smiled at Boyer.

The whole side of the casino facing the lounge was at a standstill and the audience applauded wildly. Boyer was now in a tough spot. When the noise died down he went over to the center of the stage and announced that "sometimes in show business you say things strictly for show, when you don't really mean them." Or words to that effect. It was obvious he wanted his money back, and he was going to do or say anything to reclaim it. Then a voice from the audience shouted, "Let him have the money!" And the rest of the people all chimed in, and the roar was angry. Boyer walked over to the kid and held his hand out and said something, but the kid shook his head. Now the crowd was on the verge of lynching Boyer, security came into the lounge, and Boyer, his tanned face a shade of grey stalked off the stage. In doing so he left several people sitting in the chairs onstage with their heads down, including the young man who was awake, but still under.

Boyer was nowhere to be found, Security was at a loss as to how to wake these people up, and they had to call a doctor. They closed the curtains, and the show was over. I guess the doctor worked with hypnotism, and the only thing that happened was that some of the people had headaches for a day or so. Boyer cancelled the remainder of his gig (although they did bring him back) and the Okie went home a winner.

It was an exciting performance.

212. Vic Damone; "The Best Set of Pipes in the Business." (Per Frank Sinatra)

During the late 1950s, '60s and '70s, a plethora of singers graced the stages of Las Vegas, and quite a few of them were Italian. Such names as Tony Bennett, Tony Martin, Robert Goulet, Jerry Vale, Frank Sinatra, Julius LaRosa, Bobby Darin, Dean Martin, Andy Williams, et al. All were at the top of their game.

But when it came down to raw talent, nobody could match the voice of Vic Damone.

I heard them all, and in my humble opinion nobody came close. Frank Sinatra was quoted as saying that "Vic Damone has the best set of pipes in the business." I guess you would agree, Sinatra knew his business. Vic appeared in the theatre lounge of the Frontier Hotel in 1971, his closing number was "My Way" made famous by Frank Sinatra. When the song was over it got standing ovations, people stomping their feet and begging for an encore.

One afternoon Vic and his drummer took a ride to Willow Beach, a resort on the Colorado River 11 miles below Hoover Dam, just a 50-minute drive from Las Vegas. The resort had a small restaurant, and about 60 boat slips, launching ramp and a fish hatchery in close proximity. They were having lunch when someone spotted Vic and let the owner of the resort, one Willard "Butch" Webb, know he had a celebrity at the lunch counter. Butch introduced himself and offered to take them for a boat ride upstream to just below the dam. Vic accepted and they headed up the river. The water was swift, ice cold and crystal clear, and contained probably the best trophy rainbow trout fishery in the country, maybe the world. Vic was taken by the beauty, surrounded by 2000-ft.-high walls of rock, waterfalls and solitude.

When they returned to the dock, Vic decided to buy a boat. He inquired about the hundreds of pictures on the restaurant's "Hall of Fame." The pictures were of fishermen who'd caught a "trophy trout" of five lbs. or more. The photos showed a lot of fish in the 12 to 17-pound class. Vic was hot to trot, and Butch, knowing that Vic was appearing at the Frontier, told him that their premier fisherman—me—was also working at the Frontier and maybe would give him some pointers on how to get started.

That night, after his first set, he came out to the casino and introduced himself (no introduction necessary) and told me about his trip to the river and Butch's suggestion. I liked the quiet way he handled himself, and we made arrangements to meet at the resort on a Tuesday morning. We proceeded upriver in my boat, and I showed him how to rig his line and what bait to begin with, and we started a drift. As luck would have it, He caught a 5 1/2 lb. rainbow on the first drift and he was hooked.

Of course, when we returned to the dock, they made a production of the fish, took his picture for the "wall" and Vic purchased a boat from Butch on the spot. Vic and I fished together a few more times (I never divulged my best secrets) and then he began to fish on his own.

One day six months later, my friend and I were on our way up to do some fishing, and here was Vic, alone in his boat and waving his arms like he was in trouble. We pulled over to him and on the floor of his boat was an eight lb. rainbow, still flopping around. You'd think he won the lottery, he was so proud of that fish. He asked us to take a picture, and my friend got his camera out, and I stepped into Vic's boat, put on his straw sombrero, got up on the seat and stood behind him grinning, when the picture was snapped. Later when he saw the picture with me in it, he got kinda pissed, but good-naturedly said that if it weren't for me he never would have caught the fish. I still have the picture (see photos) and fond memories of the times we fished together. Vic was always a gentleman and humble to everyone as far as I know, and never refused an autograph. The fact that he had somewhat of a baby face made people think that he was a wuss.

Take it from me, Vic Damone is no wuss.

213. Diahann Carroll: Love's Labours Lost

Enter Diahann Carroll. She and Damone were an item, and they spent time on the river together. She was absolutely gorgeous, and famous in her own right. One afternoon I was headed up the river, and here was Vic and Diahann drifting down the river with their engine off. Vic was peering off the back of the boat, and Diahann was standing in the center of the boat trying to look out the back. When I went over to see if they were okay, I saw a huge rattlesnake swimming right behind their boat, and it *was* huge. We watched it for a minute, and then the current swung Vic's boat around and they couldn't see the snake. Not knowing that she was deathly afraid of snakes, I let out a yell, "Watch out, Vic, it's climbing up your outdrive." Diahann let out a scream, jumped up on the seat, and proceeded to run in place and make funny noises. I kept saying I was only kidding, and we finally got her calmed down. I beat it out of there, and the next time I saw Vic he told me that I ruined his amorous plans for the evening.

Poor guy.

214. Margaret O'Brien

My friend, Danny, and I were on the prowl at the Desert Inn one summer day in 1952. We had just come from the hotel drugstore, a tiny affair with a four-stool soda fountain, a few sundries and a pinball machine. Danny would put a quarter in the machine, lift it up and set it on his toes. The ball would just roll around and rack up points and free games. When we arrived at a bunch of free games, we'd put the machine back on the floor, and stand there and play for hours. The owner of the drugstore complained to Danny's father that we were cutting into his pinball income, which at the most could have been a few dollars a day.

Danny's dad was Ruby Kolod, the DI big boss, and he gave the guy a month's income, figuring that if we were playing pinball, we couldn't get into any trouble.

As we walked into the casino we glanced over at the closed lounge and, sitting in the first booth, backed up to the casino was a really cute girl, looking to be about our age (16) and all alone. Danny and I were always in there, pitching, and we tried to pick up all the girls we laid eyes on. We never scored, over the span of two summers, not once. The closest we came was a girl who pulled her bathing suit aside in the pool, and we would go underwater and take a look. To begin with, we couldn't hold our breath long enough to get a good look, the chlorine burned our eyes, and we decided it wasn't worth drowning for.

I had to go to the men's room, and Danny headed for the booth and our target for the afternoon. When I came out of the men's room and headed for the lounge I hadn't taken five steps when a hand gripped my arm and pulled me aside. I looked up and saw it was Nick "Peanuts" Donalfo. Nick was there representing some "partners" from back east. He was an easygoing guy, quick to smile, but gave the impression that it wouldn't be wise to cross him. Most of the guys who had that type of job did a favor for the Mob, sometimes "taking a fall" (doing jail time for someone, or an important "favor," maybe murder).

He was livid. He said, "What the fuck are you guys doing now?" Do you know who that is? I felt my stomach clench as I saw Danny in the booth whispering sweet nothings in her ear. His "nothings" were really "somethings." Professing that I had no idea who the lady was, and being glad I wasn't in the booth, he said, "That's Margaret O'Brien, she's here with her mother celebrating her 16th birthday as guests of Wilbur Clark. You go and get him out of there."

Margaret O'Brien was a world-famous child movie star. I walked over to the lounge, leaned over the back of the booth, and whispered to Danny that Peanuts wanted to see him *right now*! I then beat it out the door to the pool. A few minutes later Danny came strolling out and said that Peanuts hurt his (Danny's) neck. I asked Danny if he said anything bad to her, and he told me he said, "I'd like to get my penis between us." She didn't reply. In those days she may never have heard the word.

I didn't know whether to believe him or not.

215. Johnny Mathis; A Lesson in Manners

Charles "Chazz" Walsh was the assistant casino manager at the original MGM Grand Hotel, opened in 1973. Ten years before, in 1963, he was a blackjack dealer at a Strip resort. His wife Helen was a cocktail waitress at the Riviera. Chazz was a friendly guy who had once done some amateur boxing. One night, Chazz went to pick up his wife after work and inquired after her whereabouts.

They told him she was sitting at a table in the corner of the lounge. She was in tears and said that Johnny Mathis had given her a real rough time and hurled some nasty insults her way. I don't know what he said, and I never asked Chazz. Chazz caught up with Mathis at the elevator and knocked him cold with one punch. Then he and Helen calmly walked out the door. Mathis's manager said that Johnny was a singer, not a fighter. Mathis cancelled the rest of his engagement, saying he was afraid to stay in Las Vegas and flew back to Los Angeles.

Nothing ever came of the incident, but maybe Johnny's manners improved.

216. Bob Hope

Joseph Magnin was the only real upscale women's store in Las Vegas, located just a few hundred yards south of the Desert Inn on the Strip. You had to turn off the Strip and navigate a narrow driveway to get to the store as it was behind two other buildings that fronted right on the Strip behind a narrow sidewalk. The buildings were so close to the street that you literally had to inch your way out, as you wouldn't be able to see anyone on the sidewalk until they were a few feet away. One day I was creeping out of the driveway an inch at a time, and I looked to the left to see if there was oncoming traffic on the strip. As I turned my head I heard a tap-tap on my fender on the passenger side. I stopped, and here was Bob Hope with a walking stick passing in front of me.

He smiled, tipped his hat and kept on walking.

217. Carmen Miranda

In the mid-1950's, Carmen Miranda was the headliner in the Painted Desert room at the Desert Inn. Circulating around town was a photo of her with her fruit bowl hat and in full costume kicking one leg up during a dance onstage. She wasn't wearing any pants. It was taken from directly below so it didn't leave any room for conjecture. It seemed like everyone in town had the picture. Without today's computer technology, you wonder where so many copies came from. Some said it wasn't really her (possible), some said the focal point of the picture was superimposed, but it sure looked real. Adding to the fact that there were so many, everyone wondered where they came from. In those days just looking at smut could get you in a lot of trouble, distributing it was jail time. I don't know if she was aware of the picture.

Today it would be a collector's item, probably go for thousands at auction.

218. Betty Grable and Harry James

Betty Grable and Harry James were residents of Las Vegas. You could run into them anywhere. She the famous actress and pin up girl for all the GI's in WW2, he the famous band leader.

We were all sitting at the bar at Musso's one early A.M. and Harry was sitting with us. There was a latticework divider covered with artificial ivy between the dining area and the bar. Betty stuck her face through one of the openings and started nagging him to come to the table. He turned around and said, "Cool it baby, you're beginning to bug me." We all thought that was one of the greatest things we'd ever seen.

Harry was a womanizer and we called him the iron man as he could drink and go without sleep for days, and still do his show in the lounge. My boss at the Flamingo, Dick Meade, a good friend of Harry's used to say, "Poor Harry, if he doesn't score, he has to go home and screw Betty Grable."

One night I was standing on an empty Blackjack table and Harry came in the front door. He stopped to talk to Dick at the far end of the pit, and I heard Dick start to howl with laughter. I'd never heard him laugh so long and hard. Harry headed for the lounge and he had to walk right past me to get there. I noticed he had a bruise on his cheek and a cut on the bridge of his nose along with a lump on his forehead. It looked as if he'd been in a fight. I asked Dick what was going on, and he said he couldn't tell me.

Later that night, after work, we made camp in Musso's and Dick made me promise not to say a word, and he would tell me what happened to Harry. Seems like Harry was inebriated and fell in love with some local lovely at one of the dives he patronized. They wound up in her apartment, and she confessed that the only way she could climax was to lay in the bathtub and let the water beat down on her most sensitive areas. Harry, who was game for anything, said okay, and while she was laying in the tub and enjoying the cascade, he kept trying to get his head under the spigot to kiss her "sensitive areas" (I'm sure he didn't use the expression). This resulted in his injuries as he kept bumping into the plumbing. Not being faint of heart, he kept trying different angles, which resulted in his various cuts and bruises. It was everything I could do to stay on the stool, but true to my word, I didn't snitch until I found out that everybody seemed to know. Somebody blabbed, probably Harry. Betty finally gave him the pitch.

219. And So On

On so many occasions people would ask me about celebrities I would meet in the course of my work, or just celebrities in general. Let me try to classify some of them. The nicest celeb I had the pleasure of meeting was Bob Newhart. His wife would play blackjack waiting for the show to end at the Frontier, and they were really nice people. She would comment on my ties and tell Bob he ought to let me pick his.

The most electrifying performer I've ever seen on stage was Lena Horne. In a closed-in, smoke-filled night club atmosphere where a lot of drinking was going on, she would come onstage and for the rest of the evening you could hear a pin drop. She played the Sands in the mid-50s.

The funniest is hard to pick. Shecky Greene and George Carlin were the funniest, in my opinion. Driving down the Strip one morning at 5AM, it was getting light, and in front of the Colonial House Motel was a naked man, bending over and reaching into the back seat of an open car. The motel was next door to the Desert Inn, and the man wasn't ten feet from the Strip. He straightened up, put on a bathing suit and ran in to the pool area. It was Shecky Greene. Shecky was nuts, and when he was drinking and gambling he was physically thrown out of every joint in town at one time or another. There were several who wouldn't let him in the casino if he looked drunk. On one occasion when he had lost all his money he jumped up on a craps table and laid down flat and announced, "Everything goes on the hard eight."

The most beautiful entertainer is also a difficult choice. I had dealt to, or had conversations with, quite a few of them and, to me, it was just like talking to anyone else. However, the only one who ever left me speechless was Mitzi Gaynor. She headlined the Flamingo Showroom in the late '50s and early '60s. On her first night, while her husband was talking to some people, she came over to my table and sat down to play a few hands of Blackjack. She smiled at me and said "Hi" and I tried to answer but it was a good 10 seconds before I could get a word out. She was drop dead gorgeous. Her skin was a perfect example of "peaches and cream." I was OK after that but she was literally stunning. Runner-ups would probably be Cyd Charisse, married to Tony Martin, a legend in his own mind, and Barbara Eden who became famous as “Jeannie” on Television.

220. The Unbelievable Jimmy Grippo

Of all the entertainers and celebrities that I had the good fortune to meet (some, the bad fortune), the one that stands out in my mind is Jimmy Grippo. Jimmy is in the International Hypnosis Hall of Fame and was probably the greatest magician and sleight of hand artist that ever lived. His life was legend. He worked as the house magician at the Desert Inn for a short time, and in 1966 when Caesars Palace opened they made him an offer and he became their house magician for over 20 years.

Prior to that he performed for royalty and Heads of State all over the globe. Among them, Presidents Roosevelt, Carter, Ford, Nixon, Kennedy, and Prime Ministers Winston Churchill and Anthony Eden, and of course, the King and Queen of England. During World War two, it was said that he worked with General Patton hypnotizing soldiers about to go into surgery and motivated those about to enter combat.

He also used hypnotic suggestions on those privy to classified and confidential information, so if they were captured and tortured, they would remember nothing of value to give to the enemy.

Jimmy got interested in boxing and groomed one Melio Bettina who was to become the light heavyweight champion of the world. He (Grippo) claimed it was done through motivational therapy and hypnotism. Before every fight he would hypnotize Bettina into believing he was invincible and could feel no pain. He fought a title bout against "Tiger" Jack Fox and, at the final weigh-in, Fox said as he was getting on the scale he glanced over and saw Grippo staring at him, and he felt weak. After losing the fight, Fox claimed that Grippo put the "evil eye" on him and he couldn't perform in the ring. Of course, a couple of good left hooks would probably have the same effect.

At a party, he so amazed Rocky Graziano with a card trick that Graziano and two other guys insisted he do it again, totally nude. All this, according to Graziano, who probably had his conception of time and space altered by Sugar Ray Robinson.

My personal interaction with Jimmy was brief, but memorable. In 1967 I was having a late bite with my father at the DI's Skillet

Room, a favorite after hours destination for celebs and show people. My dad was sitting at the table with Jimmy Grippo, whom I recognized but had never met. As I approached the table, Grippo jumped up, extended his hand and said "Mike, I'm glad I'm finally getting to meet you." He grabbed me by the shoulder, squeezed the back of my neck and said, "Sit down and tell me about the fishing." As we were shaking hands, I looked directly in to his eyes, and had a sensation that I still can't put a word to. Incapacitated? Vulnerable? In later years I've thought about it and still can't find a proper word, and yet it couldn't have lasted more than a second.

He made me feel like I was ten feet tall, and the whole meal was enjoyable. When I went to check the time, my watch was gone, and thinking it may have come off my wrist, I looked down at the floor, and it wasn't there. Figuring it was gone forever, I reached into my pocket for tip money, and all my money was gone. As I hurriedly patted myself down, Jimmy reached inside my shirt pocket and handed me my watch and money. He said he was holding it for me, as I had downed a few drinks prior to breakfast. With that he thanked my dad for breakfast and told me he hoped we'd meet again and took his leave.

I looked at my dad, and he said, "I've seen him do things that are incomprehensible." I wonder if he hypnotized me during that brief glance. His story is one that should be read.

Jimmy Grippo died at the age of 95. In a lot of ways, he remains a mystery.

221. Looking Back

Old people look back, young people look ahead. That's the way of our world. Since arriving in the "old people" category, I find I reminisce quite a bit of the time and that is one reason I wrote this book.

Many years ago, we were discussing the death of a popular casino boss, and lamented that, in spite of the money he made, he died broke. Which wasn't an uncommon occurrence in Las Vegas. A wise old pit boss who happened to hear our conversation said, "What difference does it make how he died?" "How did he *live*? That's what counts." I've thought about that statement over these many years and it's had an effect on how I look back on my life.

I wonder what would have happened if my family had never moved west. I would have lived a totally different life. Would I have gotten an education, a profession and made a lot more money? Maybe. I could also have wound up delivering dry cleaning. The gambling business gave me an opportunity to do the things I loved, and although it wasn't mentally stimulating, it was a means to an end, especially after I married and had a family. The business was good to me. I loved being able to see the mountains all around the city, the fresh desert air (which hasn't been fresh for many years), the lake and the Colorado River, both pristine, uncrowded, and teeming with fish. That was my main love. So many memories of days and nights with nobody within miles and the desert sky solid with stars. The mornings taking breaks at the Flamingo Hotel, sitting on the front steps and watching the sun coming up, looking into the desert where Caesars Palace sits now. There were huge sand dunes and a family of coyotes whose pups would chase each other up to the top of the dunes and roll down to the bottom on top of each other. Driving down the Strip after work in my convertible with the top down and the warm desert air across my shoulders like a cloak. I feel that I made the right choice as to how I lived my life. Trying to figure what *could* have been is a waste of precious time. Looking back, I like the way I lived.

And how I die is immaterial.

222. Beginning of the End

The end came quickly. I drove under the porte cochere at the Boulder Station where I was the day casino shift manager, got out of my car and headed for the front door. The rock music was blaring from the overhead speakers, and I felt my stomach churn. When I opened the door to enter the casino, the smell of cigarette smoke hit me, the noise of 2,500 slot machines in "attract mode" assailed my ears. It sounded like bells, calliopes, and the oompahs of a thousand tubas all mixed together. The graveyard shift manager had left early, and there were several beefs waiting to be settled. I handed out comps to the ladies who stood there with bloodshot eyes and cigarettes dangling from their lips. They looked like zombies after playing all night, and some had a distinct urine odor.

I proceeded into the pit. The building's piped-in music featured Whitney Houston. If you ever wondered what the sounds from a torture chamber during the Inquisition were like, buy her records. As I glanced at the desk, there was a memo from the GM saying, "Effective immediately, all casino shift managers and assistants must eat in the employee dining area."

This was never a practice at any hotel in Las Vegas. Execs ate anywhere they wanted to. Not only was it a slap in the face, but while you were eating you had to get up numerous times to handle contentious situations, or to answer the phone, and the help's hall was a long way from the casino.

I stared at it for a minute and knew the time had come.

I picked up the phone and called my wife. When she answered, I said, "It's over. I'm through. We'll sell the house and build on Whidbey Island. I don't care if I have to box groceries part time, I just can't do this anymore."

That evening I drove to the Palace Station corporate offices and gave notice.

Two weeks later my unique career in Las Vegas was at an end.

When you look at the proliferation of casinos world-wide, in every state, every major city, and tribal casinos everywhere, if you stop and think, you will realize that it all started with Las Vegas, the only place in the United States and most of the world that you could gamble legally. I watched it happen and was part of the beginning. There aren't too many people who can make that claim. I take pride in that fact.

In retrospect, I came to realize that after 40 years in a profession like the gambling business, memories don't just disappear. I was fortunate to find a place as far away from a casino as it's possible to get these days. After spending my working life laced with noise, smoke and drunks, I thought I had found my own little piece of paradise.

On a visit to Seattle in 1982 we took a side trip to Whidbey Island to visit friends who had moved from Las Vegas where he'd been a prominent contractor. After he gave us a tour of the South end of the island, we bought a lot in a development that had yet to have a home on it and held on to it for 14 years.

This is where I live today. In spite of the population increase of 2,000 percent and the addition of four traffic lights, it's still a laid-back community.

Though I still have a connection to Las Vegas, I'll never return. Let it remain in my memory as I have described it to you. I check the Las Vegas obituaries daily to see if I know anyone who recently joined the ranks of the dearly departed. I confess that I get pleasure out of seeing the names of those I've outlived; especially the ones I didn't like. Some I will miss, having kept in contact all these years.

Last, but hardly least, are the casino dreams. They recur nightly and in each dream, I'm working in a casino in different capacities. One night I'm dealing, another, I'm a boss. They're not limited to places I worked. Some, I *never* worked in. They all contain faces and names that were real, some as far back as 50 years ago. The faces are real, but the names often elude me.

It's come to the point that every morning my wife will ask me, "Where did you work last night?" One morning I replied, "The Riviera." She said, "But you never worked at the Riviera." I said, "I have now."

They just won't let me go.

It was a great experience. I cherish the years I lived in Las Vegas, raised and educated my family, and had the best the town had to offer. But nothing good lasts forever, and I've found relative peace and quiet in which to spend the twilight of my life.

Lady Luck has treated me well.

Glossary

ACE DEUCE: A term used to mean death or dying. For example, Joe threw Ace Deuce last night. Funeral is Friday. Ace Deuce is also Craps (a loser) on the Craps table.

ACTOR: A casino employee, usually a pit boss, who moans, groans and curses when the casino or a game is losing. This is generally done when the big boss is around.

AGENT: A player in cahoots with the dealer. There are any number of ways to do this. They meet later and split the money.

APRON: A cloth apron the dealers wear to keep their pants from rubbing against the table. It straps on at the waist. Also, the area on a Roulette wheel where the chips are kept.

BACCARAT: Generally, a game for high rollers. The highest hand is nine and is usually dealt by a crew of four dealers. Most of the real high action is on Baccarat. The word Baccarat means "nothing."

BAG MAN: The person who delivers money skimmed from the casino to the Mob.

BANK: One of two sides you can bet on Baccarat. The other is "Players." Because of how the game is designed, the Bank has an edge so if you bet on the Bank and win, you pay a 5 percent commission or "vigorish" back to the house.

BEARD: An individual representing someone who doesn't want to be recognized. As in "He won a big bet at the sports book and sent in a beard to collect the money." Many large sports bettors use beards.

BENDING: A method of bending cards so they can be identified on top of the deck. Even if they're straightened out there's still a detectable wave in the card. The practice is all but extinct.

BIG SIX: The Wheel of Fortune. The large wheel the dealer spins, with quite a few stops. The table in front of the wheel has 5, 10, 20, 50, and 100-dollar bills under glass. You bet on the bill and if the wheel stops on the corresponding bill you win whatever denomination you bet on. For example, if you bet $1 on the $20 bill under the glass, you will get paid 20 to 1 if you win, etc.

BLACK BOOK: The list of excluded persons. A composite of undesirables and mobsters forbidden to enter a Nevada casino. If they're caught in a casino, the owner could possibly lose his license. The person in the book goes to jail.

BLOCKER: An individual who positions himself to block the view of a surveillance camera or dealer while an accomplice proceeds to cheat a machine or game. Sometimes there can be more than one blocker.

BLEEDER: An actor who emotes when a game is losing.

BOILER FACTORY: A casino busy all the time with mostly players who don't wager a lot. A lot of work and not a lot of money in tips.

BOX: The box located under the table where the cash goes when a player purchases chips. A.k.a. "drop" box, located under a narrow opening on the table with a plastic "paddle" in it. The cash is spread over the opening and pushed down into the box with the paddle.

BOX MAN: The person on the stool in the middle of the Craps table who deposits the cash in the drop box. He also directs the game.

BREAK DOWN THE DECK: When a dealer reshuffles before all the cards are out.

BREAKING IN: Learning to deal.

BUSTING OUT: Cheating by the casino.

BUTCHER: A Blackjack dealer paid to cheat for the casino.

BUY BUSINESS: When a casino pays to bring players into the hotel. It may refer to junkets, buses or invitational promotions.

BUY IN: The money a person exchanges for chips.

CAGE: The cashier's cage.

CALL BET: When a person makes a wager by stating how much he wants to bet. If he wins, he's paid. If he loses he must pay the house. If he can't cover the wager he could be jailed for fraud or the casino may take it out of his hide.

CHASE: To lose your first bet and take money to win it back. Some "chase" it with everything they have, and then some.

CHECK: A chip.

CHECK RACK: Wooden or plastic racks that carry chips. They have five grooves that carry 20 chips each. Also "a set of false teeth," as in "He's got a full check rack, uppers and lowers."

CHUCK-A-LUCK: A game played with dice in a cage that can be turned upside down and different totals and combinations can be wagered on. It's no longer found in most casinos. If you happen to find one, don't play it.

COLD DECK or **COOLER**: When a player(s) substitutes a deck stacked against the house after removing the original deck. It's practically extinct, but possible with the help of the dealer. Some huge wins were made in this manner.

COMP: Short for complimentary, which means the house is picking up the tab.

COUNTERS: People who track the cards in Blackjack to beat the house. The subject of many books. I assure you the authors made more off the books than they did on the game.

CRAPS: The dice tables; also, the losing numbers 2, 3, or 12 on a roll of the dice.

CRIMP: A bend in a card put there by a player to see what card is on top of the deck. Even if the crimp, or "bend," is straightened out, there is still a detectable wave in the card. This practice went the way of the dinosaurs. When all the casinos were dealing single deck or double decks out of the hand, it was a regular event.

DAUBING: The art of "painting" a deck with various substances so the card can be recognized by the cheater. They usually had the "daub" on a button, or a watchband, or even face makeup. Some were only visible to ultra violet or infra-red, and the cheater had to wear glasses or contacts. The only drawback was they made your eyes look red, yellow or whatever.

DEUCE: A term used to designate a dealer taking the second card from the top of the deck. This was the primary way of Blackjack cheating by the house in the old days.

DOING SOMETHING: The term used by people in the racket to infer that they were being cheated. For example, "He did something to me." or "Watch this guy, he's liable to do something to you."

DOUBLE DOWN: A bet on Blackjack where you can turn your first two cards face up and double your bet. You receive one card, face down. It's generally done on ten or eleven, so if you get a face card, you have practically a sure winner. However, you can double down on any two cards no matter what they total.

DOUBLE ENDER: Two Roulette tables with one wheel in the center. Both tables play off the same result. The only one I ever saw in Las Vegas was at the Stardust Hotel in 1958 and 1959. The casino went on the premise that they would only have to pay the license fee for one game. When they found out they were wrong, they did away with it.

DOUBLE UP: Betting twice as much on your next bet if you lose the first.

DROP: The money dropped into the boxes on the games

DROP BOX: The box under the table containing the drop.

DRIFTER: A person who drifts from town to town and job to job.

DUTCH: Suicide, as "He lost everything he had, and went home and took the Dutch." I have no idea where the term originated.

EYE IN THE SKY: The person on a catwalk over the casino, watching through a two-way mirror in the ceiling. Replaced by surveillance cameras.

FARO or **FARO BANK**: An age-old gambling game played with one deck in a metal box, from which the dealer takes two cards face up. It's practically a dead even gamble. No longer played in Las Vegas, it was the favorite of old-time gamblers. It was the best show in town. Even in the late '50s there were no more than four or five dealers who knew how to deal it. It was referred to as "bucking the tiger."

FILL: Chips brought to a table when it runs short, or coin to a slot machine.

FLOAT: The amount of chips a casino has in circulation. Mostly in players' pockets or in other casinos that can't be accounted for.

FLOOR MAN: A supervisor on the floor in the center of the pit. Sometimes referred to as a pit boss.

GAMING INDUSTRY: A genteel name for the "Racket."

GAMING CONTROL BOARD (GCB): The enforcement division of the Gaming Commission that investigates potential licensees and resolves disputes between customers and casinos. It also controls the work cards and assists casinos in rooting out scams and cheaters. The GCB also keeps tabs on large jackpots and can recommend approval for licensing. They are a powerful and efficient entity, appointed by the governor.

GAMING COMMISSION: The Body with final say in licensing and major business decisions in the industry. Can overrule the GCB. It's happened, but rarely. Also appointed.

GEORGE: A big tipper. Also, **KING GEORGE**: The biggest tipper of all. Sometimes referred to as "The man in the white hat."

GYPSY: A switch of cards or dice or anything that can be switched. As in "He pulled a gypsy on me."

HAND (DUKE): The cards dealt to a player or several passes on the Craps table. As "He shot up a hand." (Made a lot of passes with the dice).

HANDLE: The total amount of the money the casino takes in. It does *not* denote the win.

HANDMUCK: Slipping cards in and out of a Blackjack game undetected.

HIT: As in "Hit me." ("Deal another card.")

HEAT (STEAM): When the casino is losing and the bosses are on the warpath. As "Be careful, there's a lot of steam around here."

HOLD: Not drawing another card to a hand or referring to the percentage the house wins.

HOOLY: One of the great mysteries of the gaming industry, said to have been released when they opened King Tut's tomb. It means a certain hold a player has over a game, slot machine, dealer or casino. A player who constantly wins at a certain game or machine, time after time after time is said to have "the hooly" on the game. One of the inexplicable events that take place in casinos, when all else is disproved.

HOT STAMP: A gaming chip with no center insert or logo. The denominations are stamped into the chip by machine. They still use them on Roulette chips, but not on the denominated chips on the tables.

IDIOT BAR: A contraption on a spring that fits on the inside of a slot machine. If the machine is opened illegally the iron bar comes out and the machine can't be closed. Not needed any more, but effective in stopping cheaters in its day.

IMPULSE BETTORS: People who gamble with discipline then, out of nowhere, throw a large wager on the table. They're usually accused of being notorious counters. They were around long before anyone heard of the count.

INSIDE: Generally referring to a scam by employees. As in an "Inside Job."

JACKET: A black mark on a person's reputation. As in "He got fired for stealing and can't work because they hung a jacket on him."

JUICE: Influence, as "He's got juice with the casino manager," or a term used to mean interest paid on a loan.

KEY PERSONNEL: Upper and intermediate management.

LAMMER: A negotiable chip given to a Roulette player who cashes in his wheel chips. As in "He cashed in and took it on the lam."

LAYDOWN: The term used for gambling, as in "Did you make a laydown last night?"

MARK: A sucker, or the patron of a hooker or someone being cheated.

MARKER: Credit taken in a casino, with a signed check. Not a personal check.

MARKER BUTTON: A small wooden or plastic button used to denote transactions on the table. They usually come in $5, $10, $20, $25, $50 $100, $500 and $1000 denominations, color-coded.

MECHANIC: A dealer who cheats for the house.

MINI BACCARAT: A small table where a single dealer deals Baccarat.

MONEY MAKER: The female genitals.

OUTSIDE: Anything that happens in a casino that doesn't include employees.

PAINT: A common term for a jack, queen or king.

PASS: A winning throw of the dice, as "He made eight passes on the Craps."

PAST POSTING: Placing a bet after the Roulette ball is in the winning number, or after a winning hand.

PATOOTIE: See Moneymaker.

PEEK: When a mechanic furtively looks at the top card on the deck.

PER: Percentage.

PIT: The enclosed area between gaming tables.

PIT BOSS: The person in charge of a particular section of tables.

POLE: The stick used by a Craps dealer to move the dice, or the position on the Baccarat table that handles the cards and calls out winners or losers.

PROGRESSION: The system of doubling your bet every time you lose. Very popular at one time, but the worst system you can use.

RACKER or **CHIP RACKER**: Dealer who works with the Roulette dealer in heavy games and helps pick up and sort the chips.

RACKET: Slang for the gaming industry.

RED HOT STOVE CLUB: An association of local ladies who it's said would "steal a red-hot stove if they could hold on to it long enough." It's not a small sorority, and there isn't one scruple among them.

ROUNDER: An individual out every night making the rounds of bars and casinos.

RUSSIAN LOUIS STRAUSS: A Mobster whacked by the Mob and never seen again. Rumor had it he was "somewhere" out in the desert. A common local cliché if someone disappeared was that he was "out there with Russian Louis" More on Russian Louis in the text.

SCOOTER: A person who can throw the dice and make one or both dice slide and never turn over. Thus, fixing the result.

SECTION: A group of numbers in sequence on a Roulette wheel. As 1, 13, 36, 24, and 3.

SHAVE: The altering of dice to make them act differently from perfectly square dice.

SHILL: A person who sits on a table and acts like a real player to attract customers. This is done with house money

SHOE: The box that holds the cards on Baccarat or Blackjack.

SHOOT THE LIGHTS OUT: Make a lot of passes on the Craps table. (This expression is said to be a reference to an event in Reno in the early '50s. Two businessmen from California were under the impression that a casino does nothing but make money. They opened one, and hired their own help, including a casino manager with dubious credentials. The ribbon cutting was set for 2PM The crowd outside consisted of every cheater, crossroader, grifter and agent in the area. The dealers were also suspect, and by that evening the casino was running out of money. Gaming Control was in its infancy and there were no minimum cash-on- hand requirements. Finally, at 10PM they just turned out the lights. Those holding chips were out of luck.

SHYLOCK: Loan shark.

SIZING INTO: Sliding a handful of chips into a winning bet and paying the proper amount.

SNAPPER: A common term for a Blackjack hand.

SOAPING: Running bars of soap over new bills to keep them from sticking together. Previously done on Baccarat when the game was dealt with cash.

STICKMAN: The dealer on the Craps who handles the stick and moves the dice. Also sometimes, a term for a boyfriend.

STRAWBERRY PATCH: A casino vulnerable to stealing by its dealers or other personnel.

STIFF: A person who won't tip or refuses to pay back borrowed money. Also, someone who is no longer among the living.

STRINGING: When a coin is hung on a string and inserted into the coin slot of a slot machine and jiggled up and down so as to simulate adding extra coins. You can get the maximum on a five-coin payout with only one coin. Long gone.

SUB OR SUBMARINE: A pouch sewn into a dealer's clothes where a chip can be concealed.

SUMMA CORPORATION: Howard Hughes hotels.

TAKE OFF: To steal from, as in "I heard the Riviera got taken off for $5000 last night."
TAKING THE STEAM: Gambling a certain amount of money, losing control and blowing everything you have. Happens all the time.

THREE PLUCK ONE: When three players collude to cheat a mark out of his money in a Poker game.

TOM: Someone who doesn't tip at all.

.

TURNING THE DECK: In Blackjack, dealers used to pick up all the cards after each hand and place them face up on the bottom of the deck. They would then know the bottom card. If the game was not on the up and up, they could simply roll the deck over in their hand and use the bottom card, which would now be on top. If the dealer had 15 and knew the bottom card was, say, a five or six he could "turn the deck" and make a good hand.

UNDERCUT: The act of sliding the bottom chip off of a customer's wager when paying the bet. For example; they bet five chips and should have ten if they win the bet. Instead they wind up with eight and scratching their heads. Done properly it's practically undetectable.

VIGORISH or **VIG**: A percentage of a wager paid back to the house when one bets on the bank in Baccarat and wins. It's 5 percent. Also, the interest on a loan from a shylock. (See "Juice.")

WHEEL: The Roulette wheel or the "Big Six" wheel–sometimes referred to as the "Wheel of Fortune."

About the Author

Mike Soskin is the son of the Desert Inn's first casino manager. He began his career as the youngest dealer in Las Vegas, on his 21st birthday, so history is what you'll be reading here. He worked in no fewer than seven of the most popular early casinos, starting in 1957 as a dealer and winding up as the casino boss and part owner of an off-Strip hotel/casino for over ten years. He worked as a shift manager for Station Casinos for four years until he retired in the '90s. He lives with his wife, Cheryl, on Whidbey Island in Puget Sound just north of Seattle.

93927260R00237

Made in the USA
San Bernardino, CA
10 November 2018